LAW AND THE
BEAUTIFUL SOUL

LAW AND THE
BEAUTIFUL SOUL

Alan Norrie

London • Sydney • Portland, Oregon

First published in Great Britain 2005 by
The GlassHouse Press, The Glass House,
Wharton Street, London WC1X 9PX, United Kingdom
Telephone: + 44 (0)20 7278 8000   Facsimile: + 44 (0)20 7278 8080
Email: info@cavendishpublishing.com
Website: www.cavendishpublishing.com

Published in the United States by Cavendish Publishing
c/o International Specialized Book Services,
5824 NE Hassalo Street, Portland,
Oregon 97213-3644, USA

Published in Australia by The GlassHouse Press,
45 Beach Street, Coogee, NSW 2034, Australia
Telephone: + 61 (2)9664 0909   Facsimile: +61 (2)9664 5420
Email: info@cavendishpublishing.com.au
Website: www.cavendishpublishing.com.au

© Norrie, A 2005

British Library Cataloguing in Publication Data
Norrie, Alan W (Alan William), 1953–
Law and the beautiful soul
1 Sociological jurisprudence 2 Law – Philosophy
3 Law – Moral and ethical aspects
I Title
340.1'15

Library of Congress Cataloguing in Publication Data
Data available

ISBN 1-90438-530-3
ISBN 978-1-904-38530-1

1 3 5 7 9 10 8 6 4 2

Printed and bound in Great Britain

To Peter

Thus play I in one person many people

And none contented ...

(Shakespeare, *Richard II*, V, 5)

We are such stuff

As dreams are made on.

(Shakespeare, *The Tempest*, IV, 1)

Preface

The essays collected in this book concern the relationship between law as a social and historical institution and the moral judgments it is required to make. Such judgments are necessarily, though limitedly and contradictorily, reflected in legal forms. It is this limited and complex relationship that is at the practical and theoretical core of these essays. While they draw upon my previous work on punishment, crime and responsibility, they also emphasise the search for a broader theory of law and legal method. My hope is that bringing them together will cast that work in a slightly different light and make it accessible to a wider audience. Taken together, they also reveal a theoretical development which renders their collection more than the sum of its parts. That development is explained in the first chapter, and I have reworked the last two chapters in line with it. However, I would like briefly to sketch it here in a slightly different way to help anchor the detailed arguments of the individual pieces.

There are four key ideas in these essays. The first is that Western liberal law is essentially contradictory or antinomial, so that legal concepts, troubled and oppositional, generally hunt in pairs. Secondly, this essential characteristic is shaped by the particular socio-historical context of Western liberal societies in which structural conflicts and contradictions are key elements. Thirdly, this shaping of liberal law crucially affects and limits its ethical character and implications. Fourthly, law plays a central role in structuring, shaping and limiting the ethical possibilities in Western liberal societies. At first sight, this fourth point may appear only to restate the third from a different angle; however, it seems to me to give rise to an important development of the overall theme of these essays and it introduces us to their titular figurehead, the Beautiful Soul.

To grasp the significance of the Beautiful Soul, it is helpful to identify two tendencies that a critical understanding of liberal law should, in my view, avoid. One is to dismiss such law as ethically invalid, as entirely turned away from what human being is, as 'dead' or 'bare', as morally evacuated. The other is to fall back into upholding it as being 'as good as it gets' given the nature of human being or modern politics. I seek a middle course of acknowledging liberal law's ethical validity while noting its significant structural limits and complexities. This may, however, seem to say little more than what would be claimed by many modern liberal theorists. Typically, it might be said that liberal law establishes an ethical and political basis for 'the right', and not for 'the good'. Liberalism provides a floor, not a ceiling. It is for individuals to make what they will of their lives within a framework of rights, in pursuit of their own particular versions of the good. Law prioritises the right, and thereby limits itself, in order to allow this to occur. Alternatively, in a more sociological vein, it might be argued that legal legitimacy rests not just on the forms of law, but on the complementary existence of a vibrant civil society. To be itself, liberal law must look beyond itself; what law can achieve without favourable social conditions is, it is accepted, highly limited and questionable. To talk, therefore, of the limits of law may not seem novel to the liberal mind.

These essays argue for a stronger sense of the limits of liberal legality by stressing the role of antinomy, the role of historical conflict and contradiction and, perhaps most importantly, the essentially restricted and suppressed character of ethical life within liberal society. To do this, I draw upon the dialectical tradition's more critical elements – the young Hegel, Adorno, Bhaskar and Derrida (whom I press, legitimately in my view (see Chapter 8), into dialectical service). My aim is to show how liberal law channels, contains and represses a radical Enlightenment sense of 'the good' in order to produce a modern liberal sense of 'the right'. Shaped by modern institutions of private property and contract, liberal law contains the most radical promise of the Enlightenment, but it does so in a double and conflicted sense.

'To contain' can mean two things. It can mean 'to hold within' and 'to embody' (as in 'the book contained many meanings'). It can also mean, however, 'to hold at bay' and 'to suppress' (as in 'the fire or riot was contained'). Liberal law contains the promise of Enlightenment in the first sense in that it expresses it in limited, oblique and, to use a Freudianism, 'pale' forms. It also does so in the second sense in that it checks and represses that promise through the forms of freedom it provides. This work of expression on the one hand and repression on the other is signposted by the pathologies of antinomialism that bedevil liberal thought and which reach into the finest points of its law. The chain of antinomies begins at the edge of law, in oppositions between 'the ideal' and 'the actual', and between 'social' and 'individual' justice. It reaches into law's foundations, through lines drawn between the 'internal' and the 'external', the 'formal' and the 'substantive', and the 'universal' and the 'particular'. It proceeds into substantive areas like criminal law in such forms as the 'subjective' and the 'objective', the 'honest' and the 'reasonable', 'offence' and 'defence', 'justification' and 'excuse'. What these antinomies bespeak, I argue, is confusion and dis-ease in thought, in practice, in law.

The radical promise of the Enlightenment of which I speak gets largely, but not entirely, lost in this antinomial enchainment. It is expressed in various attenuated and inchoate forms in these essays. It is there, obscurely, in the legal conceptions of responsibility and freedom that many of them discuss. It is expressed in Adorno's critique of Kant, in Bhaskar's 'pulse of freedom', in Derrida's attention to the claims of 'the Other' and, in one of its finest forms, in the young Hegel's admiration for the Beautiful Soul. Sadly, Hegel was to abandon this figure to a far off exile in order to construct the systematic dialectics for which he is known today. Yet it remained, and remains, a force to be reckoned with: an end state glimpsed 'through a glass darkly', the unfulfilled promise of modernity, the ghost in the corridors of liberal law, the absent presence lurking in its antinomies, the harbinger of what free humankind could be.

That, at least, is the argument which rounds these essays off and gives them some of their prospective unity. It would, however, be wrong to promise too much of a set of essays written over a number of years (the earliest in 1993). These essays travel from law to the Beautiful Soul, but the journey was not a straightforward one and the final destination was not known in advance. They remain individual pieces along a road and in Chapter 1 I explain how it was navigated, and how, in the journey, it changed. To essays written some time ago I returned with trepidation as to how they would stand up. Only Chapter 2 felt in need of significant development, but I decided it should be included as it was for its broad, though always sketched and now slightly dated, diagnosis of the antinomial character of modern legal theory. In Chapter 1, I explain one way in which my own thinking has developed beyond its argument while retaining its basic orientation. Chapter 5 also moves perhaps too quickly from the historical, structured understanding of the limits of criminal justice and antinomy to reflection on its experiential ethical quality. I have not sought to rewrite these or other essays significantly, though I have been through them all with a view to light re-editing as to meaning and continuity within the collection.

When these essays were first published, they were accompanied by thanks to colleagues who had read or otherwise been involved in them. I have omitted these marks of gratitude from the revised versions here, though with no diminished sense of the contribution others made to them at the time. Instead, I would like to mention those who in one way or another have helped me significantly at different times or over the whole period in developing my thinking. These include Roy Bhaskar, whose work has always inspired me, Bill Bowring, Davina Cooper, Roger Cotterrell, Kathryn Dean, Antony Duff, Robert Fine, Peter Fitzpatrick, Nick Hostettler, Nicola Lacey and Chris Thornhill. At GlassHouse, I would like to thank Beverley Brown, who is an energetic and acute intellectual presence, and Sanjeevi Perera for her production skills. I thank Michelle Dempsey for bringing the various chapters into one common format with energy, efficiency and good humour.

On a personal level, I would like to thank Gwen once more for her love and support, and Stephen and Richard for theirs, as well as for many ideas and laughs along the way. I would like to thank my father Tom, who has always been there. Thanks to Olive, Sarah, John, Catherine and Peter, my brother, to whom this book is dedicated. I also thank Kitty who, armed with camera, joined the quest for the Beautiful Soul at the Tate Modern. Though we found it, we could not capture it on film. This was as it should be.

These essays were previously published in the following places: Chapter 2 in Norrie, A (ed) (1993) *Closure or Critique: New Directions in Legal Theory*, Edinburgh: Edinburgh University Press; Chapter 3 in (1996) 5 *Social & Legal Studies* 383–404 and in revised form in Darian Smith, E and Fitzpatrick, P (1999) *Laws of the Postcolonial*, Ann Arbor: University of Michigan Press; Chapter 4 in McVeigh, S, Rush, P and Young, A (eds) (1997) *Criminal Legal Doctrine*, Aldershot: Dartmouth; Chapter 5 in (1996) 59 *Modern Law Review* 540–56 (published by Blackwell); Chapter 6 in Matravers, M (ed) (1999) *Punishment and Political Theory*, Oxford: Hart; Chapter 7 in (2002) 65 *Modern Law Review* 538–55 (published by Blackwell); Chapter 8 in (1999) 8 *Social & Legal Studies* 85–114 (published by Sage UK) and in revised form as 'Dialectics, deconstruction and the legal subject' in Joseph, J and Roberts, JM (2004) *Realism, Discourse and Deconstruction*, London: Routledge; Chapter 9 in revised form in (2004) 3 *Journal of Critical Realism* 23–48 (published by Brill); Chapter 10 in revised form in (2004) 15 *King's College Law Journal* 45–62 (published by Hart). I acknowledge copyright and permission to republish where relevant.

Contents

Chapter 1
From Law to the Beautiful Soul

… his form had not yet lost
All her original brightness …
… as when the sun new ris'n
Looks through the horizontal misty air
Shorn of his beams, or from behind the moon
In dim eclipse disastrous twilight sheds
On half the nations, and with fear of change
Perplexes monarchs.
(Milton, Paradise Lost I, lines 591–99)

But just ponder the extent to which, although we may live for the future,
we live, quite literally, in the past.
(Bhaskar, 1993, p 58)

Introduction

The essays in this collection cover topics in the area of legal theory and the theory of criminal justice and responsibility. They discuss matters as diverse as the criminal responsibility of the two boys who killed James Bulger, the guilt of Albert Speer, the nature of popular justice, problems in the law of intention, recklessness and provocation, the historical development of modern legal theory, and the nature of its critique. They were not written to a general plan, but they were written in relation to each other. The result is a set of essays that reveal a dominant theme and an emerging line of argument. Put together, I hope that the impact and significance of both is made the stronger. Since each chapter was originally written to stand by itself, I do not seek in this introduction to outline each in detail. Their titles indicate something of their content, and the next section begins by locating each one briefly within the overall argument that develops through the collection. I have focused on what holds these essays together as a whole, and this introduction is designed to bring this out.

Two themes

Two themes dominate the collection; the one on its face, the other as its emergent problematic. The first is the idea that legal discourse is essentially contradictory or, as I prefer, antinomial in its form. The essays are concerned with legal antinomies which are analysed either individually or in groups, and then, finally, as a whole. The second theme concerns the nature of legal critique, and in particular the relationship between its socio-historical and ethical dimensions. In much critical legal theory, these two dimensions are in conflict with, or at least speak past, each other. Derrida's distinction between two forms of critique in his essay 'Force of law', discussed below, is a case in point. While he privileges an ethical critique, the essays in this collection privilege a socio-historical point of view. Neither finds much place for the other. The last three chapters here, however, work towards a way in which the ethical and the socio-historical dimensions of critique can be brought together as one enterprise.

This introduction has the following structure. In the next section, I say a little about each individual chapter while linking them to the collection's two dominant themes: antinomy and the nature of critique. In the following, third, section, I develop the theoretical discussion of antinomy in law while considering the roots of my own socio-historical approach to critique. At the beginning of the fourth section, I suggest that it was focusing on antinomy that led critical theorists historically to adopt diverging socio-historical and ethical approaches to critique. In that section, I then consider two modern critical philosophies which underpin the socio-historical and the ethical approaches to the critique of law, and how they might be brought together. These are the two philosophies most important to this work: critical realism and deconstruction. In the final section, I argue that the common ground I identify can lead to a critical interpretation of law in which the socio-historical and ethical approaches are brought together. Considering my two prefatory quotes, such a convergence would draw together something like the historical approach identified by Roy Bhaskar and the ethical vision of fallen divinity – of a form terribly changed yet reflecting an original ethical grace – depicted in John Milton's description of Satan. The routes into this critical interpretation are provided by an account of Adorno's view of law in his philosophy of negative dialectics and by considering the key figure of the Beautiful Soul in Hegel's philosophy and how it relates to law.

The Beautiful Soul

Before moving to the next section, it may be useful briefly to introduce the idea of the Beautiful Soul to the reader as it appeared in Hegel's thought. In the 18th century, the Beautiful Soul had been a widely deployed, pan-European figure in ethical and aesthetic philosophy, as well as in literature. As Robert Norton's excellent monograph makes clear, the precise meaning of the term changed over its 100 year history and according to the national context in which it was deployed (Norton, 1995). The core idea was the possibility of combining moral virtue and aesthetic value in the perfection of lived human being. The Beautiful Soul represented the possibility in the here and now of attaining the morally good life as 'the most profound expression of human moral existence' (Norton, 1995, p 211). To anticipate a sceptical response, Norton does go on to say that 'identifying exactly what moral beauty was had never been an easy task', even in the period of the figure's popularity. Just how we today should treat this image of human moral potential is a question for debate, and the subject matter of the final chapter. We can, however, be helped by considering two dramatically different views of the Beautiful Soul in Hegel's philosophy. His treatment of it comes at the end of the period of its currency, and its crucial and intriguing feature is how Hegel shifts in a very few years from admiration to outright rejection. In his early theological writings, he identified beauty of soul with the figure of Jesus and the need for a modern morality based upon the loving heart. In an essay of about 1799, beauty of soul involved 'Boldness and confidence of decision about fullness of life, about abundance of love, aris[ing] from the feeling of the man who bears in himself the whole of human nature'. He went on:

> Such a heart has no need of the much vaunted profound 'knowledge of men' which for distracted beings … is indeed a [useful] science; but the spirit, which is what they seek, always eludes them … An integrated nature penetrates the feelings of another in a moment and senses the other's harmony or disharmony … (Hegel, 1948, p 240)

The morally full life of the Beautiful Soul is, however, not an easy one. To maintain a loving heart in the face of the conventional existence of one's people is to invite isolation and run the risk of worse. The crucifixion of Jesus, the quintessential Beautiful Soul, illustrates what may happen, yet his was a noble fate consistent with the best that human being can be. Contrast this view of the Beautiful Soul with Hegel's depiction only eight years later, in his *Phenomenology*:

> It lives in dread of besmirching the splendour of its inner being by action and an existence; and, in order to preserve the purity of its heart, it flees from contact with the actual world, and persists in its self-willed impotence to renounce its self which is reduced to the extreme of ultimate abstraction … In this transparent purity of its moments, an unhappy, so-called 'beautiful soul', its light dies away within it, and it vanishes like a shapeless vapour that dissolves into thin air. (Hegel, 1977, p 400)

In various places in this later work, Hegel describes the Beautiful Soul as 'empty', 'hollow', 'evaporated', 'mad', 'impotent' and 'consumptive'. With all the charm modern life can muster, this figure would now be described as a 'loser' who needs to 'get a life'. The moral purity of the earlier vision has been exchanged for a vainglorious purism that fails to involve itself with the world, and is therefore the subject only of pity and scorn. At one level, this is simply intriguing: why should Hegel in so short a period of time have changed his view so radically? Why 'kill' the Beautiful Soul? The answer to that question must await the final section of this chapter and, of course, the final chapter itself. My suggestion in brief, however, is that its significance is in equal parts historical, ethical and legal. Historically, Hegel wanted to contain and control a radical ethical impulse which modernity and its historical experience of revolution had set before humankind. The early view of the Beautiful Soul reflects that impulse, the later shows its containment. Ethically too, this process of containment was one in which law was to be set at the core of an evolving moral totality, whereas previously, Hegel had seen law as the site of only limited virtues, opposed to the radical impulse. To kill the Beautiful Soul was in effect to give life to the moral-legal subject – and a world replete with antinomies. A figure with both historical and ethical resonance, as well as legal reference, I shall argue that the rise and fall of the Beautiful Soul can be seen as a key to understanding the relationship between history and ethics in critical legal theory. That, however, is for later. For the present, I turn to the key issue of law's antinomial form.

For critique: from law's antinomies to history … and ethics

Throughout this collection, the antinomial character of law is traced to its historical roots in a particular kind of society. Yet the essays are also ethical in the way they contrast legal forms of justice with moral forms of judgment that lie beyond the law. This raises a theoretical question about how a critical approach handles these different dimensions. In this section, I sketch the essays and outline the emergence of this theoretical question.

These essays seek to develop a critical understanding of law. They seek to explain the structural limits involved in legal conceptions of justice. They do so by developing an understanding of what such conceptions represent and what they exclude. Legal justice takes place on a particular terrain, it develops its own 'architectonic', but what this represses is as important as what it represents. Law's conception of justice involves a process of forced abstraction, and this leads it to separate out questions of justice that cannot in truth be separated. The result is a set of false, one-sided, oppositions, and this is felt throughout law's categories as a series of antinomies. The separation producing these antinomies is not a matter of simple intellectual invention. It is social and historical in its origin and it can be traced to the beginnings of modern law in the Enlightenment and the early 19th century.

The chapters are assembled in three sections, reflecting a developing perspective in which law's antinomies are first located in Part 1 as part of a historical structure. Part 2 applies this historical-structural perspective to questions of justice and responsibility. These chapters consider how the historical structuring of law limits the justice it offers, and they reflect on how this affects the experience of justice for those coming before the law. They therefore raise an ethical dimension. The chapters in Part 3 begin to address some of the broader theoretical issues raised by a critical approach, which must find room for both ethical evaluation and historical perspective. While these are raised in the earlier chapters, the final chapters seek to address them in depth and more satisfactorily.

Legal antinomies in history

The two essays in Part 1 identify the problem, as their titles indicate, of antinomies in Western legal thinking. Chapter 2 considers the evolution of legal theory from the Enlightenment to the present, considering the relationship between natural law, legal positivism and a sociological approach to law. It charts a contradictory development in which approaches affirming one-sided views of law compete with each other. To this permanently contradictory, one-sided oppositionalism in legal theory, it gives the name 'antinomialism'. Chapter 3 then examines a particular antinomy central to law, that between the 'formal' and the 'informal' in the context of thinking about the opposition between 'popular' and 'legal' justice. Together, these chapters develop a sense of antinomy as central to law, and they relate this to the historical development of Western societies, and the underlying social relations which condition and shape law in a particular, contradictory way. They begin to develop a dialectical approach to the relation between law and society in which the idea of law's autonomy is seen as both a false and necessary denial of its inherent relationality. Together, they point to the historical structuring of legal form in a particular, antinomial way.

Justice and judgment

The four essays in Part 2 examine a set of issues relating to legal conceptions of justice, responsibility and judgment in light of the historical antinomialism of western liberal legal thought. Whilst their aim is to consider the theoretical structure of law in this area, each discussion is informed by the use of examples taken from legal doctrine or practice. Chapter 4 considers the 1993 trial and conviction of two boys in England for the murder of James Bulger, and relates this to the particular 'architectonic' of justice developed through legal categories. An antinomy between legal justice and moral judgment emerges as a result of the law's abstract individualism and is used as a way of understanding the limits and conflicts of liberal law. Chapter 5 considers more broadly the idea of liberal law delivering justice through what I call the 'penal equation', that 'crime plus responsibility equals punishment'. It considers the historical prioritising of the legal form of justice, before moving on to examine how law, despite its failings, provides a limited and ambivalent experience of justice. Chapter 6 pursues this latter theme of the experience of justice by examining the idea of guilt in modern societies, and considers the limits of any conception of individual guilt that rests upon a liberal model of responsibility. The focus is Gitta Sereny's moral interrogation of Albert Speer which, relying on such a model, fails to catch the sense of moral judgment Speer's actions invoke. Underlying the discussion here is an antinomy between 'the individual' and 'the community' and guilt is argued to occupy an ambiguous space between these options. Chapter 7 considers the 'logic of legal reasoning', where the categories of liberal legality are based upon antinomial forms. Here, two further antinomies of law are examined; those of 'form' and 'substance', and the 'universal' and the 'particular'. Underlying both is the antinomy between individual and social justice, an antinomy which also bears upon the discussions of Chapters 3 and 4. The attempt to deal with this antinomial conceptual terrain in Chapter 7 invokes a dialectic of legal reasoning in place of the standard analytical format, a 'dialectic of the universalised particular and the reparticularised universal'.

As can be seen, the essays in the first two parts of the collection are organised around the theme of antinomy within law and legal theory, but they raise a deeper question. Throughout, the injunction is to 'look to history' to locate and explain the existence of law's antinomies. At the same time, these essays indicate an ethical purpose. Chapter 3 looks to the role of movements of national and social liberation in reshaping legal form. Chapter 4 contrasts legal and moral judgment, and considers the limits of law's own particular 'morality of form'. Chapter 5 looks to the social and historical emergence of new forms of moral critique, while Chapter 6 considers how morally to judge an old war criminal like Speer. Chapter 7 shows law reaching beyond its own terms in a necessary, but necessarily failing, attempt to do a better justice. In looking to history, these essays also draw upon an ethical position. They therefore raise important questions about the relationship between law, ethics and history in critical thinking. Is our critique grounded in a move to historical issues, or does it rest upon ethical foundations? Can it be both?

Law, history and ethics: the nature of critique

The essays in Part 3 consider this issue. They examine how philosophers who have recognised the importance of antinomy (not necessarily by that name) have treated it. They think about how law in its Western liberal form fits within a broader philosophical context. The philosophers discussed in this part are predominantly in the modern dialectical tradition inaugurated by Hegel (see Chapters 8 and 10), but Hegel's particular contribution to that tradition is read alongside that of Adorno (Chapter 9) and Bhaskar (Chapter 8). These three dialecticians are also brought into dialogue with the deconstructionist Derrida, who, I argue, is himself to be located within the dialectical tradition (Chapter 8). The overall aim is to think about the conflict in critical legal theory between historical and ethical approaches. More specifically, how can questions of ethics, often treated as metaphysical, supra-historical questions, be brought together with a socio-historical analysis, which often denies the significance of a metaphysical approach? The nature of the conflict between these two approaches is addressed in discussion of dialectical and deconstructive theory. Before moving on, let us identify this conflict between a metaphysical-ethical and a socio-historical critique more directly.

History versus ethics in critical legal theory

The conflict between a socio-historical and a metaphysical-ethical critique of law can be seen in Derrida's essay 'Force of law' (Derrida, 1990), which I discuss at some length in Chapter 8 below. In that chapter, Derrida describes a 'critique of law' that is 'possible and always useful'. This is 'a critique of juridical ideology, a desedimentation of the superstructures of law that both hide and reflect the economic and political interests of the dominant forms of society' (Derrida, 1990, p 941). With these comments, Derrida is discussing what I call here a socio-historical critique of law, one that relates law to underlying historical interests and structures of power. For Derrida, this is a 'possible and always useful' way of proceeding, but it is not actually what he himself does. For him, there is a deeper critique to be developed, of what he calls a 'more intrinsic structure'. This involves the 'very emergence of justice and law' in a 'performative and therefore interpretive violence' (1990, p 941).

This second critique is metaphysical and ethical rather than socio-historical in its form. It links up with what Derrida has to say about deconstruction as a form of justice that is 'mad' and 'mystical', which points beyond 'what is' to a 'messianic' ethics of 'the other'. It participates in this way in an abstract metaphysics of justice, despite Derrida's own disclaimer to the contrary.[1] So doing, this deeper critique of law and legal justice, drawing on an ethical-metaphysical argument, is developed without reference to the idea of socio-historical critique. Although Derrida says that deconstruction operates in part by looking historically at the genealogies of concepts, he does not relate deconstruction as an ethical project to the 'possible or useful' socio-historical project he also identifies. Thus, the socio-historical critique is marginalised by the deconstructive (metaphysical-ethical) approach which comes after it.

How should the socio-historical critique react to this? A first response would be to adopt an oppositional standpoint. If deconstruction argues for a metaphysical ethics that marginalises socio-historical critique, the latter should reject the need for a metaphysical ethics within a socio-historical approach. This is in fact the position enunciated in Chapter 5 below, although it is one that the later chapters will confront and modify. In that chapter, I suggest that ethical standpoints emerge

---

1 While Derrida (1999, 245–49) refuses the term 'metaphysics', what he invokes as lying beyond the 'here and now' operates on a level that can never be actualised. As the never-to-be-actualised addition to what exists, it operates as a metaphysics of justice.

historically in society, and these give a critical purchase on legal concepts. There is no need, I argue, for:

> an abstract, ethical 'beyond'. There is no metaphysical 'other', rather there is real emergent history and developing social structure, and these generate actual difference, conflict, change, sometimes crisis … New perspectives and critical standpoints, new ways of looking at old phenomena, including the phenomena of law and justice, are produced in this process of emerging change and difference. (Below, p 80)

This conflict between two approaches to critique underlies these chapters, as I think it underlies much critical debate about law today. If these essays make a general contribution to the critique of law, it is in that they seek a way of moving beyond this opposition. The emergence, the recognition, and the attempt to deal with it represents a theme running through the collection. In Chapter 2, metaphysical-ethical and socio-historical approaches are counterposed. In Chapter 5, their opposition is made explicit, and supported by arguing for the irrelevance of a metaphysical-ethical standpoint. Chapter 8 is a first effort at rapprochement, but it ends up leaving the opposition in place. Chapters 9 and 10 in different ways then look for a way of bringing the terms of the opposition into a satisfactory relationship with each other. Thus, as the chapters move on, a more reconciliatory approach is adopted in which the socio-historical and the metaphysical-ethical are seen as part of a single critical project. Before we address this development further, however, it will be helpful to examine how the argument of these essays came together in the first place.

Social history and legal antinomy

Written from the early 1990s, the perspective in these essays was formed in the previous decade out of the different critical currents of that time. These included the sociological movement in law, critical legal studies, the philosophy of critical realism, and deconstruction. These led to an interest in four different but converging perspectives: law as socio-historical form, the contradictions of law, the need for a 'depth ontology' of law, and the relationship between law and ethics. The first two, historical form analysis and legal contradiction, are discussed in this section. They were instrumental in establishing the foundations of my approach, and they lead, through discussion of the idea of 'antinomy', to the second two, depth ontology and the relation between law and ethics. These are discussed in the following section as the philosophical perspectives which bring out the conflict between the historical and the metaphysical-ethical approaches described above.

Law as socio-historical form

My initial interest in the area of law and social theory was in the way that law was rooted in, and shaped by, its social context. The key to understanding Western law, it seemed to me, was to relate it to the underlying social relations in which it was embedded. This pointed to the importance of an historical perspective on law and, in the period in which I was developing, an older literature around this point was being rediscovered. EB Pashukanis (1978) had written a short book on the historical nature of legal form and its relation to political economy (Norrie, 1982), and Franz Neumann, a scion of the Frankfurt School, had made similar points in a significant chapter on the relation between law's form and historical function (Neumann, 1957). In this period, Neumann's doctoral thesis from the 1930s was also published in English (Neumann, 1986).

These writers developed a perspective which involved the claim that, in thinking about law, one would not take the law's own word on how it developed or should be understood. It was important to travel beyond law in order to relate it to social processes that were, according to orthodox legal theory, other than it, but which were in fact crucial in creating it. The value of this work was that it took orthodoxy head on. It was serious in its interest in questions that were generally seen as the province of orthodox jurisprudence. Questions about core legal concepts such as 'right', 'duty' and the 'subject' were of no real interest to the contemporary sociology of law. Pashukanis, in contrast, begins his book with a sharp critique of Kelsen and neo-Kantian legal scholarship and also an attack on forms of sociological jurisprudence which 'forgo an analysis of the fundamental juridical concepts' (1978, p 55) and 'exclude the legal form as such from their field of observation' (1978, p 53).

The challenge that resulted from this perspective was to see what one could do with it in specific areas of law. Could the criminal law, for example, be made to yield its deepest secrets to an historical perspective given that its core concepts, based seemingly on ahistorical, universal ideas, denied its relevance? Chapters 3–5 and 7 provide an answer, but the book as a whole seeks more generally to treat law as a socio-historical form.

Contradictions in law: the nature of 'antinomy'

In paying specific attention to legal form, however, how would a socio-historical approach orient itself? Here, one further quote from Pashukanis is relevant. Law, he said 'exists only in antitheses: objective law – subjective law; public law – private law, and so on' (1978, p 58). Such a statement, bold and brief, provided a starting point for thinking about law socio-historically, and for focusing on 'antitheses' as law's specific form of being.

This focus was also encouraged by another, more modern influence. The 'Critical Legal Studies Movement' in the US proved a fairly transient phenomenon. It lacked a sufficiently clear or deep sense of what a 'critique' of law should entail. In an important article about rationality in the criminal law, Mark Kelman (1981) once taunted orthodox scholarship that it had not got very far with its understanding of law. The comment seemed also to say something about critical legal studies, which tended simply to invert and negate orthodox positions. Nonetheless, it was prepared to look seriously at law and orthodox legal argument and to have the boldness to take such argument in a radically different direction. Where orthodoxy sought to rationalise law, to develop a sense of its intellectual coherence, to establish the 'internal' perspective upon law, it went the other way. It sought to show the contradictions within law and to show that much legal argument was an attempt to hide law's contradictory impulses. To a classical European line of argument, it contributed a more pragmatic-critical North American 'realism' as to how doctrine should be interrogated.

Two routes, then, into the idea of legal contradiction, but I have chosen the term 'antinomy'. What is the particular significance of this term? In Chapter 3, I give a definition from the modern philosopher Quine as a 'self-contradiction by accepted ways of reasoning [which] establishes that some tacit and trusted pattern of reasoning must be made explicit and henceforward be avoided or revised' (below, p 33). This is a start, but it is not enough, for any defender of analytic logic will argue that self-contradiction should be 'avoided or revised'. Quine added something more when he said that such revision would involve 'nothing less than a repudiation of part of our conceptual heritage' and this perhaps suggests the idea that antinomy is deep seated in the Western psyche and practices. Certainly, discussion of antinomy is engrained in the Western philosophical tradition, and it is there that I locate its significance.

Antinomy has its modern classical origin in Kant, for whom self-contradiction was inherent in human reason as the sign that such reason was going beyond its proper bounds. Hegel generalised the point to make antinomialism a feature of both subjective thought and objective being. The aim of reason was to demonstrate how, working through, preserving and transcending contradictions, antinomies could be unified in a dialectical totality that was modern living. In the Marxist tradition, this idea was given further force by Lukacs (1971), who argued that antinomial structures in philosophy reflected historical ways of living in Western society. Antinomies were the product of a particular, reified form of life: structures in the mind reflected the particular lived experience of modern capitalism. These different philosophical approaches converge on the deep-seated and structural nature of antinomy in western thought.

Antinomy in these essays carries the weight of this kind of implication: contradictions are inherent in Western ways of thinking and acting in a structural and historical way. They are not lightly or easily overcome because they reflect something of our overall state of being. Western law, as a primary form for the mediation of such overall being, is an integral part of this way of living and is therefore expressed antinomially.

In addition to this sense of the historical and structural significance of antinomy, something also should be said about its philosophical implication. There is a strong sense in the term that the two sides of an antinomy are both necessitated, and rendered inadequate, by the context in which the antinomy emerges. The one-sidedness of argument 'a' leads to the development of oppositional argument 'not-a', so that both reflect something of the underlying truth to be conveyed through the argument. Neither, however, is adequate by itself, and they are in contradiction with each other. Nor will a simple aggregation of 'a' and 'not-a' lead to a full sense of the issue at stake, for bringing together two one-sided, contradictory, views by no means guarantees a sense of the whole. Deploying the term antinomy thus brings a sense of partiality and one-sidedness in relation to an argument, an issue, or a phenomenon under discussion. It is not that what is represented in the terms of the antinomy is completely wrong, rather that it is stated incompletely in a rather radical way so that it invokes a further attempt at completion. This further attempt, however, proves to be in contradiction with the first, and this leads to an argumentative to and fro as first one side and then the other presses its claim. This back and forth only confirms that neither side of the argument really or fully captures what is at stake.

This describes something of the nature of antinomy, and how it might operate in modern legal thinking. The to and fro of legal argument is described below in Chapters 2–4, 5 and 7. The existence of antinomy, however, also raises further questions about the nature of critique. Having described something of the underlying theoretical trajectory, we are now in a position to link it to the problem of conflicting historical and ethical approaches to critique raised in the first section, and to see how this problem comes into play in these essays.

From legal antinomy to the conflicting grounds of critique

We can address the problem of diverging critiques of law first as it emerged historically out of the experience of an antinomial world. If neither side of an antinomy is able to achieve a sense of a whole, and nor is their aggregation, how is the whole, which is presupposed by the very notion of one-sidedness, to be approached or identified? Once we start talking in this way, we are led beyond the bare identification of one-sidedness to what it relates to. The idea of antinomy presupposes something beyond itself, expressed in it in a limited, one-sided way. How do we get at this relation between the terms of an antinomy and what lies beyond them? Most famously, the problem of what is expressed in a one-sided, contradictory way is what drove Hegel to dialectical philosophy. The sense that neither 'a' nor 'not-a' is adequate to the whole led him to the process of 'sublation' in his philosophy. In this, contradiction was noted, preserved and transcended in a move to higher levels within a greater ethical and rational totality (see below, Chapter 8). Dialectic was the sense of being driven beyond antinomy to a greater truth at a higher level of understanding and being. One-sidedness led to a sense of wholeness or totality, but what was the nature of that totality?

For Hegel, a rational and ethical whole was the end-point of dialectical philosophy. Philosophers after Hegel, however, found it difficult to accept that one could resolve the contradictions of modernity by theorising an ethical totality as he had done. As Chapter 2 indicates, dissatisfaction with Hegel went in two directions. One went into the socio-historical contexts and conditions establishing the antinomies of modernity. Where Hegel argued that conflicts in modernity could be resolved by a work of metaphysical-ethical reasoning, a socio-historical approach suggested they could not be so resolved, but that they could at least be located and explained on a broader and different, historical, terrain. The other pursued the ethics implicit in the idea of a rational totality, but refused to accept Hegel's view that reason should resolve antinomy. It resorted instead to a philosophical irrationalism such as that deployed by Nietzsche. Such philosophies refused the possibility of resolution or sublation, but maintained an essentially metaphysical-ethical approach to the problem. Thus was the conflict born between two approaches to critique: out of the identification of antinomy at the core of modern society and the failure of a metaphysical-ethical approach to resolve it dialectically. The opposition is observed in these chapters between two modern philosophical positions which prioritise either the socio-historical or the metaphysical-ethical standpoint: critical realism and deconstruction. I turn now to discuss these.

Grounding the socio-historical: a 'depth ontology' of law

If antinomy lies at the heart of law, pushing in one direction to the socio-historical as its basis, a philosophy is required that can explain this. The philosophy I find most able to do this is critical realism with its emphasis on the idea of a 'depth ontology'. This idea explains the ways in which social phenomena are grounded in underlying processes, structures and conditions. Critical realism also has a developed dialectical form (dialectical critical realism) which is well-suited to deal with the contradictory, antinomial quality of law while retaining a focus on its socio-historical grounding. Here, I will say something about the idea of a depth ontology and dialectical critical realism.

The idea of social depth or a depth ontology (see below, Chapter 9 for the fullest statement of this idea) is in part just the philosophical expression of the general idea that in understanding a phenomenon such as law, we need to move beyond it, to the social structures and relations which underpin it, and which it mediates. Legal forms appear as the surface phenomena which are explained by underlying social relations. For example, the form of the individual legal subject, which is discussed in several chapters here, could be seen as simply the expression of the biological singularity of the individual human agent. It is just a fact that humans are (in the vast majority of cases) born into the world as single, bounded persons with an individual consciousness, and legal concepts reflect this. However, whatever their biological make-up, individuals are also constituted by underlying social relations that assist them in creating their identity, language and being. They always exist in this broader context so that the emphasis on the individual subject begins to look one-sided. Historically, too, the emphasis on the individual subject needs to be addressed as it emerged in the early 19th century as a way of achieving and legitimating a particular system of rule. More sense is made of legal individualism in the light of these underlying issues of human relationality and historical development. The philosophical method is to look behind the legal individual to the social relations, often hidden from our immediate experience, which engender it. To view a phenomenon in history, to account for it in terms of deeper social relations, is to operate with an idea of what underlies, causes or conditions it, and gives it presence. Recognising such processes involves commitment to a depth ontology.

This is a fairly straightforward idea, but it is sometimes lost sight of by those who adopt a certain kind of criticism. This is the argument that such an ontology draws too strong a contrast between the 'appearances' of a phenomenon and an 'underlying reality', where the latter expresses what the phenomenon is 'really' about in contrast to its 'mere' appearance. The phenomenon becomes simply an adjunct to a deeper movement or truth. It is, of course, possible to argue for this kind of relation between 'appearance' and 'reality', but it would normally be wrong to do so.[2] The relationship between phenomena and their underlying conditions is one of complex co-relation and constitution, not one-sided determination. It is also a bowdlerisation of the critical realist argument. Consider the possibility of choosing between two rival explanations as to why a phenomenon exists. When one tries to explain why or how something happened, one account may be better able to

---

2　An example of where it would be appropriate would be where a person deliberately misrepresents a situation or lies about it.

explain it by reference to the underlying causes and conditions which brought it about. Identifying such causes and relating them to what is happening involves a process of exploring the depth of phenomena, not substituting a 'real' movement for them. A critical realist depth ontology asserts that both how things appear to agents and the underlying causes and conditions which make them possible are crucial to understanding. That there is ontological depth in the social world is an injunction to take history and structure seriously as real, underlying elements in our understanding of things, not to substitute those elements for the thing that is to be explained.

On this basis, critical realism has also developed a dialectical approach. This involves an insistence that, if we are looking at antinomies, we ought to see these as not just a product of the mind, but of a specifically shaped historical world. As Roy Bhaskar puts it, it is important 'to understand that when logical contradictions are committed, they are real constituents of the *Lebenswelt*' (1993, p 58). Dialectic is a supple way of thinking which forces one to think about the further implications of any statement. It constantly presses against the barriers raised by analytical thinking to ask what lies beyond them. It is present in these chapters in different ways. One is in considering the limits of legal concepts and how they lead beyond themselves to their opposites. A particular view of a legal concept (intention, recklessness or provocation, see Chapters 4, 5 and 7), or of a school of thought (eg, orthodox subjectivism, see Chapters 4 and 7) proves inadequate. This invokes a correction which, it transpires, is in contradiction to it. Another is in seeing how law establishes itself as law by erecting a boundary between itself and things 'outside' it. However, those matters that are within law are unconvincingly shielded from those that are not: for example, the positive from the moral law (Chapter 2), legal formalism from the informal (Chapter 3), legal from social justice (Chapter 7) and the internal from the external (Chapter 10). Dialectics proposes the intrinsic connectedness of things that appear to be separate and distinct, and that therefore challenges formal-logical ways of thinking.

Dialectical arguments of this kind can be handled while relating law to the socio-historical on the basis of a depth ontology that asks us to look beyond law to its conditions of existence. They make for a more subtle and complete understanding of how surface and depth fit together. This however still leaves open the question how this socio-historical approach deals with the question of ethics. How do we ground our ethical concerns within an historical approach? As I argue in Chapter 8 below, it is unclear that dialectical critical realism has as yet a satisfactory answer to this question. While I will not provide a full one here, I will at least seek to indicate what kind of answer might be given. To do so, I must turn to the fourth influence on these essays, Derrida's account of deconstruction.

Deconstruction and law: placing ethics

Unlike the first three influences on my thinking – form analysis, critical legal studies and (dialectical) critical realism – my response to deconstruction has been more ambivalent. It operates as an underlying, often uncomfortable engagement in these chapters, and one that has evolved through their course. I shall begin by explaining the grounds of my ambivalence, and then say how my view has changed.

Despite his marginalisation of the socio-historical critique of law (discussed above, and below in detail, Chapter 8), my reaction to Derrida has never been completely negative. I have always valued his insistence on the need to deconstruct law, meaning the need to chart its 'logico-formal paradoxes' (Derrida, 1990, p 959), and to trace these back to its 'aporias'. The concept of an aporia seems quite closely related to the idea of antinomy. An aporia is a 'perplexing difficulty' or a 'doubtful matter', coming from the Greek 'without passage'. It has something in common with antinomy which, from the Greek, means 'against the law'. Aporia is perhaps a vaguer term, more used in rhetoric, and without the baggage of antinomy. It seems to represent Derrida's notion of a matter being 'undecidable'. In both aporia and antinomy, there is a sense of blockage, for every contradiction by its nature indicates a lack of passage. Whatever their precise relationship, Derrida's aporias of law are all versions of what I call the antinomy between the universal and the particular (see below, Chapter 7). Since they are linked to the search for 'logico-formal paradox', there is significant overlap between the terms. Deconstruction wants to read legal language for its difficulties and contradictions, just as I do. In the intellectual context of the legal academy, where making rational sense of law is the rule, deconstruction offers support to anyone who pursues an alternative line. I have always valued this aspect.

Nonetheless, I have also written against the idea of deconstruction as a general philosophical basis for critique. In Chapter 2, I argue for the importance of deconstruction as a critical tool, while suggesting that its reliance on an abstract metaphysical-ethical foundation leads to an unbalanced approach to critique which is either over-critical (too negative), or under-critical (too positive) in that it reinstates law in its present liberal forms. The move to a 'mad' justice beyond law either leads to a nihilism of law, or, in its more 'constructive' moments, to law's re-accreditation. I have therefore argued for a separation of deconstruction's 'method' of looking at law from its underlying philosophy. This certainly takes me outside the Derridean camp, for it is clear that deconstruction is more than just a 'method' for reading texts. It is deconstruction as 'mad', 'mystical', 'messianic' justice that I have tended to avoid. However, it is just this element in deconstruction that I now believe needs to be addressed if the ethical dimension in my argument is to be understood alongside the socio-historical perspective that has always been present. How, then, can we elaborate this ethical dimension without either evading the socio-historical, or collapsing it into it?

Derrida writes of an ethical position that informs law without being fully instantiated in it; of an ethics which lies beyond law but constantly disturbs its presence. He writes of a 'universal structure of experience … of the most irreducibly heterogeneous otherness' (Derrida, 1999, p 249). This sense of a philosophical moment of absence-presence, I argue in Chapter 8, represents a moment of ideal 'unreason' (the 'mad', the 'mystical') in his thought to set against Hegel's conception of ideal reason. Both operate as further moments beyond the antinomies (aporias) of the present, and both are related back to them. Derrida, of course, refuses the reconciliation claimed by Hegel, but he remains a powerful modern thinker in the tradition of dialectics, and of Hegel. In terms of the split in critical thinking begun after the rejection of Hegelian dialectics, Derrida is one of those who decidedly followed the Hegelian pattern of linking the metaphysical-ethical to the world, while refusing the soothing resolution that reason would bring. He brings an ethical irrationalism to bear on the antinomial workings of the world and its law.

How does this relate to the socio-historical? In boldly stating an ethical ideal that is always still to come, Derrida makes a strong case for a metaphysics of the absent within the present, produced by an originary act of cutting that he calls an 'interpretive violence' (Derrida, 1990, p 941). At first sight, this seems no more than an evasion of the socio-historical, and it does, I argue, play that role. However, there is another way of looking at this resort to metaphysics, as itself an element in the socio-historical. Certainly, as an argument, it has its own historical presence. Derrida's metaphysics operate powerfully within his philosophy and they resonate with many people today. They occupy their own place in the world, and they must be understood as so doing. The question is therefore raised how they might be given credence and validity in the kind of socio-historical approach I see as central to critique. Can the 'mad', 'mystical' moment be relocated in a way that does not repudiate a socio-historical approach, but rather becomes a significant, irreducible, part of it?

The answer to which the final chapters in this collection push is to say that Derrida's way of stating the ethical dimension in legal thought needs to be recast as the metaphysical moment associated with a specifically developed historical setting. The metaphysical-ethical dimension in modern philosophical thinking about law exists as a misplaced, but nonetheless historically and ethically valid, expression of the moral character of modernity and its law. We live in a socio-historical world which produces a highly limited ethics of the present alongside, as its displaced complement, a necessarily utopian and other-worldly ethics of the future. What Derrida presents as an abstract metaphysics of what is still 'to come' is in fact a necessarily vague and inchoate indication of what *could* come under different social and historical conditions.[3] One deep antinomy of the modern world is that between the metaphysically 'ideal' and the socially 'actual', and this is not because the ideal is by definition a metaphysical abstraction, but because modern liberal society is founded on a split which produces it in that form. Such a split is represented philosophically by Derrida as the metaphysical gap between deconstruction's justice and the justice of the here and now, in their opposition and relation. Historically, it was represented at the dawn of modernity by the rise and fall of the figure of the Beautiful Soul in Hegel's philosophy. That figure, I shall argue, inaugurated a typically modern forcing of humankind's ethical possibilities into a metaphysical realm disconnected from the presently possible.

---

3 Derrida's response (1994, 1999) to this is to turn the tables. Instead of seeing metaphysics as the placeholder for a particular historical relation, history, he says, is the placeholder for a subterranean metaphysics. While it is correct to say that interpretations of history may involve this kind of operation, it is surely not necessarily the case that this be so. If we observe the development of social forms such as law over historical time, recognise determinate changes in those forms in different periods, relate these changes to underlying social relations or emerging social structures, are our interpretations driven or structured by a particular metaphysical project? From a critical realist standpoint, the idea of a depth ontology accesses real developments in time and space. Interpretation is always part of historical research, but history is not reducible to it, thereby forming the basis for a secret metaphysics of the interpreted world.

Law, history, ethics: towards the Beautiful Soul

The final two essays in the collection seek in different milieux to combine a metaphysical sense of the ethical inside and outside the law with a sense of its specific socio-historicity. Chapter 9 considers the place of a metaphysical ethics with regard to law in Adorno's *Negative Dialectics*, and argues that his account of ethics is better read as involving a specifically historical yet real and emergent impulse underlying, but also repressed by, modern law. Chapter 10 considers the Beautiful Soul in Hegel's early and mature philosophy. It argues that this figure assumes an ideal metaphysical form for Hegel because modern social institutions like those of private property and law cannot sustain or actualise its radical moral implications. However, such implications were themselves historically emergent within Western societies as a result of the 18th century experience of social revolution. As revolutionary possibility was snuffed out by property and law, so did the Beautiful Soul retreat from being a harbinger of present possibility to become, first, its tragic victim and, then, its pathetic outcast. The moral possibilities associated with it therefore had nowhere to go but into the realm of the metaphysical. In both Adorno and the young Hegel, an historically emergent promise of freedom underlies the forms of liberal legality, yet is stifled, repressed and contained by it. Forced in the socio-historical present to be a shadow of what it could otherwise be, it assumes the ideal, metaphysical form of a promise of something that is always still, as Derrida has it, 'to come'.

In *Negative Dialectics*, Adorno adopts an ambivalent attitude to modern juridical freedom. In the main, he sees it as a form of repression, a means of containing human being within forms that rigidly control it. However, he also sees in such law the possibility of a limited, formal freedom. Underlying this ambivalent (antinomial) vision of law, Adorno glimpses a conception of free humanity, which he refers to in metaphysical terms as an 'archaic' or 'untamed impulse', a 'jolt' of freedom, or even a 'flash of light between the poles of something long past'. This protean, ahistorical vision underpins modern law with a sense of human freedom existing before time or sociality. This metaphysic of freedom is however accompanied by an historical view of how the emergence of modern society produces genuine moments of freedom that are encased within and limited by a general environment of unfreedom. For example, Adorno says Hamlet's early modern existential choice, 'to be or not to be', represents a real historical advance in the cause of freedom. However, at the same time, one can add, it is a tragic choice that only delivers Hamlet up to a fate he cannot control. Modern freedom expresses an underlying sense of what it means to be free, but this is glimpsed 'through a glass darkly', inchoately, in a world characterised by unfreedom.

My suggestion in Chapter 9 is that Adorno's different and conflicting views of freedom can best be understood if one adopts a view of freedom as historically emergent rather than the ahistorical, metaphysical view he also deploys. The latter sense of an 'archaic' impulse to freedom can be seen to represent nothing other than the metaphysicalisation of an historically emergent moment. As such, it operates as a place marker for what lies implicit, but cannot be brought out, within the present. It is a way of idealising and falsely universalising a specific socio-historical development, the limits of which we need to interrogate. The difficulty with Adorno's negative dialectics is that, in their own way, they conflate the socio-historical and metaphysical-ethical directions in modern critical theory, and this is seen in the conflicting (historical/ahistorical) origins of his impulse to freedom.[4]

The idea is of an historically emergent freedom, repressed and constrained by modern law, and consequently passing into the form of a metaphysical ethics beyond the here and now. From Adorno, we move in the final chapter to Hegel and his account of the Beautiful Soul. In his early theological writings, Hegel admired this figure for its uncompromising assertion of a morality of love and non-alienated being. As his philosophy developed through the *Phenomenology* to the *Philosophy of Right*, he came to dismiss it as a 'sad loser' who refuses to take its place in the world. The backdrop to this change in attitude was Hegel's acceptance of modern forms of private property and law which institutionalised separation and alienation in the world. To accept these forms was to reject a morality of the Beautiful Soul, as Hegel came decisively, and cruelly, to do. So doing, he represents its radical morality as, first, an 'ideal' operating in conflict with the 'actual' world, and he then proceeds to idealise the actual (modern) world by making it the home of reason and ethics. These moves are only possible if the Beautiful Soul is banished to oblivion, yet it can never be forgotten since its image remains as the repressed other of modern institutions and life.

If the loser in Hegel's evolving philosophy was the Beautiful Soul, the primary winner was an image of individual moral consciousness not unlike the modern-classical model of the legal subject. Hegel defends an individual in his *Phenomenology* who takes its moral place in society by virtue of its formal capacity to will its ends, rather than because those ends have a specific moral content. The gap between this figure and modern legal personality is not so wide, so that legal subjectivity with its particular legal-moral duties comes to stand where once there was the radical ethical figure of the Beautiful Soul. However, I argue, that figure was never completely erased from the scene so that it remains as an ideal 'other' to legal subjectivity, present and absent within it, and producing antinomies wherever it goes. Legal arguments, based upon the capacities of the legal subject, push one way and then the other as they strive for a moral content they cannot reach.

Law's antinomial forms represent a socio-historically produced, limited and partial, morality which invokes broader moral conceptions beyond itself. These forms seek out a morality they cannot express, but which is glimpsed at the core of what they are. That fuller possibility was represented, and then repressed, by Hegel as the figure of the Beautiful Soul. The ethical move beyond the law is towards such a figure, though the journey remains necessarily incomplete. While it may be represented in metaphysical terms, this is only because metaphysics is the philosophical language in which interrupted historical possibility expresses itself. Balanced between ethics and history, law indexes how far morally humanity has come, and how far it still has to go. Antinomy becomes liberal law's sign, socio-history its context and condition, ethics its force and impossible goal.

---

4 The opening line of *Negative Dialectics* argues for a socio-historical approach: 'Philosophy, which once seemed obsolete, lives on because the moment to realise it was missed' (Adorno, 1973, p 3). In Chapter 9, I argue that he does not sustain it in a work caught between conflicting idealist and realist standpoints.

Part I
Legal Antinomies in History

...mbols must always express the life within us with absolute precision; ...ey do otherwise, since that life has generated them? Therefore we must not bla... poor symbols if they take forms that seem trivial to us, or absurd, for ... the natur... of our life alone has determined their forms. A critique of these symbols is a critique of our lives. (Carter, 1977, p 6)

[P]hilosophical thinking, if pursued far enough, turns into historical thinking, and the understanding of abstract thought ultimately resolves itself back into an awareness of the content of that thought, which is to say, of the basic historical situation in which it took place. (Jameson, 1971, p 345)

Introduction

There can rarely have been so much diversity in legal theory as there is at the present time. The 1980s saw a blossoming of novel approaches to the subject in a way that was quite unanticipated, and which has added much to what has not always been a rich tapestry. But this development brings with it a number of questions: what accounts for it? What is its nature? What are its strengths and weaknesses? What overall assessment does it merit with regard to its ability to explain, illuminate or contextualise the nature of law?

In sketching a framework in which to locate these questions, I shall treat this phenomenon of theoretical regeneration as both an intellectual and a social issue, claiming that these two aspects are inseparably intertwined to provide the theoretical developments of the last ten years. On the one hand, the movements of legal theory respond to the inner logic of earlier positions within the field. Theory orients itself, or rather is oriented, within an already established set of intellectual practices and paradigms, which it works to repeat or change. Theory responds to what already exists, revealing, with the benefit of hindsight, an inherent logic, whether of continuity or discontinuity. In one sense, the production of theory, as described, is already a social process, for it occurs within a tradition provided by a community of intellectuals (Bhaskar, 1979, Chapter 1; Outhwaite, 1978, Chapters 1 and 2; Bourdieu, 1988). However, there is also a broader sense in which the intellectual is social, for the production of ideas occurs within given socio-economic conditions, at two different but connected levels.

At the most fundamental level, the basic ideas of a tradition are historical products emerging out of a particular social period or epoch. Thus, the idea of abstract individual freedom as the apogee of human history in 18th century Europe was only possible in a world in which, as Hegel (1952; 1956: pp 438–57) put it, the principle of human subjectivity had been realised, and this could only occur because of the breakdown of feudalism and the emergence of bourgeois civil society. Different societies – the muslim world, the world of the state socialist societies – generate different basic ideas. At a more specific level, the ideas of a period are social and historical in that the basic intellectual structures, which are handed down from the past and engaged with in the present, are mediated and redirected according to the preoccupations of the here and now. Thus, to be a legal theorist today in the muslim world or in Eastern Europe, is to engage with the available theories in a way that is quite different from even the relatively recent past.

Thus, history and society are both fundamental and conjunctural elements in the composition of legal theory, but the work of legal theory remains an intellectual practice engaged in and given life by past and present generations of theorists. History provides the structure and the colour of theory, but it is the intellectual who works on the material and produces the accomplished product. There is, in analytic terms, both an internal and an external element to the historical location, comprehension and critique of current developments and, in what follows, I approach these both as products in themselves, and as products in history.

The developments of the 1980s can be understood in a way that can genuinely be termed dialectical. On the one hand, the flourishing of theory can only be seen as a strength; on the other hand, it is the product of fundamental intellectual weakness. This theoretical efflorescence has all the appearances of vigour and vibrancy, yet it is the product of profound and longstanding intellectual crisis. The developments on view are interesting and exciting (they are our world!), yet flawed and depressing. They derive from a tradition that has grappled over and again with what are basically the same problems, that provides us with insight and understanding, but which also obscures and occludes.

I make a division for historical and analytical purposes between two periods of intellectual development. The first, classical, period of the 18th and early 19th centuries established two sets of theories and schools which were in conflict with each other, and in which nothing was resolved other than the incommensurability of the two approaches. This period is discussed in the next section. The second, modern, period, discussed in the ensuing section, is that of the post-war political and intellectual reconstruction which reassembled the same intellectual armies on the battlefield, in somewhat different garb, but brandishing similar weapons. In both periods, we witness processes of decline and destruction as established positions unravel before us. The difference is that the process of unravelling in the classical period is reversed in the modern period. In the former, it is classical natural law which unravels in the face of legal positivism; in the latter it is positivism that comes under fire from natural law – in its modern distilled and fragmented forms. In this context, the so-called postmodern critique of law represents, in jurisprudential terms, one final throw of the natural law dice. Although it would view Enlightenment and modernity in the context of a longer philosophical tradition, and would see itself in its relation to modernity in a quite different way, its concepts are those of Enlightenment ethical jurisprudence, turned against, but remaining within, that tradition.

The breakdown of the Enlightenment tradition

The modern classical period of jurisprudence was the child of the Enlightenment, and died with it. It established a method for understanding law that was profoundly alien and unacceptable in the 19th century. Traditional accounts present this as the redefinition of the province of jurisprudence (Austin, 1861), as theorists began to separate out sets of different questions: of fact and value, of law and morality, of what the law is and ought to be, of natural and positive law. However, the demise of classical natural law was essentially much more than a matter of definitional or logical refinement. It was a profound intellectual and political shift, from which there emerged the redefinition of jurisprudence (cf Halevy, 1972; Marcuse, 1941).

First, the rise of legal positivism accompanied the political securing of the well-ordered bourgeois state. Bentham sensed the need to control and contain the restless social impulses generated by the call for intellectual and political freedom (Steintrager, 1977; Rosenblum, 1978). Once the conditions for industrialisation had been achieved, it was more important to consolidate 'what is' than to dream dangerously about what might be in an ideal world of metaphysical abstractions. What 'ought to be' should be no more than a deduction based upon the facticity of what had already been achieved. What was there was what there was, its positivity only requiring amelioration, not fundamental change (Cotterrell, 1989, Chapter 3). Accordingly, the 'nonsense on stilts' of natural rights theory was better shut off in favour of sober evaluation of the concrete (cf Waldron, 1987). The source of the evaluation had changed too. No longer was the moral standpoint that of the free individual; now it was the standpoint of the state itself through the aggregative logic of 'the greatest happiness of the greatest number'. The shift from individual egoism to general utilitarianism was the result of a major historical development (Halevy, 1972), closely connected with the positive theory of law. It was only an organised state that could posit a coherent, rational legal system.

Secondly, the same development that strengthened the hand of utilitarianism also weakened that of classical natural law. The latter's *raison d'être* was the establishment of a synthesis of the moral and the practical, the universal and the particular, the rational and the real, the ideal and the positive. Law's importance is only seen in the light of a general metaphysical stance on the nature of the social and political order. Law is seen in terms of an ethical other, is always understood in the first place in terms of its *heteronomy*. This is the moving intellectual force of modern classical natural law, from Hobbes to Locke, to Kant, to Hegel: to establish an adequate methodology for the comprehension and rationalisation of law in terms that extend beyond its phenomenal appearance and practical self-understanding.

Different cultures naturally yield different political and intellectual approaches. In the work of the British natural lawyers, moral-juridical and positive-legal concepts are promiscuously intermingled, so that one is never clear whether the argument is a direct juridico-political intervention or an abstract ethico-philosophical reflection (Strauss, 1953; Habermas, 1974, Chapter 1; Neumann, 1986, Chapters 7 and 8). The metaphysic of the social contract to establish the sovereign is also the practical basis for the powers and duties of the constitutional monarch in Locke's programme for the 'nightwatchmanstate' (Locke, 1960); in Hobbes, the philosophical constitution of sovereignty on the basis of metaphysical misanthropy is the immediate justification for contemporary political absolutism (Habermas, 1974). There is, in short, no clear method for affirming legal positivity within a universal moral theory of society and polity, no adequate synthesis of the two. The natural and the positive appear to be confused, so that when the master sceptic Hume (1898) pointed out the flaws in the contract philosophy, and the reducibility of political philosophy – that which concerns the 'artificial virtues' – to a consideration of the practical and the useful (Hume, 1888), he brought philosophy down to the same level as legal positivity and the way was opened for the triumph of the utilitarian-positivist axis in British intellectual life under Bentham and Austin.

The German route was more profound. If the philosophical materialism of the contract was an inadequate method for legitimating positivity, the answer lay in the firmer establishment of rational metaphysics, not its discarding. For Kant (1965), law was posited as the bridge between the speculative and the practical. Law was viewed dualistically as both a rational truth embodying a priori concepts of right and as a necessary element of regulation in a world governed by empirical necessity. Law embodied rational Will (*der Wille*) and controlled private egoistic will (*Willkür*). However, this did not go far enough, for, as elsewhere, Kant only succeeded in establishing an unbridgeable duality between the two sides of law. Law was positive and law was rational at the same time, but the philosophical method of abstraction employed by Kant could never achieve a true synthesis (Norrie, 1991b, Chapter 3). What was needed, as Hegel (1952) saw it, was a means of reconciling the two sides through a dialectical-rational elucidation of the universal within the particular, of synthesising what had been posited with the universality of spirit. Law was in this view both a mechanism of civil society, and an emanation of reason within ethical life. Law was one moment in the movement of the rational within the social (Marcuse, 1941; Norrie, 1991b, Chapter 4).

Thus, for both Kant and Hegel, the separation of 'is' and 'ought' was a profound mistake revealing a lack of understanding of the workings of reason in and through the natural and the social. Law was never just 'law': it was always comprehended as part of a rational 'other', and the movement of classical natural law was towards a refinement and development of what the 'other' was, reaching its final highpoint in Hegel's philosophical system. However, in the end, this grand theoretical edifice turned out to be no more than a rationalisation of the status quo, with the Prussian state as the terminal point of history (Hegel, 1952, pp 179–88; Marcuse, 1941; McLellan, 1969). Recognising the inability of the forms of individual right and self-interest (property, contract, civil society) to generate institutions entailing a genuine ethical unity of the people, Hegel was forced to stipulate the rational necessity of ever more positive statal and para-statal agencies as the basis for Ethical Life. The culmination of his grand dialectical method was a set of extremely 'profane', historically specific, institutions. Their historical particularity proved to be both the cause of the *Philosophy of Right*'s fall into disrepute, and an important opening for positivist methodology from within the heart of its main adversary. Hegel's dialectical method increasingly embraced actually existing (posited) political and legal institutions (Marx, 1975; and see below, Chapter 8).

Hegel had rationalised the real, but the real turned out a sore disappointment, so that when the Prussian state began to act in authoritarian ways in order to quell the growing crises of civil society, Hegelianism, which had predicted the end of history in a rational, liberal social order, had no means of analysing what was happening, and therefore collapsed (McLellan, 1969, Chapter 1; Engels, 1968). The result in German intellectual life was a void, which was filled by positivism in social philosophy (Marcuse, 1941, pp 360–74), and the weak abstractions of the historical school in law (cf Therborn, 1976, pp 178–86). The particular history of the German polity, with its relative economic underdevelopment (Cullen, 1979), did not permit a stable and pragmatic intellectual development as occurred in Britain, and its very metaphysical sophistication made it clear that a grand intellectual synthesis of the ideal and the actual was impossible on the conceptual terrain provided by modern social conditions. Thus, at the very moment in which positivism was given a boost by historical developments, classical natural law was fundamentally undermined, in a moment from which it is yet to recover.

The problems were not, however, all one way. If, under the weight of socio-historical development, natural law was threatened by the development of a new intellectual approach, positivism too was soon to be in the position of looking over its shoulder, in its case, at the rise of sociological approaches to the study of law. Positivism flourished under the socio-political patronage of the consolidated bourgeois state, which affirmed the possibility of social construction according to the 'universalistic' criterion of the 'greatest happiness of the greatest number'. Positivism was formed out of the heady optimism of the early days of industrialism, and underpinned by a conviction of the eternal and natural character of contemporary developments. It relied on the support of the well-ordered economy as the counterpart to the well-ordered state and legal system, so that its intellectual partner in the elucidation of the nature of social order was the theory of the classical political economists (see, eg, Bentham, 1975, p 265). The subsequent developments of social life in the nineteenth century revealed that the abstractions of political economy could not be a reliable basis for continuing good order, and that a more concrete sociological investigation of social ills was required (Abrams, 1968; cf Corrigan and Sayer, 1985, Chapter 6). This conclusion led to questions about the nature of law that threatened the depoliticisation and formalism, the certitude that law could be understood as an *autonomous*, self-grounding regulative system, achieved under positivist theory (cf Cotterrell, 1993).

In Britain, positivism managed to remain fairly stable because of the strength of the socio-economic developments of the period, and the resultant growth of a legal profession that theory could feed off, legitimate, and in turn be legitimated by (Cotterrell, 1983). In the rest of Europe, where these developments were less even and successful, the problem was more stark. Whether the underlying political project was conservative, liberal or radical, it was necessary to think more historically and sociologically not only about the nature of social order but also about the nature of law itself. Thus, France could give rise to a Durkheim (1964) with his investigations of the nature of social solidarity, with legal obedience seen as a dependent factor and indicator of social health, and with his analysis of the historical evolution of modern legal form (Durkheim, 1973). Germany produced Marx, with his diagnosis of both the class basis of law (Marx and Engels, 1968) and the economic basis of legal form in generalised commodity exchange (Marx, 1973), and Weber with his historical-ideal typifications of different types of law (Weber, 1978). While modern law was attributed, in neo-Kantian style, a status independent of capitalist economic developments, Weber insisted upon an historical and sociological mode of investigation which both emphasised the contingency of legal developments and threatened – in his discussion of the 'England problem' (Hunt, 1978) and his study of Islam (Turner, 1974) – to undermine his formalism.

Thus legal positivism was itself threatened by another approach that emerged out of the social-historical developments of the 19th century. Law should be comprehended neither in its positivity nor as a metaphysical correlate, but as a social phenomenon, comprehended within sociological theory. A sociological approach shares with positivism an insistence on shearing away the metaphysical baggage of natural law, but having done so, has this much in common with the natural lawyers: a shared belief in the impossibility of seeing law as an autonomous, self-standing institutional force. Law in this view, as with natural law, was regarded as essentially heteronomous, but this was to be comprehended in sociological terms, in its intrinsic relationship with other social and historical forms and relations. Law's heteronomy resides in its existing in social relation: to attempt to portray it in terms of a projected autonomy, while acceptable as a means of cutting out metaphysical speculation, may be deeply misleading as a means of understanding it.

Modern trends in the wake of the classical breakdown

I have identified a historical period of development and decline which lies at the root of the modern developments in legal theory. Having established three actors on an intellectual stage, I now wish to indicate the basic scripts that they will read and the strengths and weaknesses in the characters that they will play. It will be noted that this is a genuine play, for as we proceed, we will see that the actors' lines are always in dialogue with each other. The play's dynamic is provided by interplay between the three characters because they exist in relational tension, and in a sense need each other in order to fill out their own roles. The essence of legal theory is a grouping of intellectual ideas in a set of one-sided ways. It will also be noted that through dialogue, the different actors come to assume some of the characteristics of their opponents, for, some of the time, their competition is of a somewhat 'friendly' nature. Broadly, three connected intellectual moves can be discerned in this play.

Positivism and the attack on legal closure

For the positivist, history, in the well ordered polity, is on her side. The establishment and expansion of a legal profession in the UK provided the positivists with a set of professional practices and intellectual problems that were legal in a narrow sense, and on which they could feed and in their own way thrive (Cotterrell, 1983). The existence of law as a social practice in itself encouraged the development of a legal theory that would define law intellectually as an autonomous practical phenomenon. However, at a deeper level, the search for the autonomous essence of law proved chimerical. In the standard positivist texts, the theorist always buys certainty at the cost of limitation. Austin's sovereign is a juridical master for the purpose of legal theory, but at the cost of hiving off the interesting questions about power and social relations to other disciplines (cf Fitzpatrick, 1991a, on the work of Hart). The province of jurisprudence is circumscribed from the beginning. What, then, is the positivist left with? The answer is a set of 'technical' materials, which can do no more than replicate and refine an existing social practice, but which can never get beyond it. Furthermore, as American legal theorists have pointed out from the time of realism onwards, even the technical certainties of the legal positivists are hardly so certain. Law is about what judges do, not what they say they do (Llewellyn, 1951; Frank, 1963); it is about conflict and social interests, about rationalisation in the pejorative sense of covering political goals in a 'show' of formal impartial reasoning (Kelman, 1987). Positivist legal theory reflects the self-understanding of legal practice, and cannot move beyond it. For this reason it can be designated as what Bhaskar (1979) calls a 'praxiology', a term to which I return below (see p 30).

This battle between positivism and a sociologically inspired realism is fought out all the time, with the argument swinging first one way and then the other. At present, both sides have some strong weapons in their armoury, for there has been a revival in forms of positivism as its theorists come to terms with the onslaught of first the sociological movement in law, and then the Critical Legal Studies movement in the US and the UK. In this context, MacCormick's work (1976, 1983, 1993) has been exemplary because of its willingness to take on, and to take on board, the criticisms of positivism's opponents, while Dworkin (1986) has sought a more dogmatic, unconvincing closure of the debate with critical approaches to law (Cotterrell, 1993).

This dialogue about law's heteronomy is not just between the positivist and her sociological and realist critics. It is also one that one branch of the descendants of natural law have been keen to join. To understand the nature of this further intervention, it is necessary, first, to understand the process of fragmentation that occurred after the collapse of the classical doctrine. The Hegelian system had combined deep philosophical abstraction with a close focus on the positivities of law, politics and economics. When the synthesis of these elements achieved no more than a glorification of the present, the intellectual world was sundered into a strict positivism on the one hand and a variety of one-sided theoretical, ethical and irrational abstractions on the other. Within the latter realm, theory was more or less unbounded by the 'discipline of positivity', that is, the need to explain and analyse 'what is'. Freed from this obligation, it was able to engage in radical, sometimes wild, philosophical speculations about the nature of law. In this process, law as an object of study became of secondary importance, to be pulled along on the coat tails of a master abstraction. The neo-classical world of these different writers was a world where 'anything went', and where fragmentation was the order of the day.[1] In this situation, intellectual stability was impossible, indeed undesirable, and the latest abstraction would reflect the political or ideological colour of its period and place. It is within this context that the current attempts by postmodern legal theory, from a diverse and varied set of perspectives, to take over the field of legal theory can be located. Postmodernism is a one-sided response to the breakdown of the classical syntheses of law and rationalism, turning the post-Enlightenment irrationalism of the declining and fragmented natural law school against the proclaimed achievement of legal positivism: a theory of law as a more or less closed and autonomous system of rules, norms, or regulation.

---

1 For a helpful account of the intellectual development from romanticism to Nietzsche, and beyond to Heidegger and Bataille, see Habermas, 1987.

Thus, positivism is always under attack from different sides because of its claim about the autonomy of law. These attacks are more or less well grounded, sometimes in realism, sometimes in sociological critique, sometimes in postmodern theory. From whichever side, the claim is that law should be understood in terms of an 'other', in terms of its social or philosophical reliance upon and instantiation of practices and ideas beyond itself: in terms of its heteronomy. Positivism must always walk the line that it has chosen for itself (and that a particular historical period has generated for it) between two different approaches to legal phenomena which, in their different ways, seek to ground and explain legal phenomena in relation to what lies beyond them, whether this is comprehended in terms that are predominantly metaphysical or material.

Natural law distillations and filtrations

For the natural lawyer, a variety of responses has emerged to the breakdown of the classical tradition. First, there is the neo-Kantian response, which replaces the transcendental basis of the categorical imperative with a scaled down, prosaic *sollen* ('ought': cf Rose, 1984; Lukacs, 1971, pp 108–09). This is then attached directly to the categories of law, producing an 'ethicalised' legal positivism, as in the work of Kelsen and, in quite different ways, in that of Weber (cf Schluchter, 1981; Murphy 1993), Fuller (1969; cf Summers, 1984), and even, through Weber, the Marxist, Lukacs (1971, pp 83–110). The problem with this approach is that, in its purest Kelsenian form, it gets the worst of both worlds. On the one hand, the diminution of the 'ought' required by the theory's reduced transcendental quality provides an unconvincing account of law as a series of logically linked but empirically unspecified oughts, which suffer for their 'purity' in a parallel way to the original Kantian metaphysic; that is, they remain barren. The unbridgeable gap between Kant's moral law (the noumenal) and the world of nature (the phenomenal) (MacIntyre, 1967, pp 197–98; Wolff, 1973, Chapter 2) is replicated in the gulf in Kelsen's work between the form of law and its content (cf Pashukanis, 1978, p 52). On the other hand, where Kelsen does say something about law, it appears as little more than a mystified *doppelgänger* for its positivist counterpart – for example, in the employment of the *Grundnorm* in place of the sovereign's command. More broadly, the problem with neo-Kantianism, even in its sociological form, is that it fails to get 'behind', or to penetrate into the nature of law. It takes law on its own terms, as in Weber's embrace of the legal paradigm as a rational practical form (Albrow, 1975; cf the discussion of Weber below in Chapter 9), or in Teubner's affirmation of the self-closing character of the juridical sphere in an autopoietic system (Teubner, 1987; cf Cotterrell, 1993). Neo-Kantianism is no more than a scaled down version of Kantianism itself in which the antinomies of the noumenal and the phenomenal are replicated in a narrower ambit.

A second response, one that has been partially described already, is to break away from the rationalism of the classical and neo-Kantian discourses, and to replace them with one of the many varieties of irrationalism which stem from the radical conclusions drawn by Nietzsche and others about the value of classicism. From this viewpoint, the pretensions of law are swept away as its discourse is hitched to a 'will to power' (Foucault, 1977, 1980), or the vagaries of an historical text (Foucault, 1972), or its suppression or denial of 'the other', however that might be conceived (Derrida, 1990; Lacey, 1993b; Barron, 1993; Goodrich, 1993; Land, 1993). One danger with this response to the demise of classicism is that the object of study (law) remains secondary to the motivating theoretical impulse, and underdeveloped in its specificity. This may be claimed to be no more than a function of the newness of approaches that have only recently sprung up, and require time to attain a synthesis, but there is also an inherent methodological tendency for such approaches not to engage thoroughly with law, for two reasons. One is that the perspectives that are developed in this mode are necessarily fragmentary, and therefore lack the concepts necessary to engage in a full critique of law. Where they do make the effort of engagement with law, they are likely to replicate its self-image, like the neo-Kantian. Thus, in Goodrich's work (Goodrich, 1986), it is not clear whether bringing a hermeneutic critique to bear on legal discourse does more than affirm the recognised practice of lawyers (Norrie, 1989b), while a positivist appropriation of hermeneutics is possible (MacCormick, 1983). Similarly, the representation of law as a system of technical and bureaucratic rules (eg, Goodrich, 1993; Land, 1993) that is closed off against authenticity or wholeness is not that far from the positivist's own stance. The second is that in these approaches, the 'critical' is out of balance with the 'analytical', so that the theorist is motivated by the kind of thoroughgoing negativity that makes 'trashing' a satisfactory and sufficient response to law (cf Kelman, 1984). Instead of seeking the intrinsic specificity and modalities of the legal enterprise (which is not thereby to accord them the positivist's claimed autonomy), the tendency may be to dismiss these elements as epiphenomenal, and to reduce the critical enterprise to one of full-blown negation. To make these criticisms is not, however, to deny the value of postmodern critical tools such as deconstruction to our understanding of law, or the possibility of using them to investigate the nature of law as a social phenomenon; my concern is that, pursued to their full extent, such approaches may miss as many legal targets as they hit (see further below, Chapter 8).

Is so ambivalent a reaction to postmodernism possible? Only a brief answer to that question can be made here. If we take Derrida's work as exemplary, he would deny the charge of nihilism, yet his account of deconstruction is hitched to the affirmation of a justice so 'mystical' that it beggars description. Justice 'would be the experience that we are not able to experience ... an experience of the impossible' (Derrida, 1990, p 947). Justice is at best a negative moment defined against all that positively is, an outside, a beyond, that cannot be expressed, only felt as an 'impulse', an 'unsatisfied appeal' (*ibid*, p 957). However, this irrationality, this 'madness' (*ibid*, p 965), this 'anxiety-ridden moment of suspense' (*ibid*, p 955), this upturning of the moral rationalism of the Enlightenment[2] is allied to the prior, in my view more valuable, deconstructive tasks of seeking out the contradictions within discourse and tracing the 'historical and interpretative memory' of the concepts. One must 'do justice' to the historical and political concept of justice, interrogating its 'origin, grounds and limits', attending to 'the theoretical or normative apparatus surrounding' it (*ibid*, p 955). This genealogical investigation into justice can then go two ways. Either it can go back into the moral-philosophical

---

2   Derrida's self-expressed orientation to classical thought is that, while he might not be 'in the race' (*dans la course*), in an inside lane, deconstruction 'keeps him running' (*fait courir*) 'faster and stronger' (*ibid*, p 966).

tradition that it is deconstructing, in the process seeking some precarious foothold on the classical terrain it has already deconstructed, or it can probe more deeply the historical and social relations within which the concept has flourished. Either it can go back to natural law, or it can go forward to a sociological understanding of the nature of the concepts at play. Derrida's deconstructionism does the former, but his deconstructive project strikes important chords with anyone who, as I will indicate below, wishes to follow the latter course.[3]

A third response is to attempt some kind of return to the classical tradition, and this is in many ways still the most popular approach. From Hart's 'minimum content of natural law' (Hart, 1961), to Dworkin's view of the animating values of the Western polity (Dworkin, 1977; cf MacCormick, 1978a), to MacCormick's 'ethical positivism' (MacCormick, 1989), to Habermas's discourse ethics (Habermas, 1984, 1989; see also Alexy, 1989), to Rawls's original position and contractarianism (Rawls, 1972; cf Rawls, 1985), to Nozick's Lockean natural rights theory (Nozick, 1975), to Rose's reading of Hegel (Rose, 1981), to Beyleveld and Brownsword's Gewirthian, and Kantian, rationalism (Beyleveld and Brownsword, 1986, 1993), a host of different 'back to the Enlightenment' approaches have been adopted. The difficulty for all these approaches, which exhibit a wide variety, is to know whether they have been able to achieve what their classical predecessors were not, ie, the resolution of the difficulties of combining the ethical and the positive. It has been said that 'positivists are not so positivist as they were', but the question is whether any of these approaches achieves a synthesis between their positivism and classicism. Positivism has been under attack for many years from many directions, and this return to natural law premises is part of a response. But in reversing the historical process that saw positivism triumph on the back of a natural law in decline, it is doubtful just how much mileage there is in these neo-classical syntheses.

Locating legal specificity sociologically

It will already be clear that in separating off three approaches to the study of law, it is only possible to construct models for analytical purposes since our three main characters are so frequently the product of intellectual crossover. Thus, in considering a sociological approach, it must be noted that one of the main theoretical traditions, the Weberian, has already come under scrutiny for its neo-Kantianism. However, for those who believe that the study of law is a matter of building theoretical concepts out of the observation of a social phenomenon, in its relatedness to other such phenomena, a sociological approach does offer the possibility of breaking out from the one-sidedness that either leads to the pure reduction of law within an analysis stressing heteronomy, or its secular deification through the stress on autonomy. In recent times, there have been attempts to view law in this synthesised way through a legal form analysis that combines an insistence on the historicity of all social forms with a regard for their particularity in

---

3 This argument is pursued below, in Chapter 8, where I press Derrida into service in the ranks of the dialectical tradition. According to Habermas (1987, p 97), this division within deconstruction is already present in Nietzsche as the two paths of (1) sceptical unmasking of 'the perversion of the will to power, the revolt of the reactionary forces, and the emergence of a subject-centred reason by using anthropological, psychological, and historical methods', and (2) the initiate's critique 'of metaphysics [which] pretends to a unique kind of knowledge and pursues the rise of the philosophy of the subject back to its pre-Socratic beginnings'.

different historical periods. In this way, form and content are merged on the basis that law is a specific social form emerging within certain social relations, and mediating them. To name two such attempts, there has been the work of Unger (1976) in the US, and the rediscovery and use of the legal form analysis of Pashukanis in Western Europe (Pashukanis, 1978; cf Neumann, 1986; Neumann and Kircheimer, 1987).

These approaches have been important for their ability to re-establish broad historical-conceptual frameworks for the study of law, both in its juridical specificity and as a social phenomenon. However, both remain somewhat isolated within the intellectual traditions of which they are a part and exhibit certain weaknesses. This may be for a variety of reasons that are extrinsic to the theories themselves, but there are also internal problems with them that should be mentioned.

The major problem of the Ungerian analysis is that it rests on an idealised conception of the economic and political processes underlying the Western legal polity. Resting on a theoretical basis of sociological pluralism and evolutionism, the dynamics of liberal society are founded upon abstractions that are themselves liberal in their conception (group pluralism, the impartial state) with the result that the predicted future of 'post-liberal society' (based on welfarism and corporatism) can only recapitulate the developments on the surface of Western social life, which the last 15 years of neo-liberal backlash have shown to be highly contingent, reversible, and by no means necessary. Unger's account is shown by the current historical period of conservativism and authoritarianism to be unable to grasp the real underlying trends within which the development of legal forms must be located, and within which they perform their socio-political roles. Nonetheless, his work is an important attempt, utilising impressively broad comparative and historical analysis, to comprehend different legal forms in particular historical periods (cf the important but now dated essay by Kamenka and Tay, 1975).

The problem with the second approach is that legal form analysis in the Marxian tradition has been hamstrung by certain assumptions, the most important of which is the indefensible claim that law and capitalism are coextensive on the basis of the commodity form. This view has been promulgated by those who are particularly critical of Pashukanis's work (Collins, 1981, pp 108–11; Warrington, 1981). I do not think that so crude a view can be attributed to him (Norrie, 1982), but the charge appears largely to have stuck, discouraging further work. It is necessary to discard this view through a deeper awareness of the nature of the theoretical premises which underlie form analysis (Sayer, 1987). A more flexible approach to legal forms is required which can locate different kinds of law in different kinds of societies, starting from a deeper analysis of the social relations which constitute particular social formations (see, eg, Fitzpatrick, 1982; Norrie, 1990a, 1993b).

There remains much strength and potential in such an approach, both in terms of its comparative and historical dimensions, and in terms of its ability to understand the nature of modern Western law. The focus of a sociological approach should be the specificity of law, and to explain such specificity as a particular, historical form of practice. The aim should be to steer a path between the autonomisation of law sought by positivist and neo-Kantian approaches on the one hand, and reductive heteronomising accounts, such as those suggested by postmodern analysis on the other. Law is to be understood neither as the fruit of a regulative system which can achieve, by its own efforts, closure and autonomy (cf Teubner, 1987), nor as the pale reflection or negation of forces beyond it that it can never embrace. Law must be seen in its specificity as a historical practice which operates through particular forms and mechanisms which are real, effective and differentiated, and which are related but irreducible to broader social relations.

One way to capture this duality of law is through Roy Bhaskar's concept of 'praxiology', by which he refers to any theoretical account of some form of action that is tied to, and limited by, a set of possible practices and outcomes. The range of concepts available within a praxiology is governed by the set of social practices that they represent, inform and legitimate. To the extent that the social practice represents a partial or particular mode of intervention in social affairs, to that extent are the knowledge forms that it generates also limited. A praxiology may best be regarded as a normative theory of practical action, generating a set of techniques for achieving particular ends, rather than as an explanatory theory capable of casting general light on actual events (Bhaskar, 1979, p 37; see my use of this approach in Norrie, 2001b, Chapter 11).

A primary example of a praxiology would be neo-classical economic theory, but also other theoretical accounts such as that provided by different kinds of game, rational and public choice theories in the social sciences, by utilitarianism, and by political liberalism. All such accounts seek to explain and guide action by reference to abstract ahistorical criteria while remaining rooted in particular, historically given, social relations they seek to bracket off or deny. Positivistic theories of law, which attempt to explain the nature of law and to provide guidance for legal practice, share many characteristics with these praxiologies. The essence of a praxiology is that it takes the part represented by the practice to be the whole, and in so doing both obscures the whole and misrepresents the practice. By ignoring the relationship between the practice and its broader social context, the need for a radical reinterpretation of the nature of the practice in the light of its social context is hidden. Praxiologies both describe real social practices and obscure and mystify their deeper foundations, where recognition of those foundations would force a reappraisal of the practices themselves.

I will illustrate this position with a brief discussion of the descriptive and normative concept of the legal subject as a responsible agent which lies at the heart of the 'general principles' of the criminal law (for a general critique, see Norrie, 2001b). Such a concept is instantiated through the doctrines of *mens rea*, *actus reus* and the general defences which go to make up the 'general part' of the law. The concept of a 'responsible legal subject' is constructed through ideas of intention, recklessness, voluntariness and rationality, which refer to real characteristics of human agency as it has evolved in modern Western societies (Harré, 1983). Modern Western agents are constructed as, and understand themselves as, agents in terms that correspond to those of the law. Nonetheless the law's conception of these terms remains partial and mystificatory because it seeks to abstract the actor from the context of social conflict and deprivation which generates crime, and to exclude that context from the judicial gaze.[4] Human agency is intentional, but, in the way these

---

4   This argument and its implications are developed below in Chapters 4 and 5, and most fully in
    Norrie, 2000.

concepts are differentiated, intentions are always linked to motives which are socially constituted and normatively determinative for agents. In order to exclude this broader social context of agency, legal responsibility formalises the distinction between 'intention' and 'motive'. Were these to be seen as combined in the creation of agency, the responsibility of the individual would dissolve into, or at least require a very different articulation with (Norrie, 1990b, discussing Lacey, 1988), society's own responsibility for criminal actions. Similarly, legal praxiology abstracts the 'factual' question of awareness of risk in the law of recklessness from the socio-political and 'normative' question of the justifiability of risk in order to locate criminal responsibility individualistically in the law of recklessness (Norrie, 1992); while in the law of causation, it attributes causal responsibility individualistically by socio-political *fiat* in order to separate off the consequences of individual agency from the broad flux and structure of social causation (Norrie, 1991a).

Thus, the praxiological explanation of juridical subjectivity takes the modern social fact of individually constituted mentality as the basis for a descriptive and normative account of criminal responsibility, but takes it in an entirely one-sided way: individually instantiated social agency is translated into individualistically constituted, desocialised, responsibility. Recognition of the social dimension of individual agency transforms our knowledge and understanding of the implications of such agency. Legal knowledge, tied to the criminal law practice of punishing individuals, is founded upon the denial of the social relations which inform agency where their recognition would radically challenge its legitimacy. It is this tying of knowledge to a particular, partial, mystificatory view of agency that justifies the designation of legal knowledge as praxiological.

One starting point for the sociology of law would thus be the investigation of the various ways in which legal praxiologies operate to govern social conduct and mediate social relations, informing practices that are in the same moment real and unreal, ie, represent practical but distorted, particular, non-necessary interventions within the social world. Such an approach can recognise the specificity and particularity of legal forms at the same time as it relates them to, and explains them by, the broader social processes of which they are a part. Law must be understood methodologically, at the same time, in itself and in its otherness, and this is only possible by regarding it as a specific, historical, socio-political practice.

Conclusion

My brief conclusions, or perhaps alternatives to a conclusion, on the basis of this largely inadequate account of its development, are presented in the light of the two contexts within which I have sought to understand legal theory.

First, the problems of legal theory are to be located in a historical-intellectual development that established a framework for future positions which contained important defects. Legal theory came out of a period of intellectual crisis, in which theoretical unities were sundered, leaving a mixture of approaches which, for all that they are in dispute, have one thing in common: a one-sided approach to the phenomenon of law. Those theories that emphasise law's heteronomy fail to account for its specificity; and those theories that emphasise its autonomy fail to account for its relatedness. Thus, no one theory is adequate. However, to combine different theories will not produce a synthesis, only eclecticism. In approaching theory today, it is paradoxical that the exciting diversity of the modern scene is a product of this process of fragmentation and decline occurring in the last century, so that the variation of the present comes out of and is caught up in the problems of the past. The tendency is usually to one-sided understandings of the nature of law.

This is the first context within which I seek to understand modern developments in legal theory. At the same time, I would stress as a more specific context the nature of the current conjuncture within which particular theories are constituted. We live at the end of the period of post-Second World War reconstruction, and it is this which provides the present with its more specific colouration. What we have witnessed in this period is the construction, and then crisis, of a theoretically hegemonic project. That project was largely positivist, but with a minimum of ideas strained from the natural law tradition, and buttressed by the normative argumentative approach of modern Anglo-American political philosophy. The iconic works in this tradition, which reached its head in the mid to late 1960s, were those of Hart (1961) and Rawls (1972). However, no sooner had this modern liberal project been consolidated than events in the form of the social strife of the late 1960s and early 1970s overtook it. The response to this was a critical approach which began in legal sociology and the sociology of deviance, and reverberated in different forms through Critical Legal Studies and postmodernist approaches to law. It is this counter-tradition that has opened up the theoretical debate in the present period, albeit within the broader historical confines we have identified. The interest in legal theory today stems not just from the vibrancy of the counter-tradition but from the responses to it that have been elicited from those whose ideas have developed out of legal positivism. There has on occasion been a willingness to defend and renew the older tradition in more intellectually interesting ways, so that on all sides the level of theoretical engagement has been increased.

In this dual context, it is notable that the current period replicates the classical period – in reverse. Whereas then, positivism emerged from the downfall of natural law, today the postmodern residues of natural law have begun to take their revenge. Meanwhile, lurking somewhere in the wings, temporarily eclipsed by the bright lights of postmodernism, and not, perhaps, clear as to its future agenda, sociological approaches rooted in classical sociology await their return to the centre-stage. The result of all this theoretical endeavour may not be more satisfactory answers, but certainly it has produced a more stimulating set of questions in an area of the social sciences that has for too long been marked by 'leather tongued' sterility. I have sought to uncover the foundational and conjunctural historical elements behind this repetition in reverse of classical jurisprudence, and to suggest, in a necessarily limited manner, a way forward that can move beyond the different reductionisms perpetrated by attempts to autonomise (positivism, neo-Kantianism) or heteronomise (natural law, postmodernism) law. What is required is a historical and sociological approach which can grasp the duality of law as a specific form of historically constituted sociality.

Chapter 3
From Law to Popular Justice: Beyond Antinomialism

Popular justice: in search of a concept

The sociology of law has long failed to understand the nature of popular justice. Boaventura de Sousa Santos has viewed it as central to the discipline, but he notes the increasing vagueness of discussion, so that 'the core debate is increasingly a debate about what is being debated' (1992, p 132). He further notes the failure to emphasise the challenge that popular justice makes to liberal political and legal theory, in particular to the understanding of the state and law as autonomous forms. My argument will be, inverting and extending his point, that the failure to understand popular justice itself also results from the failure to challenge the liberal idea of law. Until we interrogate fully a certain way of understanding law, we will not understand popular justice. The latter term covers a number of different phenomena, but what governs its conceptual possibility in the sociology of law is the relationship of 'otherness' that is established between it and a liberal conception of law. If we challenge the concepts of liberal legality, moving from a critique of law to an understanding of popular justice, we will find a more adequate way of talking about the latter. If we do not do so, our comparative understanding of different systems of rule, particularly those we call popular justice, will remain imprecise.

The conceptual failure at the heart of the debate over popular justice has a longstanding Weberian form and a more recent Foucaultian one. The central problem is a falsely dichotomising tendency, an 'antinomialism',[1] which has its main expression in the formal/informal opposition in Weber's sociology of law, and which ramifies into a series of dichotomies. These include form and substance, the legal (or bureaucratic) and the popular, the indigenous and the statal, the local and the national, the rational and the irrational, and the individual and the social. My argument will be that antinomialism places Western law on an imperialist pedestal, and sets popular justice up to fail. There is a need to cut Western law down to size (which is not the same thing as dismissing it, either theoretically or politically) and to give popular justice its due. This is done by a method which can explain what Western law and popular justice have (and have not) in common as differentially constituted juridical modes.

I begin, however, by illustrating antinomy. In their book on community mediation in the US, Sally Merry and Neil Milner write that popular justice is 'less inclined to rely on legal forms of discourse and more on the discourse of the world outside the legal system'. However, they also claim that 'many of the procedures, symbols, rituals, and forms of language used in popular justice derive from state law' (Merry and Milner, 1993, pp 4–5). They write that popular justice 'provides a stark contrast to the violence and coercion of law', yet also that it 'does not

---

1 The sense of antinomy I wish to convey is something like 'a self-contradiction by accepted ways of reasoning [which] establishes that some tacit and trusted pattern of reasoning must be made explicit and henceforward be avoided or revised' (Quine, quoted in Honderich, 1995, p 40). Antinomy, I argue, is deeply embedded in Western thinking about law.

necessarily produce a non-violent justice' (*ibid*, p 7). They claim that popular justice does not 'typically challenge the hegemony of state law', but also that it 'confronts the legal system with a persistent critique' (*ibid*, p 9).

Merry argues that popular justice may involve a 'counterlegal order' arising from 'spontaneous acts of collective judging and violence' (*ibid*, p 31), but she also characterises it as a 'judicial institution located on the boundary between local ordering and state law' (*ibid*, p 32). She characterises popular justice *culturally* (ie, in the way it is represented) as similar to indigenous or local ordering, but *practically* as homologous to state law (*ibid*, p 35). Her four-part typology of popular justice forms identifies two types (the reformist and the socialist) that are 'more closely tied to state law than to indigenous law' (*ibid*, p 45), and two types (the communitarian and the anarchic) that are closer to indigenous ordering (*ibid*, pp 45–49). Within this typology, the experience of Papua New Guinea is represented as falling under both the 'statal' reformist form and the 'local' communitarian form. Merry concludes that 'by and large, popular justice tends to reinforce and entrench relations of power rather than to transform them'. She also claims that 'the argument that informal justice is an expansion of state control by non-state means is only one side of the story' (*ibid*, p 61).

Merry and Milner may claim that the ambiguities in their approach result from the ambiguous character of popular justice itself, but it is surely the test of a theoretical method that it can adequately locate the phenomena it investigates. It should explain rather than simply embody, or reflect, ambiguities. In the authors' account, popular justice is trapped on a borderline between the statal and the local, forcing it to look both ways at once, but that borderline is itself a theoretical construct, and it needs interrogation and critique if we are to understand the phenomena under investigation.

My focus in the next (second) section of this chapter will be on the form of the antinomy that has been most central to the popular justice debate: the dichotomy between the formal and informal. I shall take this dichotomy to be central to Weber and the product of the neo-Kantian, essentially juridical, worldview that informs his work (see above, Chapter 2), and which therefore informs the popular justice debate. Since Weber's view of law is fundamentally skewed, any view of popular justice that starts out from it will also be skewed. I shall argue that a Weberian conception of law and legal formalism generates a correlative antinomial conception of informalism and it is this that lies at the heart of the problem of popular justice.[2] My argument will be that in order to conceptualise the idea of popular or informal justice, we need to develop a methodology that can displace the concepts of formal law and justice that govern our thinking. The failure to understand informalism stems from a prior failure to understand formalism.

---

2   There is a problem specific to critical analysis in using concepts such as 'law' and 'popular justice', or 'formal' and 'informal' justice, because such analysis must both use such categories as they are presented in experience (for what they are), and seek to establish their historical conditions of existence and limits (what they are not). The latter problematises the concept to reveal its inadequacy and incompleteness, while not denying its practical significance. Hence every use of terms like these should carry the academic equivalent of a government health warning, perhaps in the form of scare quotes, to show that one is handling them critically. For exploration and explanation of the methodological issues raised by a critical realist analysis of social forms, see Bhaskar (1979), Outhwaite (1987) and Sayer (1987).

What is to be put in the place of this antinomial problematic? One possibility is Foucault (Fitzpatrick, 1987, 1992a). I also suggest in the next section that the Foucaultian position does not possess the theoretical resources with which to explain the phenomenon either. The use of Foucault, indeed, only replicates and sustains the problem of false dichotomies. In this regard, a Foucault-inspired approach tends to repeat *mutatis mutandis* the mistakes of the Weberian approach it purports to supersede. Whichever approach is followed, we are left with an untenable sense of 'the informal', and it is this that leads to the kind of falsely dichotomous and contradictory approach exemplified above.

In opposition to these two approaches, I shall argue in the third section for a dialectical approach which draws upon Roy Bhaskar's recent critical realist renovation of dialectic (Bhaskar, 1993, 1994), and my own work on criminal law and legal theory.[3] It is true that the idea of dialectic has already been canvassed in the popular justice debate and found wanting, but I shall argue that the concept that was employed was in fact itself antinomial and failed to take dialectic seriously. It was the attempt to apply a concept of dialectics that was at fault, not the concept itself.

Ultimately, I wish to argue for what I think is a more subtle, historically *and* structurally more viable, account of the character of *both* legal and popular justice: one that is more sensitive to the phenomena in question than an approach that is governed by antinomialism. I shall argue for an approach that recognises social control systems as involving different, historically and structurally particular, dialectically constituted, architectonics of law and justice: an approach that can supersede the antinomialism of formal/informal dualisms and thereby locate the 'in-betweenness' central to the character of law (Darian-Smith and Fitzpatrick, 1999; see also below, Chapters 5, 6 and 8). In the fourth section of the chapter I will seek to illustrate my approach with discussion of the debate on popular justice in one society, Mozambique, in order to show what I think to be its strength. It must, however, be stressed that the primary aim of this chapter is theoretical, and it is not possible to clarify all the questions it raises, or apply its perspective broadly, in relation to an extensive and differentiated empirical field. My argument will be that there exists a plurality of popular justice forms. The aim of the chapter is to make headway on a theoretical position which can adequately ground that plurality.[4]

One consequence of the failure to understand popular justice, save in antinomial terms, has already been indicated: that it becomes virtually impossible to think the concept at all. A further result, more directly practical and political, is that popular justice is seen as fundamentally concerned with *social* goals rather than *individual* aspirations in the mediation of social relations. If form is opposed to substance then, before long, individual rights are opposed to social interests, and a simplistic opposition between the values of individual and social justice is established. This particular form of antinomialism has both a radical and a conservative version. In

---

3 See below, Chapters 4, 5 and 7. The argument here rests on Norrie 1993b/2001b and also on a comparative and historical essay on criminal justice (Norrie, 1993b). The linking of criminal justice thinking to dialectical theory was developed further after this essay in Norrie (1998b and 2000).

4 Cain (1985) is a bold attempt to develop such a position, but it suffers from an over-emphasis on standpoint and political function, and an insufficient analysis of the essential forms of, for example, 'professionalised justice'.

the former, popular justice is portrayed positively, as affirming popular and collective over individual ends. In the latter, it is viewed negatively, as a kind of 'mob rule' (cf Spitzer, 1982; Cain, 1985; Allison, 1990; Sachs and Welch, 1990; Scharf and Ngcokoto, 1990). Either way, popular justice is portrayed as separate from and inimical to individual justice, but this, I shall argue in my conclusion, is a result immanent in the theory deployed, rather than in the phenomenon itself. Popular justice forms may or may not be, as a matter of historical account, anti-individualist, but this should not be theorised as a logically necessary characteristic.

The false antinomies of popular justice: Weber and Foucault

The Weberian problematic

The 'original sin' is Weber's. Steven Spitzer, in his seminal investigation of law and popular justice, sets out to 'decipher the *dialectics* of formal and informal control' (Spitzer, 1982, p 171, emphasis added), but he does so armed with the following *Weberian* standpoint:

> 'Equality before the law' and the demand for legal guarantees against arbitrariness demand a formal and rational 'objectivity' of administration ... If, however, an 'ethos' – not to speak of instincts – takes hold of the masses on some individual question, it postulates *substantive* justice oriented toward some concrete instance and person; and such an 'ethos' will unavoidably collide with the formalism and the rule-bound and cool 'matter-of-factness' of bureaucratic administration.

> The propertyless masses are not served by a formal 'equality before the law' and a 'calculable' adjudication and administration, as demanded by 'bourgeois' interests. Naturally, in their eyes justice and administration can fulfil this function only if they assume an informal character to a far-reaching extent. It must be informal because it is substantively 'ethical' ('Khadi-justice'). Every sort of 'popular justice' – which usually does not ask for reasons and norms ... crosses the rational course of justice and administration ... (Weber, 1991, pp 220–21)

'Formal and rational' justice is opposed to 'substantive' justice, formalism to informalism, and substantive ethics become a matter of the masses' irrational instincts. Weber's legacy was to link radical social change to what he called informalism, and to oppose popular justice to formalism, defined as the giving of 'reasons and norms'. In Weber's account, the connection between popular justice and mob rule is also foreshadowed.

Weber's disdain for popular justice is not shared by Spitzer, whose aim is a non-juridical, non-alienated state of being, but the use of the Weberian antinomy still structures his 'dialectical' account. While his formal definition of dialectics reflects classical analyses (Spitzer, 1982, 169–70), his method ends up repeating the Weberian antinomies in order to chart 'the ways in which movements toward *formalism* and *informalism* contain *dynamics* that transform them into something very different from what they appear or are proclaimed to be' (Spitzer, 1982, pp 172–73, emphasis added). Spitzer's dialectic is in fact Weber's antinomialism dynamised, and since the Weberian approach portrays popular justice as beyond 'reasons and norms' – beyond *form* – this generates an inchoate basis for Spitzer's conception of popular justice. Thus, when he comes to consider popular change in Maoist China, he is forced to talk of the 'attack on "old" legal form and the search for "new" legal substance' (Spitzer, 1982, p 169).

The problem with this approach is that it artificially separates out issues of form and substance. The old form/new substance formulation elides the question of substance in relation to the 'old' form, and the question of form in relation to the 'new' substance, and this is not just a question of shorthand description. Weber's approach sanctions the view that form and substance can be separated and set against each other, that popular justice is a substance, an 'ethos', that 'does not ask for reasons or norms'. It lacks precisely *form*, that which constitutes rationality. Spitzer's antinomial conclusion, that either we risk sticking in the reassuring mud of formalism or ride the tiger of informalism, is set up by his Weberian methodology.

From Weber to Foucault

In the light of Weberian antinomialism, Fitzpatrick's prefatory quotation from Blake is appropriate: 'Unorganised innocence: an impossibility' (Fitzpatrick, 1992a, p 199). 'Unorganised innocence' is precisely what a concept of formal rationality posits as its other, whether this be viewed favourably or not. It is in either case an impossibility, and this is the thrust of Fitzpatrick's Foucault-inspired critique of accounts of the Community Boards Program in San Francisco (1992a). However, how successfully would a Foucaultian approach avoid the false dichotomy of the formal and the informal that Fitzpatrick rightly criticises?[5]

In Foucault, the informal is also constituted as the other side of a formal juridical realm. The juridical conception of action and actors operating with responsibility under law necessarily establishes as its opposite a non-legal dimension in which multifarious powers, relations and agencies operate. However, this is not a realm in which the state lacks control. The informal is the area in which the disciplines operate, and in which power produces actions. The realm of law establishes formal controls upon a juridical subject, but these controls are supported both within and beyond the juridical realm by the productive power of the disciplines. Thus, the informal aids and abets the formal. Far from being opposed to it, the informal secures the formal by offering other mechanisms of control; the two 'are distinct but the same ... what is involved here is a homology' (Fitzpatrick, 1992a, p 202).

The immediate problem with this approach is that once again the possibility of popular justice is ruled out. Law backed by the disciplines squeezes out alternative counterlegalities so that we are driven beyond the modern state's realm of control to the nations of 'the periphery', so called, to find such things 'in places where the vitality of alternative traditions and the relative absence of disciplinary power have restricted the ability of state law to present an adequate synopsis of power and society' (Fitzpatrick, 1987, p 196). Fitzpatrick ultimately suggests the necessity of 'the denial of alternative law in Western societies, not because it has been rendered insignificant in modern society, *but because it is so significant*' (*ibid*, p 197, emphasis added). However, it is hard to see why this should be, given the dominance of

---

5   Fitzpatrick's more recent work (1995b) makes clear his own current distance from these positions. They remain important, however, within the theory of popular justice, and that is why I consider them here.

disciplinary power. Popular alternatives appear to be only possible in 'the periphery' because of the dominance of the Western lifeworld by the disciplines, and therefore impossible under Western conditions. How can it be otherwise in a world in which people are only the effects of power, the 'elements of its articulation' (Foucault, 1980, p 98), unless the alternative is conceived, precisely, as the expression of 'unorganised innocence'? Where power is all consuming, all that remains is either the 'acceptance of the system' or an 'appeal to an unconditioned event' (Foucault, 1991, Chapter 2).[6]

The deep reason for this impossibility, I suggest, is that Foucaultianism, while apparently opposed to Weberianism, in an important way operates as its mirror image. For Weber, the formal or legal constitutes *the* mode of social organisation in modern society, while the informal constitutes its logical and political opposite. With Foucault, there is a parallel dichotomisation, albeit in different terms. Law-and-discipline repeat in different guise the form-and-substance antinomy. For Foucault, disciplines *underpin* the juridical forms, whereas for Weber, substantive rationality *threatens* formal rationality. The terms of the opposition are different, as is their relationship (the one complementary, the other antagonistic), but the opposition remains in place. In both, the defining term is *form*: form of law as guarantee of individualism, markets and rationality (Weber), versus form as mask of individual rights and liberties (Foucault). Foucault replicates Weberian antinomialism.[7] Both in their different ways involve the kind of oppositions which marginalise and render inchoate oppositional agency.

---

6 These are the invidious alternatives posed to Foucault by an anonymous questioner (*ibid*). Foucault's argument is that a progressive politics does not meet this choice if it is devoted to examining *inter alia* the 'possibilities of transformation' accorded by the 'mode of existence of discourses' (*ibid*, p 70). However, what transformation is possible if discourses, like individuals, are inscribed by the workings of power? Either discourses conform to the laws of their own production, which means acceptance of the system, or one must have recourse to an outside, unconditioned event.

   Foucault wrestles with different aspects of this dilemma in several places in his later work. Freedom, for example, is explained as the internal condition for the working of power, but in his description of its 'intransigence' and 'recalcitrance', he places it tantalisingly beyond power's reach. When he writes of an 'agonism' between power and the 'intransitivity of freedom', and describes this as 'inherent in all social existence' (Foucault, 1982, p 223), as part of an argument for promoting 'new forms of subjectivity' (*ibid* p 216), he comes close to undermining his own premise that subjectivity suggests 'a form of power which subjugates and makes subject to' (Foucault, 1982, p 212). A similar ambivalence seems to be at work in Foucault, 1984, pp 45–50. With regard to resistance, Foucault claims that 'great radical ruptures' are possible, yet resistance 'is never in a position of exteriority in relation to power' (Foucault, 1981, p 95). See further Dews, 1979; Fitzpatrick, 1995b.

7 In his 1972 discussion of popular justice with Maoists, Foucault writes that the 'idea that there can be people who are neutral in relation to the two parties, that they can make judgments about them on the basis of ideas of justice which have absolute validity, and that their decisions must be acted upon, I believe that all this is far removed from and quite foreign to the very idea of popular justice. In the case of popular justice you do not have three elements, you have the masses and their enemies. Furthermore, the masses ... do not rely on an abstract universal idea of justice, they rely only on their own experience [and] purely and simply carry [their decisions] out' (Foucault, 1980, pp 8–9). This is no different from Weber's position, although Foucault is an enthusiast for popular justice; indeed, he rather heroically 'out-Maos' the Maoists in this discussion, who argue, correctly in view of what I say below, that a state apparatus, and controls on it, are a prerequisite for popular justice in a third world revolutionary society.

Beyond antinomialism I: taking law dialectically

Others have remarked upon the failure of a 'dialectical' approach to popular justice because of its 'mechanistic' character (Cain, 1985; Fitzpatrick, 1987). Spitzer's work exemplifies the genuine problem of what a dialectical approach means and how it can overcome Weberian and other dichotomies. It will not be enough either to paint form and substance, or the formal and informal, with the colours of history and politics, or simply to invert one's political viewpoint – to shift one's commitment from 'form' to 'substance'. We need to develop and apply a mode of dialectical analysis that forgoes antinomialism if we are to progress. In this section, I begin by outlining in schematic fashion what a concept of dialectic means, and then move to consider in the following sections what role it can play in a theory of the formal and informal, law and popular justice. As I have already stated, the key to unlocking popular or informal justice will eventually be found in an understanding of its Weberian antonym, legal formalism.

Dialectic and critical realism

The concept of dialectic has recently been developed by Roy Bhaskar (1993, 1994) as an elaboration of his critical realist philosophy. A limited and necessarily schematic digression is necessary to locate this development.[8] The ramifications of Bhaskar's work are many, and are only now beginning to be taken seriously (Collier, 1994, Chapter 7). For my purpose, the significant elements in his conception of the social sciences are those of *relationality* and *totality*. The former entails the possibility of discovering the internal connections, the relations, between apparently disparate phenomena such as forms of economic, political and legal life. Sociology, looking for relations amongst phenomena, seeks through totalising theoretical strategies to understand the nature of social totalities. Such a relational approach gives rise to a conception of sociology as 'concerned with the structure governing the relationships which are necessary, in particular historical periods, for the reproduction (and transformation) of particular social forms'. This approach entails a view that sociology is never 'sociology-in-general, only the sociology of particular historically situated social forms' (Bhaskar, 1979, p 56), which means that the totalising tendency in sociology is always towards the totalities embraced by and understood in history.

The aim of Bhaskar's most recent work is to develop this position by marrying it with the Hegelian dialectical tradition, but with the intention of going beyond the idealism and the unitarianism that govern and limit Hegel. Bhaskar seeks a fuller understanding of the role of dialectics in thought but also in history. For Hegel, dialectics involve a process of differentiation and negation, the positing of contradiction which is resolved in a further moment of integration. However, in Hegel's approach, the new and deeper unity is always a return and restoration, for it is always already present in the initial separation. Hegelian dialectics never escape their starting point in an idealist monism which posits as the end state of the dialectical process a unity-in-diversity which is the product of mind.

---

8 The key books leading to his work on dialectic are Bhaskar (1975, 1979 and 1986). See also Outhwaite (1987) and Collier (1994).

An important starting point in Bhaskar's account is the decentring of mind and the insistence on ontologically real, emergent dialectical processes operating in society and history. To Bhaskar's existing account of (*inter alia*) the nature of social scientific knowledge and of social relationality and totality, he now adds what he calls a 'second edge of development' which includes characteristically dialectical categories expressed in ideas of negation and negativity, contradiction, becoming and development (retrogression and decay), spatiality and temporality, mediation and reciprocity (Bhaskar, 1994, Chapter 1). These represent only one part of a profound account of the role of dialectical thinking,[9] but it is the combination of an historical, relational approach to sociology with an insistence on the importance of dialectical processes (and understanding of those processes) that I wish to carry into the analysis of law and popular justice. In particular, I want to employ a concept of dialectic in the sociology of law in place of the antinomial approach I have described. To this end, I take from Bhaskar his account of *dialectical connection* and *contradiction*:

> The essence of dialectical connection is the idea of the internal relatedness of elements, their inherent, 'molecular', connectedness. A *dialectical connection* exists between entities or aspects of a totality such that they are in principle *distinct* but *inseparable*, in the sense that they are synchronically or conjuncturally *internally* related, ie both ... or one existentially presuppose the other ... (Bhaskar, 1994, p 58)

It is the sense of existential presupposition that is missing in Weber's antinomial account of formal rationality. In that account, an ideal typical methodology insists upon the empirical and historical links between, and therefore the coexistence of, different conceptions or aspects of law, but not their real bonding in necessary social connections. The ideal-typical methodology of abstraction hypostatises (and thereby misrepresents) one element in an internally bonded, real social relation, rupturing its fundamental interconnectedness. Formal rational law is wrenched apart from its substance in a way that denies an essential linkage; in the process the ideal type of rational legal form is both made possible and prioritised, while other forms, such as 'popular justice', are both denegated and denigrated.

Linked to the idea of dialectical connection is that of *dialectical contradiction*. Contradiction *per se* involves a situation in which a premise or end cannot be satisfied save at the expense of another. Contradictions can be internal or external. Where they are internal, 'a system, agent or structure, S, is *blocked* from performing with one system, rule or principle, R, because it is performing with another, R1' (Bhaskar, 1993: 56). A *dialectical contradiction* is a form of internal contradiction where the contradictory elements are inherently interconnected in the sense described above. Such a contradiction involves both internal relatedness and opposition in that one element of the dialectically related entities negates an element in another, or in their common ground. This sense of the internal relatedness or necessary interconnection of contradictory elements is, I shall argue, central to an understanding of Western law. Of course, it is denied by any theory that portrays law's base in formal rationality, but once we have seen the difference

---

9 Beyond this second level of analysis, Bhaskar also proposes third and fourth levels, concerned with 'totalising motifs of totality' and practice as 'active and reflexive engagement within the world'. These levels do not concern us here.

that a dialectical understanding of Western, so-called formal rational law makes, we will be in a much better position to understand informal or popular justice.

Dialectic and law

To return to where we started with Bhaskar and his relationship with Hegel, there is an important parallel between his project of decentring mind in order to establish a realist conception of dialectics, and the decentring task that needs to be performed with regard to law. The positivism of the modern legal worldview was given sophisticated expression in the neo-Kantian thought of writers as (apparently) diverse as Kelsen and Weber. Legal neo-Kantianism took up the characteristics of unity and rationality threatened by the collapse of the Hegelian system, and read them directly into law. Rather than seeing law as part of a dialectical progression of rational spirit through historical society, law became the immediate locus of reason. This non-mediated identification was understood philosophically through Kelsen's 'pure theory', and was given a sociological turn by Weber. It is the ideal-typical, formal rational conception of law, on which is based the formal/informal antinomy, that we need to decentre.

What is required is a socio-historical approach which can grasp the duality of law as a specific form of *historically constituted sociality* (see above, Chapter 2, and also Norrie, 1997a). Such an approach reflects law's own claims, but at the same time critically explores and decentres them. It involves a respect for the 'internal' presentation of legal concepts (their treatment *as if* they were formally rational), coupled with a historical and deconstructive exposure of the limits of such an approach. Such a deconstruction takes us into the 'external' social and historical conditions of possibility of the internal presentation. It asks: what claims does law make and how does it sustain them; what is wrong with the claims that law makes and the means of sustaining them; and in what social conditions and contexts does it become possible to seek to make and sustain them?

Central to this deconstructive and decentring project is the concept of dialectical connection. The very idea of law as a *specific form* of *sociality* endorses the idea that law can only be understood dialectically, in its intrinsic relatedness to what it is not. Law is generated by, and is an expression of, broader social and political relations, but in the image presented by lawyers, it is seen as independent, autonomous and formally rational. In its practice, it is presented as possessing its own specificity, but there remains an important difference between self-image and purported specificity on the one hand, and the law's reality on the other. The insistence on fundamental interconnectedness, keeping falsely abstractive methodologies at bay, is one important means of holding onto *both* sides of this difference: of recognising law's claims to specificity, while denying its independence.

A second key idea is that of dialectical contradiction, for it is this that both directly challenges the claim to independence, autonomy and formal rationality, and reveals the interconnectedness of law and its social context. It is through tracing law's contradictions that we expose the claims of formal rational law and disclose the relations which underlie it. In this way, we get to understand the deeper historical logic that underlies the flawed self-understanding of law and legal ideology. So-called formal law is a contradictory, hence irresolute (Darian-Smith and

Fitzpatrick, 1999), 'molecular' compound reflecting the dialectically contradictory structure of the socio-political context which generates it. If we start from this point, we will find that our understanding of both formalism and informalism are qualitatively enhanced.[10]

I have already suggested that the formalism/informalism dichotomy can be traced back to the late 19th century positivist and neo-Kantian traditions in Western thought, which posited a conception of formal closure as the basis for stable and legitimate legal practice (Cotterrell, 1983; above, Chapter 2). Because of this nexus between theoretical argument and legal practice, the academic construction and defence of legal formalism does no more than take the self-understanding and self-presentation of the lawyer, law's self-image, as the basis for a scientific theory. The law, as Stanley Fish (1993) puts it, 'wishes to have a formal existence', but there is a fundamental gap between the wish and its fulfilment. Law needs to see itself as complete, as immune from social and moral interpretation, as 'normatively closed', but the closure it achieves is always and only fictive. Legal formalism in this sense is never achieved. It is manufactured and needs constantly to be maintained - in part by legal theorists who, like practical lawyers, act as if legal formalism were true. In Fish's account, the 'amazing trick' of the law is achieved rhetorically, by the actions of lawyers who continually act 'as if' formal legal interpretation were possible, even as their own arguments reveal the 'as if' to be the fiction it is.

In contrast to Fish's rhetorical resolution of the problem of law's formal possibility, I have developed elsewhere the argument that legal formalism is organised around the figure of the abstract legal subject. It is this figure that permits the instantiation of one moral and political discourse, the repression and exclusion of alternatives, and the denial that this is happening (Norrie, 1993a, 2001b; see also below, Chapters 4 and 8). Repression and exclusion are intrinsic to legal subjectivity and rationality, but because that which is repressed continually returns, these need to be worked at constantly. This is a role of legal actors, including academics who seek to rationalise law's necessarily contradictory texts. One can understand the conjunction of academic reconstruction and legal practice that constitutes modern legal science as 'praxiological', that is, as knowledge that is inherently tied to a particular historical practice, and therefore limited by the character of that practice (Norrie, 1993a, 2001b, Chapter 11; cf Bhaskar, 1979).

It is this praxiological character that involves lawyers in bridging the gap and contradiction between law's self-image and its socio-political reality. Formal law is concerned with achieving normative closure, but this involves discursively elaborate exclusions of alternative social, moral and political discourses. Legal form is the imposition of one moral and political narrative about how people ought to behave, dressed in a language of formality and universality that has to be constantly safeguarded against alternative moral and political possibilities. Judges and academic lawyers, in the name of legal subjectivity and formal rationality, operate as the border patrollers of this moral-political discourse. Its fictive character is revealed by the constant need to repair the boundaries against the corruptive

---

10 What follows is a limited account of certain core concepts. A more developed approach would recognise the additional enhanced 'social' roles of the state in the 20th century Western state and the fragmenting effect this has had on legal forms (see, eg, Cotterrell, 1995).

invasion of alternative moral-political accounts – of legitimate and illegitimate uses of property, of violence, and of sexuality.

The key concepts in maintaining the possibility of closure are those of legal form and formal rationality: concepts organised around the ideology of the juridical individual. This homuncular figure's abstraction and generality is the basis for maintaining law as a seemingly general and universal system of social control that is nonetheless politically, normatively and historically specific and partisan. The 'logical integrity' of the system, as opposed to its historical and practical stability, rests upon a decontextualised conception of the individual subject that stands at the centre of its discourse. Through the manipulation of the individualist forms of the law, it maintains an appearance of universality in the face of the social, political and moral conflicts in which it participates. To take two examples: in the area of criminal law, it is the idea of the abstract responsible subject operating within a legal code which blocks discussion of conflicting moral and political issues generated by that code (Norrie, 1993b, 2001b, generally); and in different contexts, it is the abstract rights-bearing subject within a liberal private property system – introduced by violence and deceit – who blocks the 'customary' or 'traditional' land and environmental rights of 'first nation' or local peoples. These rights become 'additional and competing' claims superimposed upon a system which largely excludes them in favour of an apparently more 'complete', more logical, system of property tenure (see, eg, Kelsey, 1993, Part 4; Higgins, 1995; Fitzpatrick, 1992b, pp 82–85, 89).

Legal individualism and formal rationality are modes of exclusion and repression. At the same time, it is through these conceptions that law establishes itself as the basis for a realm of freedom, in which the individual's rights and interests are constituted and guarded (see below, Chapter 5; Norrie, 1993b, 2001b, Chapter 11). At the heart of law is a set of contradictions in which the abstract juridical individual stands 'in the place of' socially contextualised individuality on the one hand, and 'against' general social and political interests on the other. The liberal subject of law, the responsible citizen it instantiates and which formal rationality adumbrates, represents both a figure of inclusion (the bearer of rights against the state) and exclusion (the bearer of imposed duties to respect laws to which 'he or she has agreed'). Thus, a system that blocks and excludes particular moral and political voices with one hand gives something back with the other: rights subjectivity within a liberal legal order.[11]

From formal law to popular justice

This limited sketch of the complex individualist core at the heart of Western legal systems indicates a contradictory combination of elements of form and content, in which the specifics of juridical form are dialectically related to the social and

---

11 Vivid examples of this process often emerge in colonial and postcolonial contexts in which liberal capitalist institutions are introduced to replace existing social orders. Thus in British India, colonial law conspired with Indian patriarchal power to exclude the moral and political voices of women, as in Guha's powerful account of 'Chandra's Death' (Guha, 1987). However, it also sought to protect women in the name of liberal values, as in the efforts to abolish *sati*, the ritual immolation of a widow on her husband's funeral pyre (Stein, 1988). Today, Indian feminists utilise the law as a means of developing and protecting women's freedom, while recognising the social and political limits associated with that freedom (Stewart, 1995).

political context of liberal capitalist societies. Form is already inherently, 'genetically', a mode of establishing and maintaining a particular social and moral content, and of barring alternatives. Thus, legal form is set up as an exclusion of other forms and other contents. The crucial point for thinking about popular justice, however, is that this conception of law is also the basis for the exclusion of other *combinations* of form and content. So-called legal or formal justice is dialectically connected to the exclusion of what comes to be called 'informal' or, sometimes 'popular', justice, and what comes to be described in these 'other' terms can only be so described because of the work of exclusion and construction that goes into the manufacturing of the particular form/content relationship that is modern Western formal law.

So-called formal-rational law is one way of organising social control processes around the presentation of particular moral and political norms under the figure of the abstract individual subject and the rule of law. Formal-rational law is *one* form, with its own particular organisational modes, an *architectonic* (see below, Chapter 4; Norrie, 1998b), of a dialectical form/content relationship. However, it sets itself up as something rather different: as 'legal formalism' in contradistinction to other non-formal modes. In so doing, it denies that it is the embodiment of particular contents, that it is a particular historical embodiment of a form/content relationship, and that its casting of other such embodiments into the wilderness of the inchoate and incomprehensible is a deeply political act.

If we permit the Western lawyer's 'claim to form' to define and to exclude, different architectonics of justice, judgment and law are understood only as negations of Western law, as its antinomy. Formal-rational law is part of a particular, historical practice that is underpinned by a specific philosophical (neo-Kantian) conception of rationality, one that apparently separates form from any particular content. Its claim to universality seeks to evade the charge that it is a particular, historically constructed, dialectical combination of formal *and* normative elements operating to exclude differently constituted architectonics of form and content. Weber's conception of law must be located as much in the camp of analytic jurisprudence as the sociology of law. However, the popular justice debate operates and applies his constrictive historical categories as the basis for a supposedly adequate elucidation of the phenomena of popular justice. The irony in this should be clear: the popular justice debate utilises concepts for understanding a phenomenon that were originally developed to exclude and deny its very significance. Modern writers generally, although not uncritical, see more in popular justice of value than Weber did, but they work with one hand tied behind their backs because they continue to employ his scheme. Small wonder, then, that the very idea of popular justice should prove elusive.

Beyond antinomialism II: dialectics and popular justice

I have argued that there has been a hijacking of the ideologically resonant conception of 'formalism' by Western law, a conception which in this manifestation embodies social, economic and political interests in one particular form/content architectonic. Popular justice must be seen as its antinomy, as what Western law is not, that is, as 'informal'. This means that it becomes impossible to think seriously about the organisational architectonic of form/content relations in so-called popular ·

justice systems, and about their disparity and diversity. Popular justice is always defined against a fiction, and therefore is taken fictionally in itself. Only occasionally do researchers who are thoroughly immersed in the social relations they investigate, together with the particular mediation mechanisms that they generate, comment on the inappropriateness of the Western epistemology. In a study of popular justice in Mozambique, Gundersen makes the point very well when she writes that:

> very few, if any, of the systems described under the heading of 'informal justice' are informal in the sense that they are formless. What have sometimes been labelled 'informal' systems of law may be systems which exhibit *different* forms in comparison with one type of system which is used as a reference, namely Western-style formal courts of law. (Gundersen, 1992, pp 260–61)

She rightly cautions against the 'ethnocentrism' in such an approach, although less polite words could be used. It is the idea of differential juridical architectonics embodying particular dialectical form/content relations that I see as the key to developing an understanding of popular justice, and *different* popular justice forms. It is beyond the scope of this chapter to apply such an idea in detail to any particular version of popular justice, but I will indicate with an example the force of this method in comparison to the antinomial approach adopted by one leading writer.

In Albie Sachs's account of Mozambiquan popular justice, the phenomenon is cast in the form of a moment of ideal innocence:

> The people solve their problems, applying progressive new kinds of norms, and it's the people themselves, organised, that do this, they express power ... and they achieve a very large degree of involvement and support from the community in general ... [It is] a very rich experience, and a wonderful one ... to see justice transformed into a true instrument of community expression. (Sachs and Welch, 1990, p 123)

Sachs does not, however, integrate this identification of a 'truly' popular moment with his acknowledgment of the role of the Frelimo-organised (and therefore state-sponsored) 'dynamising groups' in sponsoring and promoting popular justice, or the leading role of the vanguard party in establishing the social and democratic principles of the popular tribunals, although he acknowledges the importance of both (*ibid*, Chapter 5; cf Isaacman and Isaacman, 1982). Nor does he explain why creating popular justice in Mozambique should require a synthesis of *three* distinct and contradictory dimensions: the 'liberating and freedom-enhancing aspects of community-based law' (the moment of true community expression), the need for strictly imposed state law 'to defend the gains of independence and the new society', and the application of 'what some refer to as internationally accepted norms of justice', that is 'procedural rights and guarantees, commonly referred to as human rights' (Sachs and Welch, 1990, pp 15–16). Sachs points out that the demand for procedural rights was initially generated by the theory and practice of the Frelimo party-state, and not by self-interested Western liberal institutions,[12] but he

---

12 However, Sachs does not point out the co-determination of current rights discourse by Western self-interest and a technocratic elite within the Mozambiquan state (Hanlon, 1984; Utting, 1989, pp 15–16). In 1989, Frelimo formally abandoned its Marxist-Leninist ideology, supported IMF backed economic recovery plans and the principle of a mixed economy. These developments took place against the backdrop of a brutal, externally sponsored, civil war which closed down democratic participatory options, forced reliance on Western economic aid donors, and encouraged market reforms (Brittain, 1994).

does not explain how the experience of a Third World revolutionary state could give rise to so contradictory an amalgam of state-encouraged social action ('popular participation'), state imposed power and state controls on itself. The result is a set of paradoxical conclusions about law, the state and emancipation.

In the wake of the taking of state power by a Third World revolutionary party, idealist talk of popular justice is perhaps to be expected. However, it must be tempered by the recognition that there will be, to the extent that the new state can exercise power, a necessary interconnection between the state and popular social relations. Lines of political power will exist, will be created and maintained, between the people and the state. State power will be exercised in particular and contradictory ways in relation to the social forces and movements which give their support to and/or are governed by it. The social forces which give their support to the new state are at once the historically placed agents of social change, partners in progressive social struggles for development and against colonialism, and the objects of what may become a centrist bureaucratic power with its own interests, capable of acting both against and with its people (White, 1983; Norrie, 1993b). In this contradictory context of co-operation and conflict, procedural rights appear paradoxically as both a necessary protection *against* the state, and as barriers to progressive and liberating change led *by* the state. Similarly, as I shall argue below, community-based law (popular justice) can genuinely have a liberating quality, but only because it is not wholly community based, but comes in significant part *from the state*.

Law and popular justice in Mozambique had a necessary but ambiguous place shaped by the context of Third World revolution. They lay between the urban and the rural, the 'traditional' and the 'modern', the politically progressive and the reactionary, the authoritarian and the liberatory aspects of a complex social context. Popular justice was not pre-social, primary, or innocent. It was always complexly located in relations with the state and the underlying social structure. To say this, however, is not to say that it was compromised, captured, or that it failed to 'escape' the state, because such judgments measure the concept of popular justice against what is an impossible, ideal standard.

The apparent paradoxes of popular justice in Mozambique were a product of its dialectical situation within a contradictory field. It was exercised in and through a relationship with the state and the conflicting social forces at play. It is only if we can see that popular justice in such situations involves a combination of 'popular', 'statal' and 'legal' mechanisms that we can see that popular justice is always situated and particular, and often what its name suggests it ought *not* to be: dialectically combined with law and state. That is what popular justice is, so that to talk of it as either a form of state power or as a locus of local power is to miss the point: that state and local power were inherently inseparable. There was no 'borderline' between state power and indigenous order on which agencies of popular justice were located: such agencies always-already instantiated dominant social and political relations in the society as a whole, expressing them in particular form/content architectonics of mediation and judgment.

Consider the Mozambiquan experience of popular justice in the liberation of women. For Sachs and Welch, popular tribunals (or, as they also describe them, 'state courts' – *sic*!), 'drawn directly from the local community' have been important in supporting women's rights by 'balanc[ing] out to a considerable extent the advantages which men enjoy in the society' (Sachs and Welch, 1990, p 17). They include at least one woman, and are related to the work of the OMM, the Organisation of Mozambiquan Women. New socialist principles of marriage affirming the freedom and equality of the woman were applied, according to the authors, 'without strain' on the basis of the:

> concept of a voluntary union based on equality and the free assumption by the partners of rights and responsibilities. Although the judges might not always have expressed themselves exactly in these terms, these were the principles that underlay their decisions ... (*ibid*, p 101)

However, in a society in which traditional social relations governed 90% of the population living on the land, and where the authors acknowledge the need to eliminate 'the structures of women's oppression' (*ibid*, p 97), it is not possible that the popular tribunals would not reflect the contradictory social forces at play. A propaganda and practice of modern marriage generated in the early liberated war zones by Frelimo, and later in the urban centres, had to compete with arrangements reflecting the ideas and structures of the traditional patriarchal peasant society. In later fieldwork, Gundersen (1992) confirms that popular justice tribunals operated to provide mediatory *compromises* between traditional and new views of the roles of husband and wife; that there accordingly *was* strain in their practice; and that *women* members of tribunals, appointed by the OMM, often reflected traditional values in their assessment of how women should behave. The strain produced by this process of mediation and control was evidenced by the coercive, state-enforced character of these 'popular' decisions.

Given the ideal understanding of popular justice as 'a true instrument of community expression', it is hard to grasp the fact that tribunals could only embody emancipatory norms because they reflected principles established and promoted *by the Frelimo party-state*. Thus, the transformative and liberating aspects of the popular tribunal came from the state. This seeming paradox can only be understood in terms of the structures, forces and ideologies in operation in the society at large, and therefore embodied and expressed through its forms of mediation and control. Popular justice as a progressive social practice in Mozambique was rooted in a set of social relations which were mediated by a particular architectonic of form and content at the level of the tribunal. That architectonic was marked by procedural informalism[13] and dialogue, with coercive mediation available, and it was coupled with (and enabled) the clash of contradictory political and social positions which were expressed and contained, not resolved or overcome, within it. Popular justice, although never popular in the ideal sense suggested by Sachs, was progressive and evolving. It conjoined social forces and political power to produce a developing complex combination of juridical forms and contents. The three dimensions of socialist legality which Sachs identified, with all their contradictions, can only be understood if we discard the innocent, pre-social conception of the popular, and put in its place an historical and structural understanding of social relations within the Third World revolutionary state. Only from such an understanding can we move to

---

13 While it is necessary to hold onto the idea of informalism as an empirical description of a particular kind of procedural context, it is crucial to separate this usage from that which designates a particular form/content architectonic as informal (cf Gundersen, 1992).

contemplate the contradictory forms of regulation such a society instantiates. This involves thinking relationally about the social and historical totality which constitutes the contradictory crucible in which the juridical – *any* set of juridical relations, 'first' or 'third' world, 'East' or 'West' – is formed.

Conclusion

I began this chapter by opposing an abstract method of looking at issues of legal form that is only able to see issues of form and content, the formal and the informal, and so on, in antinomial terms. I argued instead that a better method would insist on the differential, internally organised, character of form/content relations in different contexts. Such a method would recognise the dialectical relationships within such architectonics of law, justice and judgment, and also between them and the social, political and historical contexts whence they arise and which they mediate. Such a view can then lead to a mode of analysis that can better understand the phenomenon of popular justice in itself. What emerges is the idea of specific, internally related, combinations of form and content, locally moulded as they relate to, and develop from, particular moral and political contexts and histories. Law is always to be read, therefore, in terms of what it defines itself against, as always occupying the relational space between its self-definition and its definition of what is other to it. It is this relationship of 'in-betweenness' that accounts for its antinomial irresolution (see below, Chapters 5 and 6).

What I am arguing for is the concept of a dialectical understanding of architectonics of form and content as a means of understanding both popular justice *and* Western law. Such a conception would be the basis for a wide-ranging comparative analysis of what we understand as law. With regard specifically to popular justice, such an approach would give a much more nuanced analysis of its character and dynamics than we are at present able to provide. The diversity of contexts within which different 'popular' architectonics of justice occur means that popular justice cannot have the homogeneous quality that the antinomial approach necessarily gives it. Once we get beyond 'either/or' thinking, we can give credit to the crucial differences between different popular justice forms. It has always seemed odd that forms of justice generated by quite different social contexts such as exist in late capitalist, revolutionary socialist, post-revolutionary and post-colonial societies should all be lumped together under the same heading of the 'popular'. However, if we define Western law as legal formalism, this is encouraged and has profound effects on our ability to understand other 'non-Western' juridical relations. Attempts to typologise will inevitably lead into the kind of problems outlined above in relation to Milner and Merry. Understanding popular democratic forms through an antinomial prism, we are driven to a theoretical characterisation of them as informal, whereas they are better understood as 'differently formed'.

The legal pluralist nomenclature in particular adds confusion to a difficult area. Even Gundersen, in her exemplary Mozambique study, falls foul of this terminology. She is alert to the importance of holding onto an empirical concept of the informal (meaning a minimum of procedural requirements, see fn 13), while insisting that to describe what is merely different in its form as informal is misleading. She also correctly stresses the connection between form and content in assessing the character of a system of justice. However, she still endorses the term 'informal' to describe 'a normative system outside the formal legal system'. This leads her to argue that:

> [t]he local popular tribunal [in Mozambique] can best be conceived as an institution located in the borderland between the formal and the informal systems of law. (Gundersen, 1992, p 261)

If popular tribunals should be seen as differently formed from the Western-style formal court of law, how can they also be said to exist *between* the formal and the informal? How is the metaphorical terrain between the formal and the informal to be described or delineated: what is the specific character (form?) of this borderland?

What is at stake here, however, is not just our understanding, although that is clearly a first step to anything, but also practice. If we see popular justice as simply informal, then it can be portrayed as incipiently authoritarian, for there are no formal mediations to protect the individual from the collective. Popular justice becomes equated with 'mob rule', a position central to the old Weberian standpoint, as we have seen. There is no means of protecting people from the revolutionary monster they have created; in Spitzer's phrase, it is a matter of 'grabbing the tail of a passing tiger' (Spitzer, 1982, p 200). Accepting this dichotomy, one is then drawn back uncritically onto the terrain of Western legal formalism, as in Sachs's call for 'respect for human rights', what he grandiosely calls 'part of the patrimony of humankind as a whole'. In the process, as he says, socialist legality 'becomes less rather than more demarcated from bourgeois legality' (Sachs and Welch, 1990, p 16), and, one might also suggest, socialist society becomes rather less demarcated from bourgeois society.

However, as Sachs himself recognises, the need to rule through consensus meant that citizen's rights were already on the agenda for a socialist Mozambique, and such rights could therefore be understood as part of the practical patrimony of the Mozambiquan revolution, not as something to be parachuted in from outside to an otherwise 'informal', non-rights-based system. To portray citizen's rights as exogenous to a socialist system is clearly to delegitimise that system in the name of other social and economic systems, which are unlikely in the long term to advance or empower the majority of the people in a Third World society like Mozambique. That, after all, is what popular justice is supposed to, and can, be about.

Western legal concepts, like other forms of Western aid, do not come without strings attached. Societies seeking to encourage development on the basis of self-determination encounter many difficulties. There is no need to add to these by a Western mode of analysis that fails to understand, on the juridical level as regards the concept of popular justice, what self-determination might mean. I return to where I began, with de Sousa Santos (1992). If we are to understand popular or community justice, we must interrogate the liberal concept of autonomous law, which not only places itself on a pedestal, but also ordains that other modes of social regulation must fail, conceptually and practically. The conceptual vagueness in our understanding of popular justice is a corollary of liberal law's understanding of itself as firm and clear. If we tackle that understanding by placing relationality, infirmity and unclarity at law's centre, we can move beyond it to open up the different geo-historical and socio-legal worlds that have existed, and will continue to exist now and in the future.

Part 2
Justice and Judgment

Chapter 4
Legal and Moral Judgment
in the 'General Part'

[I]ntentional agency provides the paradigm of responsible agency. This is why intention is the central or paradigm determinant of moral culpability ... As with morality, so with law. (Duff, 1990, p 102)

We possess indeed simulacra of morality, we continue to use many of the key expressions. But we have – very largely, if not entirely – lost our comprehension, both theoretical and practical, of morality. (MacIntyre, 1985, p 2)

Introduction

In the dominant view, criminal law contains a 'general part' containing principles and rules which reflect a philosophical understanding of the relationship between the individual, law and the state. This liberal and Kantian understanding is elegantly expressed by Andrew Ashworth in the idea of respect for individual autonomy, from which stems desert for punishment (Ashworth, 1991). Criminal law is, or should be, reflective of the idea of individual choice, and penal sanction should only follow a freely chosen act. From these premises is born the subjective approach to criminal law principles affirming the need for intention, foresight, knowledge and belief concerning actions and their consequences. These constitute, in Ashworth's terminology, the 'positive fault requirements' which have to be established in order to prove an offence (*ibid*, Chapter 5). Beyond these, however, there exist certain 'negative fault requirements' which operate to supplement and qualify judgments of responsibility that might otherwise be made on the basis of the positive requirements (*ibid*, Chapter 6). Into this category, there fall the various 'defences' – 'excuses' and (on some analyses) 'justifications' – which may negate responsibility otherwise established on the basis of the positive criteria. It is this relatively simple picture of a general part consisting of acts and mental elements, qualified by justificatory and excusatory defences, and based upon principles of individual autonomy, that I wish to examine.

The picture does, however, have one complication worth mentioning. Ashworth notes 'how individualistic, even atomistic, are the assumptions implicit in the liberal theory which underlies the subjective principles' (*ibid*, p 132). No person is an island, and the subjective approach must sometimes be restricted in the light of the demands of social defence 'which one can expect to suffer in a society based on mutual co-operation' (*ibid*). Restrictions of this kind in the criminal law directly affect the 'general part', for example in the law of recklessness, where obviousness of risk supplements foresight as a ground of liability. Nonetheless, this approach is attractive both for its image of a society resting on individual autonomy and social co-operation, and for its simplicity. It seems to provide a relatively straightforward basis for organising the criminal law, and it is also compelling because of the relationship it posits between legal and moral judgment.

At one level it is an axiom of liberal theory that there is a division between law and morals, so that legal and moral justice are essentially different. Max Weber expressed this in terms of the distinction between law's formal rationality (decisions deduced from existing rules) and substantive rationality (decisions based upon substantive ethical ideas: see above, Chapter 3). However, it is important to note that the separation of 'legal form' and 'moral content' does not mean that legal judgments of responsibility are lacking in moral significance. On the contrary, legal justice, although separated from 'substantive' morals and politics, is still regarded as morally legitimate and legitimating because it is based upon a universal respect for individual autonomy in a world based upon social co-operation. There is, therefore, as the prefatory quotation from Antony Duff proposes, a homology between the principles of the general part and broader principles of moral justice. The spirit of Kantianism within the criminal law informs this overlap between judgments in law and in morality. Legal judgment is understood as a particular form of moral judgment – a morality of form – in the liberal tradition.

I want to question the adequacy of the liberal tradition in relation to those aspects that I have said make it attractive. I will argue that the image of individual and social life that it produces is in fact partial; that the simplicity of its schema is ultimately simplistic; and that a key problem stems from the Kantian nexus between legal and moral judgment. I shall make three arguments against the idea that legal judgment shadows or reflects moral judgment. The first is that legal judgments based upon the responsibility of the subject fail fundamentally to capture the nature of moral judgments about responsibility for wrongdoing; indeed, they act as barriers to such judgments. The argument here (which is in the spirit of the prefatory quotation from Alasdair MacIntyre) starts from the same critical observation as Ashworth, that liberal theory is too individualistic and atomistic in its conception of human subjectivity, but it takes it in a different direction. Rather than moving to 'social policy' ideas as an alternative justificatory basis for legal judgment, I ask in the next (second) section how this individualism and atomism structure legal judgments of guilt. I argue that they lead to a hardening and narrowing, a sclerosis, of judgment that drives a wedge between legal and moral judgment and, in the extreme case, paralyses society's ability to judge crime. I illustrate this by discussing the recent trial of two small boys for the killing of James Bulger.

My second argument, developed in the third section, is that the legal sclerosis of moral judgment is the result of a historical and political process of suppression of alternative moral and political judgments to those that ushered in our modern world of private property and crime. The modern legal combination of formalism and individualism (the 'atomism' to which Ashworth refers) is based on the figure of the responsible individual deserving punishment under formal law. The abstract legal individual appears to 'rise above' morals and politics, and therefore to constitute a legitimation for judgment and punishment.[1] I will argue that the legal

---

1 It is the presentation in liberal criminal law theory of a separation between (a) law as the embodiment of a formal morality and politics, based on the abstract individual subject, and (b) substantive moral and political concerns, together with the impossibility of that separation, that constitutes my main object of investigation here. Law's 'trick' through this separation is to present itself as a form of politics that is apolitical, as a morality purely of form. Thus, liberal criminal law theory both acknowledges and denies its politicality. Matthew Kramer (1994, pp 111, 118–19) misunderstands this crucial point in his criticism of an earlier essay on the law of recklessness (Norrie, 1992, p 45).

individual is not morally and politically neutral. It is the site of inclusion of certain moral and political views and exclusion of others. The moral and political neutrality of the legal subject, on which is based the formal morality and legitimacy of modern legal judgment, is only an appearance, although one which has important practical effects. I will illustrate this in the third section by focusing on a primary separation that occurred in the criminal law at the end of the 18th and beginning of the 19th centuries, a separation of motive and intention, which helped induce the sclerosis within legal judgment.

My third argument is that the peculiar division between legal and moral judgment, whose practical moral effect and historical roots have been examined, informs and undermines the logical structure of the law's general part, and especially the combination of mental element, justification and excuse. This conceptual trinity, examined in the fourth section, is central to law's 'architectonic of judgment'. It is a historically specific combination of elements which operates to suppress deeper moral and political issues within the law, and to maintain a morality of form. These deeper issues, however, are only artificially repressed and therefore continue to irrupt within sophisticated analyses of the law's logic. In this section I consider in particular Duff's work on intention, justification and excuse (Duff, 1990, p 102), which I see as an attempt to rationalise and defend legal judgment, but one which exposes in the process its fragile, irrational and repressive character.

Finally, in a concluding section, I will relate the discussion of the nature of legal and moral judgment to broader questions of the possibility of judgment in modern society with reference to themes in the work of MacIntyre (1985). I begin, however, with a case which illustrates in a practical way the ethical difference between legal and moral judgment, and the significance of legal judgment in our society.

The guilt of children and the sins of their fathers

Sentencing two 11 year olds for the murder of two year old James Bulger, Mr Justice Moreland described their crime as 'a cunning and wicked act of "unparalleled evil and barbarity"'.[2] Echoing this condemnation of the boys, a senior policeman stated that 'These two were freaks who just found each other. You should not compare these two boys with other boys – they were evil'. As they were driven from the courtroom, their departure was accompanied by shouts of 'kill them' and 'hang them' from an awaiting crowd. In a rare show of moral and social solidarity, a discourse of individual wickedness and evil had united the bench, the police and the crowd in judgment against two boys who, at the age of 10, had committed so terrible a crime. Such a judgment is sanctioned by the law, which allows a 10 year old to be found criminally responsible, and normal rules of *mens rea* apply.[3] Such a person can be as guilty in the eyes of the law as any adult of the most serious offence. England has a low age of criminal responsibility compared with France (13), Germany (14), Norway (15) or Spain (16) (although not with Scotland where

---

2 All reports are drawn from *The Guardian* (1993) 25 November and *The Observer* (1993) 28 November.

3 The law has been subject to recent reform in part as a result of the Bulger case, leading to the abolition of the *doli incapax* presumption by the Crime and Disorder Act 1998.

the age is eight). However, there was some concern expressed after the trial that the age of responsibility might not be low enough, for, had the boys been eight months younger at the time of the killing, they could have escaped punishment altogether.

These categorical judgments of guilt and wickedness were undercut as soon as they were uttered. Mr Justice Moreland undermined his own view of the boys' wickedness with his accompanying evaluation (presented as a non-judgment) of their families. 'It is not for me to pass judgment on their upbringing, but I suspect exposure to violent video films may be part of an explanation.' Similarly the Detective Superintendent in charge of the investigation could say both that the boys 'had a high degree of cunning and evil' and that why the boys committed the killing 'will not be known for some time'. However, if believed, the former view can be a complete answer to the latter question: the boys killed precisely because they were 'cunning and evil'. Another policeman contrasted what he saw as the chilling coldness of one of the boys in the police station with the evening he went with three other burly officers to pick him up, and found only a small boy in pyjamas coming down the stairs. In order to interview and 'take instructions' from this boy, his solicitor had to sit and play a Gameboy with him for hours.

The legal attitude evinced in these judgments permits a narrow, essentially unreflective attitude to the question of individual responsibility and guilt. It does not look beyond the individual and his or her act. When a person viewed in this way does something terrible, there is no need for recourse to anything other than an abstract metaphysical conception of wickedness to explain what happened. A disembodied concept of responsibility for crime calls forth an equally disembodied explanation of its genesis. In the legal gaze, the boys in this case can be 'evil', yet their childishness evokes a sense of their innocence as victims themselves. They are constructed as juvenile Jekylls and Hydes – unconnected embodiments of good (as children) and evil (as killers).

Of course, other judgments abound in this case. There are the judgments of the child care experts who see 'disordered and emotionally inadequate families' and educational problems, problems of inadequate parents breeding inadequate children in a cycle of deprivation. There are the judgments of the environmentalists who see inner city living, social deprivation and poverty as the root causes. However, none of these judgments seems entirely adequate either: many families would be classified under the headings of the child care experts, and an increasing number of children live in deprived inner city conditions, yet few commit the kind of crime that these boys did in Liverpool. Somehow, a convincing account evades us. In these circumstances, it is tempting to follow the line argued by some in government and the media[4] that this was an isolated event from which there is nothing to be learnt. Yet surely this is also unsatisfactory. The problem is that all these judgments try to understand an event that can only be judged in terms of its synthetic combination of social levels and individual factors united in one incident. It is a 'one-off case' that paradoxically is not a one-off case because it mixes social, educational and familial circumstances with individual chemistry in a way that turns two not uncommon boys into killers. In the words of another 10 year old

4 For example, the then Minister of State David Hunt, and the BBC's Home Affairs correspondent Polly Toynbee both made comments along these lines.

Walton child: 'They were just your average scruffs – like the rest of us.' Sometimes 'your average scruffs' do cruel, violent things, which is to say neither that most do, nor that those who do are in some way fundamentally different from the rest.

The situation calls for a form of judgment that can unite appreciation of social and political environment with individual agency. Such a form is extremely hard for the representatives of our various institutions – the government, the media, the law, the caring professions, the police – to arrive at. The scale of the tragedy of the death of James Bulger, and the way it happened, sits uneasily with the simplistic judgments that have been made as to the causes and who was to blame. However, the trial of the boys who killed this infant highlights a general issue of judgment about crime and punishment, one that is more starkly seen in this case because of the age and vulnerability of the killers,[5] as well as their victim. I suggest that the failure to find adequate judgments in such a case is in substantial measure a result of the primacy that society gives to law and legal judgment in the way that it looks at these matters. Law is the organising discourse for a process of judgment that ramifies far beyond the courtroom. Its easy accounts of guilt and innocence and good and bad, echoed by judges and police, and broadcast through the media, constitute society's starting point. Thus *The Guardian* front page on the day following the convictions headlines its reportage with the moment of criminal guilt ('Boys guilty of Bulger murder'), and then, at the foot of the page, begins the analysis which, potentially, subverts the banner headline ('Two youngsters who found a new rule to break'). *The Guardian* is known for its attention to social issues and does at least give these other accounts some significance, but they are afforded a secondary position to that founded upon the law.

In any case, because of law's hegemony, other accounts tend to accommodate themselves to it. Psychiatrists, who could provide an alternative account of crime in such cases, testify to the law's 'knowledge of wrongdoing' test. With other 'behavioural experts', they accept the law's standard of normal responsible conduct, from which they construct an image of the abnormal individual as the exception to the law's rule. On the other hand, social environmentalists, focusing on the conditions of crime, hardly address the question of why this person committed the crime, leaving the field of individual responsibility unchallenged by default. Politically, this may lead to a dualistic affirmation of the need both for a system of law that is hard on criminals, and a policy to address the criminogenic environment ('tough on crime, tough on the causes of crime'). Legal judgments, in other words, still set the agenda, and structure the field in which other discourses have their play. What they produce, routinely, is a kind of 'rush to judgment' in which precious few are able to catch their breath and look beyond the easy answers. We only notice this in a case like that of the two boys in the James Bulger case, for the combination of

---

5   My argument is that the issue in this case goes beyond the question of the age of the defendants, and how children *qua* children should be judged. The fact that the killers in this case were children only brings out more starkly the abstract and narrow character of legal judgment. This is not to deny that Western systems can and do differentiate child from adult killers on occasion, as the recent French treatment of three boys who killed a tramp shows. The magistrate withheld the case from the press until the Bulger case was finished to avoid comparisons. The boys were allowed to return to their families without a period of confinement. Rather than demanding more severe treatment *à l'anglais*, it might be noted, French newspapers 'generally preferred to question the wisdom of submitting Jon Venables and Robert Thompson to a full blown trial' (*The Guardian* (1994) 23 March).

their age and the horror of their acts challenges the narrow and bounded categories of responsibility we employ.

Taking all the views that have been proffered, it is not that the prime candidates for moral judgment are wrongly identified; it is rather the methodology by which they are judged, and the resultant quality of the judgments, that is at fault. The process of judgment must take in the broader environment, social policy and conditions, because these establish the circumstances under which family life occurs and children grow up. It also includes the parents of the children, the surrounding neighbourhood, and ultimately the broader society. These are not easy judgments; they are multi-faceted and particularistic, recognising general circumstance in the moment of individual agency. They must also, I suggest, include the two boys because they were actors in their own 10 year old way, and, treated with compassion, they will have to come to terms with what they did. Their crime has, as Hegel put it, a 'positive existence' for them (Hegel, 1952, p 69). However, in moral terms, this single aspect of judgment ought not to be wrenched from its broader context and the multiplex of responsibilities this involves.

Such a complex process of judgment, which involves all sections of the community, cannot be encapsulated in the finding of a criminal court on the basis of black and white categories of guilt and innocence or good and evil. The law's wigs and gowns lend only a spurious gravitas because the legal categories hypostatise rather than contextualise. They separate event from structure and history, and fragment moments of socially produced agency. This is convenient administratively, for it identifies processable individual subjects, and politically, since it produces ready scapegoats and easy 'law and order' solutions for complex social phenomena, but the judgments it produces are facile and backward looking.

If this criticism appears abstract and hypothetical, I suggest that one very concrete indication of the inadequacy of a legal discourse of judgment is the failure of a social control system imbued with it to come up with any plausible view of how one might avoid a repetition of so horrid an event as the killing of James Bulger, hence the 'wisdom' that there is nothing to be learnt. In reality, there is nothing that can be learned because the discursive categories organise out the possibility. It is true that the legal process does have its immediate effects, both psychological and political, and some of these, for the victim's family for example, are positive. A public record of wrong done seems to help the process of mourning, to achieve some sense of 'closure'. However, in the long run, for society at large, one effect is to trivialise the issues, to provide easy solutions by means of an individualistic and momentary focus upon a complex social phenomenon embodied in individual agency. Geoff Dyer has made the following point:

> Since Conrad it has become a cliché to talk of a journey to the heart of a narrative darkness, but this was the path the Bulger trial followed ... [At the end we were still] left with the tantalising question 'why?' ... Like this, with no one knowing why two unidentified children had committed such a crime, the nation would have felt thwarted. Justice may have been done but the hunger for a closure of the narrative which brought us right to the brink of some terrible insight would not have been assuaged. This is why – although he too refused to disclose his motives – the trial judge had no choice but to allow publication of the boys' names; this is why *The Guardian* ... carried a huge picture of Bobby Thompson on the front page. Narrative must not only be resolved, it must be seen to be resolved. (Dyer, *The Guardian* (1993) 12 March)

Legal judgment seeks to establish the closure moral narrative requires, but it is always inadequate, and this is apparent in the Bulger case. Superficially, the finding of guilt brings things to an end, but the deeper questions remain unanswered. The inadequacy of the conviction to close the case necessitates a further attempt at closure in terms of a demonisation of the two children – by publishing their names and photographs, and by labelling them as evil.[6] This goes beyond the law's own judgments, but it relies on the law's initial conferral of guilt to set the ball rolling. Symbiotically, it both thrives on, and compensates for, the law's failure. Like others before, the social memory of James Bulger and his killers will fade, but only until the next time, when we again witness the demonisation of lost innocents in a world they cannot comprehend.

Law's sclerosis of judgment: the separation of motive and intention

The argument of the previous section suggests the failure of law to reflect a deeper moral sense of judgment which synthesises contextual social particularity with the normative appraisal of individual agency. The James Bulger case is not exceptional, only stark in its exemplification of the point because of the age of the killers. The legal judgment fails to reflect a broader moral judgment of the wrongdoing in this case.

The general problem is witnessed in the murder cases of recent years where there is an important gap between the legal concepts mobilised to judge deaths, and the moral quality of the killings. The main legal concept is that of an intention to kill or cause grievous bodily harm (the *mens rea* of murder). However, the haphazard progress through the cases (Norrie, 1993a, 2001b, Chapter 3) suggests a deeper normative agenda that is unsatisfied by the law of intention. As Lacey, Wells and Meure put it, the legal categories of judgment operate, inadequately, in the place of moral judgments:

> Although often obscured by the conceptual apparatus of the law with its use of mental elements as a means of delineation, a moral judgment is also being made ... [T]here is an ever more desperate search for a magic formula whereby the murderer can be distinguished from the manslaughterer through the use of the notion of intention. (Lacey, Wells and Meure, 1990; see also Lacey, 1993a)

In the law of murder, the legal definition does not distinguish actions that are substantially dissimilar from a moral point of view, for example the difference between a contract killer and a mercy killer. The legal categories have to be teased and twisted to reflect the moral quality of killings in particular cases. A man who shoots his beloved stepfather in a drunken race to load a gun after a family party is not morally the same as a woman who puts petrol through a letter box and kills two young girls in order to frighten, or two striking miners who drop a concrete block

---

6 The process of demonisation and repetition was also illustrated by the case of Myra Hindley which remained in the headlines 30 years after her original convictions for murder. It seemed that she had to remain in prison for no reason connected with standard principles of penal administration, but only to assuage the sense of her evil, constructed in similar circumstances so long ago, and never allowed to dissipate.

off a bridge to obstruct a motor convoy and kill a taxi driver.[7] All three are cases in which the law of oblique intention is manipulated to produce a legal judgment that in some ways matches a sense of moral culpability. This is not possible without substantial conceptual discomfort within the law.

What is lacking in all these cases, and within the law, is consideration of the different contexts and motivations that gave rise to these deaths. There is a moral decontextualisation at work, which we can approach by examining the division between motive and intention within legal judgment. This division, I will argue, is one root source of law's moral problems, and is central to its general conceptual organisation, its architectonic, of judgment.

I begin by examining two alternative discourses which historically threatened the discourse of the responsible subject within the criminal law. The first is a discourse of need, the second a discourse of competing (counter-) right. The former states that a person broke the law because of acute personal or familial need. The latter claims that the breaking of the law was not wrong in the first place, but was legitimate in itself. If the social world was one of economic plenty and broad political and moral consensus, the law might dismiss such claims as impertinent or cranky. Where, however, processed criminality was (and is) structurally linked to social differentiation, economic inequality, and to the protection of a particular socio-political order, this is not always so easy. The problems of need and counter-right were confronted by criminal lawyers from the late 17th through to the early 19th centuries when capitalism was developing and consolidating its hold upon social relations, and when the liberal ideology of individual subjectivity was dominant. That ideology could not immediately rule out disruptive discourses of need and counter-right. The legal task at hand was to draw the boundaries of the legal subject-citizen in a way that 'respected' his or her liberty and freedom, but not too much.

One central element in the lawyers' strategy was the division of motive and intention. A modern conception of mentality conceived of the individual as a purposive actor acting in the context of his or her environment, reacting to the opportunities and constraints which surrounded him or her. This was represented as a modern subjectivity of intention and motive. Both could be taken as universal features of subjectivity: everyone forms intentions to act regardless of who they are, whence they come, what they experience; everyone experiences the force of desires and fears, and is motivated by them to action. However, motive could go further: it could contextualise the subject in his or her social and political environment. The poor and dispossessed could say that their motive was need, or could claim that they acted on right. Motive represented a threat to the law, and was therefore excised from legal subjectivity, from the juridical attributes of responsible citizenship. Abstract mental states of intention, recklessness and agency were constructed as the moments of liberal legal subjectivity, to the exclusion of motive.

Theft occasioned by hunger was known as the 'common excuse' in 18th century England. Writing in the 17th century, Hale noted the significance of motive only

---

7 These are the facts of three of the leading English murder cases: *R v Hyam* [1974] QB 99, *R v Moloney* [1985] AC 905, *R v Hancock and Shankland* [1986] 2 WLR 357. I pursued this argument subsequently in Norrie, 1999 and 2001b, Chapter 3.

once in his criminal law treatise, and that was in order to reject it. Larceny born out of hunger or lack of clothing remained 'a felony and a crime by the laws of England punishable with death' where there existed the intention to steal (Hale, 1972, pp 1, 54). At the beginning of the modern period of development of a systematic criminal law, the early Victorian Criminal Law Commissioners quoted with approval the smug judicial comment 'We must not steal leather to make poor men's shoes', and the words of the Scots criminal lawyer Hume:

> Whatsoever be the cause which impels a person to the doing of those things, which are destructive of the interest or bonds of society, his will is not on that account the less vicious or his nature the less depraved. (Criminal Law Commissioners, 1843, p 29)

Hume constructs the issue in terms of the breach of a universal social interest (the 'bonds of society'), but universality was proclaimed in opposition to the interests of the poor, for whom poverty was endemic. As an excuse, however, it cut little ice.

The second cause of the rule concerns not the denial of motive out of compassion, where compassion threatened to undermine private property, but the squashing of alternative definitions of right and wrong. The poor might not just claim an absence of malice, but the positive existence of rightful or good motive on their side. The late EP Thompson makes the point well with regard to the trauma of enclosure:

> Viewed from [the commoners'] standpoint, the communal forms expressed an alternative notion of possession, in the petty and particular rights and usages which were transmitted in custom as the properties of the poor. Common right ... was local right, and hence was also a power to exclude strangers. Enclosure, in taking the commons away from the poor, made them strangers in their own land. (Thompson, 1991, p 184)

A new universal definition of right and wrong was sought that could legitimate property expropriation within new relations of production. It was the political success of these classes in forcing their interest and will that ensured that the legal reformers could express legal rules, which were the product of sharp social conflicts, in terms of consensus, good common sense and opposition to anarchy. The rule of private property became the 'rule of law', so that attacks on the former could be condemned as attacks on a universal social good. Instrumental in this process was the creation of an abstract and formal definition of human subjectivity that would cut off reference to substantive moral argument. This abstract and formal conception of human subjectivity was central both to the philosophy of the period, and to the criminal law:

> The motive by which an offender was influenced, as distinguished from his intention, is never material to an offence. If the prohibited act be done, and be done with the intention by law essential to the offence, it is complete, without reference either to any ulterior intention or to the motive which gave birth to the intention. To allow any man to substitute for law his own notions of right, would be in effect to subvert the law ... [A] man's private opinion could not possibly be allowed to weigh against the authority of the law ... 'though he (the offender) thought that the act was innocent, or even meritorious' ... (Criminal Law Commissioners, 1843, p 29)[8]

---

8   The last sentence in quotation marks is from Hume.

However, legal formalism cuts both ways. In choking off alternative social and political voices through the adoption of abstract legal categories, legal formalism constricted its own potential for moral judgment. It is that constriction that lies at the heart of the criminal law today. We see it, as I have said above, in the law of murder, where a reliance simply on intention to kill or cause grievous bodily harm provides an ineffective basis for the judgment of the moral quality of killings. James Bulger's killers, under the law's definition – its formalistic morality – are as guilty as anyone who intends to kill or do grievous bodily harm. This is juridically simple, but morally simplistic. What is lacking is a synthetic view of the relationship between mental state, social context and criminal act; however, the possibility of synthesising different aspects of responsibility and judgment was consciously suppressed in the foundation of the modern criminal law.[9] The apparent neutrality of the criminal law's individualist concepts of responsibility was achieved at the cost of neutering the process of judgment.[10] Law represents a simulacrum, a pale and ambiguous *doppelgänger*, of moral judgment. However, in the dominant view, represented in the prefatory quote from Duff, moral and legal judgment are homologous. In the next section, I explore the way in which this relationship is presented in legal theory, and the flaws within it.

Law's architectonic of judgment

In the standard view, the structure of criminal law involves a 'general part' which applies *ceteris paribus* to the specific offences. The general part is composed of *actus reus* and *mens rea*, which occupy the central position (cf Smith, 1989). While acts and intentions are central to the establishment of criminal responsibility, general defences incorporating ideas of justification and excuse may operate where *actus reus* and *mens rea* have already been established in order to exonerate the accused according to the nature of the defence he or she has invoked. It is this conception of a general part in which *mens rea* is central to legal judgment, while defences of justification and excuse are regarded as secondary and exceptional, that I describe as the architectonic of legal judgment. It is presented in orthodox accounts as commonsensical and rational (if problematic in its detail), but I will argue that this particular shape of the categories of judgment is the result of the scleroticisation of judgment described above.

According to Antony Duff, intention is integral to human action, and intended and intentional agency form the central paradigms of responsible agency. This is true in both law and morality, so that Duff affirms this homology:

> The underlying assumption here is that criminal liability should, in principle, be ascribed in accordance with moral responsibility. A defendant should be criminally liable only for conduct for which she can properly be held morally responsible or culpable ... That is why *mens rea* should be required for criminal liability, and why intention should be the most serious kind of criminal fault. (Duff, 1990, p 103)

---

9 On the nature of this suppression in the law of recklessness, see below, Chapter 5.

10 On the ambiguous role of sentencing as a symbiotic, yet contradictory mode of judgment to that provided by the categories of legal responsibility, see Norrie (2001b, pp 45–46). Of course, mitigation is not available on a murder conviction, a contingency which serves to point up the failure of the legal categories to reflect a moral sense of wrongdoing.

Duff's analysis is, however, ambivalent. On the one hand, intention in his account is central to both legal and moral responsibility, so that he seeks to rationalise the morality of form that legal judgment entails. On the other hand, because of his commitment to an interpretivist approach to judgment, Duff ends up pushing beyond the legal categories and showing the irrational, morally suppressive, character of judgment within law's architectonic. I deal with this in relation to three aspects of Duff's work. The first concerns his account of the relationship between intention, justification and excuse; the second involves his account of the nature of intentional agency; and the third relates to his critique of what he describes as the orthodox consequentialist and dualist account of criminal responsibility. My argument will be that in all three areas, Duff's discussion reveals the impossibility of maintaining a separation of questions of intention (form) from the broader context of normative judgment (content) in which they are constructed. The morality of form, with intention as its anchor concept, is shown to be irredeemably infected with, and unsustainable apart from, the broader normative context within which perforce it operates. Law's Kantian moral abstraction proves never to be enough.

Intention, justification and excuse

A central question for any explanation of law's architectonic of judgment is why *mens rea* has pole position ahead of questions of justification and excuse. There is a *prima facie* problem, as Duff notes. Questions of *mens rea* may not be sufficient to establish criminal guilt, for an act may be intended, yet be justified or excused. This raises the question whether intended agency is truly the central question for criminal responsibility, or whether matters of justification and excuse have overriding importance. As regards justification, Duff argues that this apparent problem can be met:

> One who justifies her action is prepared to answer for it, by showing it to be right: the possibility of avoiding blame or criminal liability by justifying our intended or intentional actions, therefore, does not undermine the claim that intended and intentional actions are paradigms of responsible agency. (*Ibid*, p 100)

As regards the latter, excuses operate with, not against, intentional agency, for they 'at least qualify, even if they do not wholly rebut, the ascription of intended or intentional agency' (*ibid*). Justification and excuse issues are therefore compatible with the centrality of intended and intentional agency to moral and legal culpability. The relationship is complementary rather than contradictory so that intention's primary position is valid.

Dealing first with justification, Duff's analysis of the relationship between justification and intention hinges upon his understanding of responsibility, which is cast in terms of answering for one's actions:

> To act with the intention of bringing a result about is to make myself fully responsible for that result – I must be ready to answer for (to explain, to justify, to accept criticism for) my action of bringing it about; and I bring about intentionally those effects for which I am held responsible. (*Ibid*, p 99)

Hart has shown, however, that there are a number of different meanings of the word 'responsibility' (Hart, 1968, Chapter 9), and although he does not identify Duff's conception of 'being called to respond' as one of them, it is doubtful whether this idea reflects what is really required for either legal or moral responsibility. What Duff, I think, is looking for (or at least needs) is something like Hart's account of 'moral liability-responsibility'. For Hart too, there is substantial homology between legal and moral responsibility. Differences, he says, 'are due to substantive differences between the content of legal and moral rules and principles rather than to any variation in meaning of responsibility' (*ibid*, pp 225–26). However, Hart explains such responsibility not in terms of being 'called to respond', but in terms of being 'morally blameworthy, or morally obliged to make amends for the harm' (*ibid*, p 225). Duff's account by comparison appears to describe a preliminary situation prior to that of ascribing blame, in which the issue of blameworthiness has yet to be settled. To be 'called to answer' is not the same as to have one's answers accepted or found wanting, and it is the latter that blameworthiness requires.

Because the concept of responsibility-as-answerability does not settle the issue of responsibility-as-blameworthiness, it cannot settle the proper relationship between intention and justification with regard to culpability. At best, it gives rise to a kind of *prima facie* culpability (cf Gardner and Jung, 1991 pp 559, 587). However, even this is questionable, for even such culpability depends on a proper allocation of matters of justification alongside intention. Yet this is Duff's chosen means of reconciling justification with intention.

As regards excuse, I will focus on Duff's treatment of the twin excuses of duress and necessity, which present problems for his analysis of the centrality of intention. Duff argues that intentional actions are done for reasons, and that this means that intention is linked to rationality. Duress and necessity claims:

> serve to rebut the presumption of rational competence which ascriptions of intentional agency normally involve. Duress or necessity should excuse if the pressure to which the agent is subjected is so severe that it impairs her capacity to grasp, to weigh or to act on good reasons for action – to realise that and why she should resist the pressure, or to carry through a resolution to resist it. (Duff, 1990, p 102)

Note, first, that this is not the standard analysis of how duress and necessity operate in relation to intention. According to the standard analysis, it may be perfectly rational to intend to commit an act under duress because of the threat that has been made. There is no assumption that the agent cannot grasp, weigh or act on good reasons for action. He or she may perfectly well realise why the pressure should be resisted, and yet submit to the duress. The use of reason may be what makes the duress potent.

Duff's account, I think, recognises as much in that he introduces the idea of 'good' reasons for action, but the significance of this goes against rather than for his argument. In introducing in effect a notion of morally substantive rational agency into his conception of intention, he reveals that it is not simply the issue of intention that grounds a notion of responsibility, but intention related to a particular, morally substantive context. Thus, duress as excuse forces Duff into a position on responsibility in which a substantive moral addition is needed to supplement his analysis of intention. Intention involves acting from good reasons, not morally neutral reasons. This, however, is a 'dangerous supplement'[11] because it reveals that the matter of normative content is a central and constitutive component of responsibility alongside the factual ability to form intentions and act intentionally.

To put it another way, duress and necessity are defences which operate to deny responsibility notwithstanding the existence of intended or intentional agency, and therefore they undermine the claim that intention and intentionality are the central moral features of judgment. It transpires, in these cases, that excuses invoke broader issues of normative judgment as the basis for settling matters of responsibility, and that questions of intention and intentionality are relevant only within this broader context. While it is true that law's architectonic of judgment focuses on intention and intentionality, the extreme cases of duress and necessity reveal that the normally hidden substratum of these categories is moral and political. Duress and necessity force this normative basis into the open, revealing that intention and intentionality are only the primary categories of responsibility so long as this deeper normative element remains hidden. Intention cannot be isolated as a primary category on which to base responsibility ahead of issues of justification and excuse. It cannot be abstracted; it needs to be synthesised.

The legal concept of responsibility normally seeks to suppress this contextually synthetic account of judgment in favour of a morality of form, in which apparently neutral categories such as intention are given primacy. Potentially threatening normative issues such as those of justification and excuse are portrayed as contained and secondary exceptions. However, a sophisticated attempt to rationalise this position such as Duff's only shows the act of suppression and denial that goes into law's architectonic. Moving to Duff's concept of intention itself, we will see the continuing juridical need to suppress content in favour of a morality of form, and a vivid example of the logic of legal practice in this regard.

The normative foundation of intentional agency

Intention in Duff's account includes both 'direct' and 'oblique' forms. One either acts with the intention of bringing something about, or one brings something about not as one's intention, but as a foreseen by-product of one's actions. In the latter instance, one does not 'intend', but one still acts 'intentionally'. With regard to oblique intention a question arises as to whether we ascribe responsibility with regard to all or only some unintended but foreseen consequences. However, Duff observes that we cannot ascribe every foreseen consequence to an agent because there is a moral dimension involved:

> Ascriptions of intentional agency do not describe neutral facts: they express normative judgments of responsibility, in which we may disagree. (Duff, 1990, p 84; cf Williams, 1987, p 417)

Such normative judgments involve a potential moral issue as to what an agent should take into account as an effect of his action. If an examiner fails a student to

---

11 'To supplement jurisprudence, then, could be just a matter of making sure that valuable things are kept on board. The supplement provides what is lacking. It serves to complement and complete that which is supplemented ... But, as Derrida has it, the supplement is also "dangerous". The supplement is not fully assimilable. It remains outside, challenging the completeness and the adequacy of that which is within' (Fitzpatrick, 1991b, p 2).

the student's serious detriment, the examiner, Duff argues, is not responsible even where the consequences are foreseen. It is part of the normative role of an examiner to judge a student on performance and not on the consequences of that performance. Similarly, whether a doctor is criminally liable for aiding and abetting unlawful sexual intercourse by prescribing contraceptives to an underage girl depends upon one's moral view of the doctor's role: is it to the patient, or to the patient and the law? Depending on one's view, one will come up with a different conclusion as to whether the doctor intentionally aided and abetted the offence.

This issue of substantive normativity has emerged in cases such as *R v Steane* [1947] KB 997 and *R v Ahlers* [1915] 1 KB 616. Both were cases involving charges of intending to assist the enemy in time of war. In the former, Steane was acquitted because he broadcast for the Germans under threat of death to his wife and children; in the latter, Ahlers, a German Consul, was held not to assist the enemy by helping Germans to return home because he was only doing his duty as a Consul. Both cases involve a normative judgment about the scope of what was intended, since to broadcast and to assist repatriation were both actions that *ceteris paribus* would have the effect of assisting the enemy.

Such questions involve matters of moral and political judgment and raise centrally the question of what justifies a person in acting in a particular way. Thus, Duff's analysis of intentional agency undermines his account of intention and intentionality as simple paradigms of responsible agency. Justification is a central and constitutive component of the judgment of intention, part of its intrinsic structure. Responsibility is 'molecular', not an admixture of separate 'atoms' of intention, justification and excuse. However, this is what the law denies, for the historical reasons given in the previous section above, and it is this denial that drives a wedge between legal and moral judgment.

The denial is achieved in practice by a forced repression. While Duff shows that oblique intention involves substantive normativity, he also notes that normative disagreement is 'more typically found outside the law than within it':

> Outside the law our different normative standards (our different moral values, for instance) will generate conflicting criteria of responsibility, of relevance, and of intentional agency: but the law provides authoritative criteria which determine our legal responsibilities, the legal relevance of expected side-effects, and thus the scope (in law) of our intentional agency. (Duff, 1990, p 84)

An individual swimming naked in public view might have no oblique intention to expose herself indecently, and might insist that she is entitled so to swim. However, the law may hold that the conduct is intentionally disgusting and, no matter what the person thinks, she 'will not be heard to deny that [she] cause[s] it intentionally'. In such a circumstance the law forecloses the issue of normative disagreement by insisting that the oblique intention is present whatever the individual's own normative view. The issue of judgment is settled by the court, according to its view of what is acceptable. The normative issue of what is justifiable is finessed by the law's unilateral declaration of what the 'authoritative criteria' are to be. As with the distinction between motive and intention, or the sidelining of justification and excuse, so in relation to intentionality we see the way in which matters of normative judgment are suppressed within the law's base categories. Once that is done, and these categories have been 'secured' against moral infection, issues of justification and excuse are permitted as limited subsidiary categories within law's architectonic. Law, in separating these issues out and prioritising a psychological concept of intention, does not run with morality, but cuts against it.

A good example of how this splitting disrupts legal theory is seen in Duff's troubled discussion of *R v Steane*. Taking this to be a case of intentional rather than intended assistance of the enemy, there arises on Duff's account a substantive normative question (as with the doctor or the teacher) as to whether Steane's assisting the enemy was morally intentional. Rather than arguing the case on moral terms, however, Duff does what I argue the law does: he finesses the potential normative disagreement by positing a consequentialist argument as to why Steane should not be allowed to claim his assistance was unintentional:

> If we deny that Steane intended to assist the enemy, because he intended to save his family, we must likewise deny that one who broadcasts for the enemy in order to earn money intends to assist the enemy. However, it would be outrageous to acquit such a person of 'doing acts likely to assist the enemy, with intent to assist the enemy'. Mr Steane's defence should have been duress, not lack of intent; his intention to assist the enemy was excused by the threats under which he acted. (Duff, 1990, p 93)

There is, however, a world of moral difference between Steane and a mercenary that should, on Duff's *own* analysis, be reflected in his consideration as to whether Steane acted intentionally. This can be seen if we compare Duff's treatment of *R v Steane* with *R v Ahlers*, where he argues on the moral issue. Ahlers' intention 'was simply to do his legal duty as consul, which required him to help enemy aliens return home when war began' (*ibid*). The difference between Ahlers and Steane is that the former was not a 'private citizen' and his role and duties as a Consul constitute a moral threshold over which the known side-effect of assisting the enemy does not pass. This is, however, no more than an additional moral judgment that the role and duties of a consul are somehow more valid than those of a husband and father. In both, there can be moral disagreement on Duff's account, and in neither can the moral issue be ruled out by a consequentialist argument. In foreclosing on the moral question of intentionality in *R v Steane*, and sidelining it to the excuse of duress, Duff does precisely what the law does in order to avoid contestable moral issues around its paradigm categories of intention and intentionality. However, he does it against his own account of the moral substance of intention.

Consequentialism versus interpretivism

Law's architectonic of judgment thus privileges an apparently de-normativised (or de-politicised, de-moralised) concept of intention and intentionality, relegating the 'difficult' moral and political issues to what is constructed as a subsidiary category of justification and excuse. There, in the law's back alleys, they become relatively unimportant 'exceptions to a rule' rather than what they really are: constitutive elements of responsibility and judgment.

If Duff's work can be seen as seeking to defend and rationalise law's architectonic, his interpretive method also provides us with a theoretical tool for its critique. The most radical part of his *Intention, Agency and Criminal Liability* (which cuts against his rationalisation of law) sketches a critique of legal individualism, dualism and consequentialism. Duff argues that legal judgment entails a number of dualisms, the most important of which is the subjective/objective dichotomy within a consequentialist account of harm and blame. For the consequentialist, harm is defined 'objectively' according to principles of political utility, and separately from questions of fault which operate as a side-constraint. Fault, in turn, stresses practical issues concerning subjective individual knowledge and control over the occurrence of harm, and it is for this reason that questions of intention are central to the consequentialist theory of criminal responsibility. Consequentialism therefore depoliticises or demoralises the question of criminal harm by establishing the bounds of harm 'objectively', and by identifying subjective responsibility for harm in terms of apparently 'factual' categories of knowledge and control.

Duff's critique correctly points out that this separation of subjective and objective components misses the synthetic nature of the moral judgment of harm. Such a judgment attributes responsibility for murder, for example, in terms of the moral quality of the mental state that is linked to a death:

> Both the murder victim and the victim of natural causes suffer death. However, the character of the harm that they suffer surely also depends on the way in which they die. One who tries to kill me ... *attacks* my life and my most basic rights; and the harm which I suffer in being murdered ... essentially involves this wrongful attack on me ... The 'harm' at which the law of murder is aimed is thus not just the *consequential* harm of death, but the harm which is *intrinsic* to an attack on another's life. (*Ibid*, pp 112–13)

Criminal law, with its separation of *mens rea* (fault) and *actus reus* (harm), reflects the dualist position which Duff regards as inadequate. His argument is that the essence of murder is not the consequence of death but the intrinsic harm in the attack on another's life. That intrinsic harm is paradigmatically present in a wilful killing, and therefore paradigmatically present when there is an intention to kill. Duff still insists on the centrality of intention, but it is a morally substantive conception that he invokes in his discussion of the intention to kill. It is not the factual issue of control over one's conduct that is important, but the moral badness revealed by one's intention:

> Human actions are purposive: they are done for reasons, in order to bring something about; their direction and their basic structure is formed by the intentions with which their agents act. It is through the intentions with which I act that I engage in the world as an agent, and relate myself most closely to the actual and potential effects of my actions; and the central or fundamental kind of wrong-doing is to *direct* my actions towards evil – to *intend* and to *try* to do what is evil. (*Ibid*, p 113)

Duff's emphasis on the synthetic relation between law's subjective and objective elements opens the door to the element of moral evaluation in the establishment of any death as murder. It goes beyond the combination of result and mental state, narrowly conceived in terms of factual or psychological intention. His interpretive analysis of judgment, with its unification of moral form and content, still makes intention a central part of the judgment of wrongdoing but it at the same time decentres it. It is the 'moral colour' of the intention that is now crucial, and on which the judgment is based. It is impossible to judge intention separately from the quality of the act that is being done. If we return to the example of Steane and the mercenary who both broadcast for the enemy, it is clear that Steane's (indirect) intention to assist the enemy in no way matches that of the mercenary. The moral colour of Steane's oblique intention is provided by his direct intention to save his family. Steane does not seek in moral terms, 'to do what is evil', while the mercenary does. The interpretive account takes this into account in a way that the consequentialist cannot.

Duff quite rightly takes us beyond the narrow understanding of judgment contained within the traditional consequentialist view. However, he also takes us, despite himself, beyond the law's demoralised architectonic of judgment. The radical and critical thrust of Duff's interpretivism takes us beyond law, but beyond law to what?

Conclusion: beyond legal judgment

I have argued that the creation of a legal architectonic as a morality of form involved an attempt to demarcate a legal sphere that was immune from overt normative – moral and political – questions. The practical effects of this can be seen in the trial of Venables and Thompson for the murder of James Bulger (see the second section above). The separation of motive and intention was one central element of an apparently apolitical and amoral sphere of judgment (discussed in the third section). The prioritisation of *mens rea* over justification and excuse in the 'general part' is a corollary of this, for it was indeed matters of justification (motive of right) and excuse (motive of need) which were suppressed by the central reliance placed upon intention in the primary act of separation. However, scrutiny of the logic of this architectonic of separation and suppression reveals that questions of moral and political context are inseparable from questions of act and intention (see the last section above). Legal judgment seeks to differentiate itself from moral judgment, but fails. That which has been repressed returns. In this section, I seek to locate this return of a repressed connection to broader questions about the nature and possibility of judgment in modern society.

Alasdair MacIntyre has written of an impasse in modern thought resulting from the incommensurability of ethical claims:

> [W]hen claims invoking rights are matched against claims appealing to utility or when either or both are matched against claims based on some traditional concept of justice, it is not surprising that there is no rational way of deciding which type of claim is to be given priority ... Moral incommensurability is itself the product of a particular historical conjunction. (MacIntyre, 1985, p 70)

The problem stems from the invention of an autonomous moral individual as the source of morality in the modern world. The price paid for this 'homuncular' morality (Norrie, 1991b, Chapter 9) is a failure to establish any sense of moral bonds beyond the individual. Utilitarianism, as MacIntyre puts it, is an inadequate attempt to replace traditional moralities with a principle with which to 'contextualise' individual acts. It fails to do anything other than create an opposition between the collective interest and individual autonomy.

I agree with MacIntyre about this sense of incommensurability at the heart of the discontents of modernity (cf Norrie, 1991b), and I also agree that the problem can be diagnosed as an historical one, as a result of the way that Western societies have been constructed in modern times. This chapter can be read as supporting MacIntyre's project by showing the way in which one aspect of how we live – through the law and its judgments – crucially contributes to, as well as reflecting, the broader moral impasse. Thus, Ashworth's presentation of liberal criminal law, discussed in the introduction, can be seen to reflect the rights/utility antinomy, and the discussion of the failure to achieve a synthetic and contextual judgment in the James Bulger case, in the law of murder, and around the concept of intention, stems from the structuring of judgment according to the law's individualism.

The historical dimension is as important to the analysis presented here as it is to MacIntyre, perhaps more so. Indeed, I think it is possible, through a reading of the law's individualism as a social and historical process of exclusion, to see a way of at least beginning to address one central failing of the moral analysis in *After Virtue*. MacIntyre seeks to re-establish a moral conception of the good life for man in the face of the individualism of the modern world and the moral fragmentation that flows from it. His approach is to argue for a sense of community and tradition, implicit in all moral discourse, which we take forward into our conceptions of what is morally good. However, this leads MacIntyre into his own moral impasse because he has already argued that it is precisely the failing of the modern sense of community that has caused the loss of coherent moral vision. In grounding his analysis of the morality of individualism in the historical development of the modern community, he fails to establish the existence of an 'other' community that can found a sense of moral order. The basis for an alternative sense of community to modernity is denied by his historical method, and MacIntyre is ultimately forced into a leap of faith that somehow it will be possible to construct, out of nothing, a new community. From somewhere, we must find 'men and women of good will' who can construct 'local forms of community within which civility and the intellectual and moral life can be sustained through the new dark ages which are already upon us' (MacIntyre, 1985, p 263). How these mysterious 'men and women of goodwill' (at once a highly abstract and a very 'modern' construction) can appear is not explained, and nor can it be, given his description of the moral failings of the modern individualist community.

However, MacIntyre's quest appears legitimate. His ability to reveal the failures of the morality of modernity already implies a morality that could exist, even if he cannot adumbrate it.[12] My suggestion is that through looking quite concretely at the historical way in which modern law and politics scleroticised moral judgment, we are able to posit a sense of morality beyond the law's individualism, within our already existing communities.

My method has not been to elaborate an alternative morality to that of the law, and thence to criticise the law for its failures. I have worked out of the failures of the law adequately to capture an immanent sense of moral judgment in both practical

---

12 In his subsequent work, MacIntyre (1988, 1990) appears to slacken the historical and contextual strictures of *After Virtue* in order to argue for the possibility of reconstituting older moral traditions in the present. But it has recently been rightly noted that if he is to attach importance to the 'social embeddedness of thought and enquiry, [then] his largely negative view of modernity continually threatens to undermine any attempt to root his positive proposals in the contemporary world of advanced industrial societies' (Horton and Mendus, 1994, pp 13–14).

and theoretical settings. Thus, I have suggested the failure of a law-dominated universe of judgment to reflect a more profound sense of the complexity of wrong evoked by the James Bulger case, and I have argued that the law's analysis of intention, justification and excuse unsuccessfully represses a more synthetic methodology of judgment. The creation of our modern categories of judgment is based upon a suppression of deeper moral possibilities which remain sensible and serious even if (and because) they appear legally impossible or impractical. Duff's conception of an interpretivist moral strategy shows the inadequacy of legal judgment, even as his rationalisation of the law defends a morality choked off by homuncular forms of responsibility. Individualist legal forms repress other possible architectonics of judgment which do not go away: they lurk behind and within the contradictions of law.[13]

Part of MacIntyre's problem lies in the abstract way he uses history, representing the historical character of modern morality in vague socio-cultural terms. His main premise is that a cultural change occurred in Northern Europe in the 17th and 18th centuries from which individual autonomy and the separation of morals, religion, law and aesthetics emerged (MacIntyre, 1985, pp 36–39). Later in his analysis, he recognises as a central characteristic of modernity the existence of social conflict in modern society, acknowledging that we are 'fundamentally right in seeing conflict and not consensus at the heart of modern social structure'. Modern liberal conceptions of morality, he argues, 'furnish us with a pluralist political rhetoric whose function is to conceal the depth of our conflicts' (*ibid*, p 253). However, MacIntyre forges no real connection between the individualism and the social conflict he identifies.

On my analysis, the relationship between ideological form and structural context is stronger and more explicit. Legal individualism operates as a mode of exclusion and repression of alternative substantive views of right and wrong, and the moral absences of modernity and law are based on that repression. The forms of law scleroticise our sense of judgment not only because they stand apart from moral judgment but also because they stand in the way of alternative, immanent formulations. We are not talking only, *pace* MacIntyre, of a concealment of social conflict, but of a repression of moral and political alternatives in a structurally conflictual environment. This is achieved by virtue of the abstract individualist forms of law and morality, while the moral contents that are excluded by law's formalism keep forcing themselves back to our attention as felt 'lacks' to which we try to give names. Much of the time we are unable to articulate what these alternative moralities are, but this is exactly what we should expect given the historical experience of repression of which our own cultural imaginations are the victims. They remain necessarily inchoate.

In this context, it makes sense for us to look to alternative processes of judgment to try to understand what is lacking in our own legal and moral processes. On a personal level, we may reflect on the processes of judgment that we are familiar with with friends, in families, or sometimes in communities or the workplace.[14] As

---

13 Thus, the antinomy of the formal and the informal discussed in Chapter 3 represses the possibility of alternative modes of judgment which are cast into the darkness of 'the informal'.

14 This is not to deny that these too are structured and conflictual environments, but they are not so clearly or so closely constructed around a legal architectonic of judgment.

legal actors, we may look to systems of 'alternative' or 'popular' justice that exist in the interstices of, or in opposition to, Western style systems such as described here. This is not the place to do other than indicate in very broad terms what we find in these other places of judgment.[15] Frequently, categories of judgment are nuanced and more reflective than those of the state and the law. Judgments recognise the context of agency and measure knowledge of background and competence against action. There is not an abstract standard, but a graded sense of what a family member, a friend, a colleague, a member of the community could have done, as well as what he or she did do, and there is also a reflexive sense of the judger's own role in relationships and the outcomes that they generate. There is also a sense that the result of judgments should be constructive and developmental, not punitive and regressive. There is an emphasis on particularisation in the application of norms to individuals, and a correlative sense of the need to act flexibly with regard to the selection of norms.

I can do no more than gesture at this discussion, but I think it is clear that the rough sketch I have outlined is closer to the alternative sense of judgment evoked by the James Bulger case than the abstract conception of judgment that is generated by law, and that was predominantly and publicly applied in that case. Thus, my suggestion against MacIntyre is that a more critical historical methodology can help us to see that the alternative sources of moral judgment do not require a complete rupture with the present as a social and political reality in order to search out a community 'beyond' what exists. The other community that MacIntyre seeks beyond our own is an illusion and an impossibility, but this should invoke relief not desperation. The resources to work morally and politically against the 'new dark ages' to which he refers already exist, suppressed, in the here and now.

It is the sense of alternatives suppressed in the past and the present that burns in the late EP Thompson's last work, *Customs in Common*:

> As capitalism (or 'the market') made over human nature and human need, so political economy ... came to suppose that this economic man was for all time. We stand at the end of a century when this must now be called in doubt. We shall not ever return to pre-capitalist human nature, yet a reminder of its alternative needs, expectations and codes may renew our sense of our nature's range of possibilities. (Thompson, 1991, p 184)

Thompson reminds us, *pace* MacIntyre, that we need not go back to aristocratic Athens for a sense of moral community and tradition, for 18th century plebeian England will do just as well. Ordinary people, not extraordinary 'men and women of goodwill', sharing 'experiences in labour and social relations' generate their own moral judgments alongside 'the necessary conformity with the status quo' (*ibid*, p 11). As in the past, such judgments can constitute the basis for alternative counter-legalities in the present. Whether they will do so was something about which

---

15 Important discussions in a voluminous literature can be found in the following: Allison, 1990, pp 409–28; Burman and Scharf, 1990, p 695; Fitzpatrick, 1987; Fitzpatrick, 1992a, pp 199–215; Gundersen, 1992, pp 257–82; Sachs and Welch, 1990; Scharf and Ngcokoto, 1990; Spitzer, 1982. See above, Chapter 3.

Thompson expressed pessimism,[16] and it is indeed hard to feel anything else in the present Western social and political climate. However, we should understand that alternatives exist as part of 'our nature's range of possibilities', and not as a mystical ideal for another community, operating somewhere beyond the world in which we live.

With MacIntyre, we may agree that the dominant intellectual structures of our social, political and legal world are not necessarily immanent in human existence, but are the politically achieved artefacts of a particular society. It is this historical and political structuring of law's architectonic of judgment, represented as a 'general part' of *mens rea*, justification and excuse, that ultimately guarantees its strength and longevity. Neither its intellectual coherence nor its ability to reflect the moral character of judgment and responsibility in everyday life vindicates it.

---

16 And caution: see Thompson's comments about 'rough music', a form of law that 'belongs to the people, and is not alienated, or delegated', but which is not 'necessarily more "nice" and tolerant'. Rough music was 'only as nice and as tolerant as the prejudices and norms of the folk allow' and Thompson comments that 'Law and a bureaucratised police must have been felt as a liberation from the tyranny of one's "own"' (1991, pp 530–31). These comments are important in Britain today, where unpleasant forms of 'popular justice' have begun to emerge as a result of the perceived failures of the police and the courts to contain some forms of criminality. The value of producing an analysis of the limits of the Western legal architectonic is to formulate a clear analysis of the strengths and limitations of such law. This can then form the basis for comparison with other architectonics of judgment in different times and places. The argument of this final section makes it clear that it is possible to conceive morally and historically of the possibility of such alternative architectonics of judgment. This is a prelude to considering what role law-like regulation might play under alternative moral, social and political arrangements. It is not to argue for the abandonment of law, as the previous chapter makes clear.

Chapter 5
The Limits of Justice:
Finding Fault in the Criminal Law

Introduction: challenging the 'penal equation'

Crime is a serious social problem to which society does not have a serious answer. Loud voices say that if our stock responses fail, we need more of the same. It should be easier to detect and convict criminals, punishments should be harsher. The resulting calls for 'law and order', with increasing emphasis on the latter, rely on what we may call the 'penal equation'. This is the simple formula, 'crime plus responsibility equals punishment', that has informed our social control practices for 200 years. Crime requires punishment as retribution and deterrence, and criminal justice qualifies individuals as deserving of the state's legitimate sanctions. It is this sense of justice, responsibility and desert, justifying social control through criminal punishment, which is the focus of this chapter.

Criminal justice fixes a badge of responsibility to the individual's lapel, and thereby justifies retribution and deterrence. Yet who is satisfied with this? Retribution appears to evoke backward-looking ideas of revenge, while deterrence, *pace* almost every modern Home Secretary, hardly seems to work (Norrie, 1993a, 2001b, Chapters 2, 10).[1] Over the past 100 years, reformers have sought persistently to move the system from these tired rationales. Calls for reparation, reconciliation, and mediation, as well as for increased use of diversion, non-custodial penalties and forms of intermediate treatment indicate the need, perceived by many, for changes which can break the iron grip of the 'penal equation'. Legal justice is contrasted with reintegrative approaches (Braithwaite, 1989), with what can broadly be termed 'relational justice' (Burnside and Baker, 1994).[2] However, as Sir Louis Blom Cooper has noted, such developments remain peripheral and for that reason sustain the mainstream. Mitigating its worst features, they 'positively acknowledge the centrality of the courts and prisons as the instrument to be deployed' (Blom Cooper, 1995, p 11).

So what is to be done in terms of challenging this equation? Is it possible to move beyond it? Were we to do so, would there be loss as well as gain? It is easier to acknowledge problems with the penal equation than to solve them. As Michel Foucault (1977) noted, the history of penal reform is as old as the penal system itself, and we should be aware of the pitfalls of grand designs. Blom Cooper calls for a new 'theoretical underpinning' and a radical alternative to the criminal justice

---

1 I argue there that retributive and deterrence theories have a common root in the individualism of Enlightenment ideology, and this accounts *mutatis mutandis* for the different problems both experience. My focus here is on criminal law and justice, so the discussion primarily relates to questions that are seen as being in their essence retributive.

2 For a good summary of the contrasts and similarities between retributive and reparative ideas, see Zedner, 1994. While I use the idea of a 'relational' theory of punishment in my own work (Norrie, 2000), I distinguish a philosophical use of the concept from one that directly endorses particular practices of control and reconciliation in line with the overall thesis of this essay: see fn 18 below.

system, but he does not provide one.[3] While sympathetic to the call for a new theory underlying a new practice, I will argue that a direct link between theory and practical reform may be problematic. That is not to argue that theory does not illuminate the problems of criminal justice, or that practice is not enhanced by it. It is to claim that the relation between theory and practice is intrinsically difficult. What is needed is a theoretical approach that can encapsulate an *ambivalence* in our assessment of the legal conception of justice, one that can explain its weaknesses, but also its strengths. It is important neither to reject totally nor to accept uncritically the conception of justice established by criminal law. We need a theory which can take us beyond either wholesale rejection or broad acceptance of the present system. Such an approach would be sensitive to the unavoidable gap, as well as the links, between an adequate theory and a possible practice.

My approach will be to find a theoretical route beyond criminal law and justice, but to go 'beyond the law' by going 'through' it. So doing, we achieve a more complex and sophisticated picture of what is at stake in the 'penal equation'. It is one thing, as criminological thought from Italian positivism (Ferri, 1901) to Barbara Wootton (1963), and now Blom Cooper has done, to dismiss legal ideas of retribution and deterrence as outdated, inefficient and unenlightened. It is another to engage with law to show *through that engagement* the limits, but also the strengths, of legal justice. It is important to stress the double-sided character of law. A legal approach contributes to the failure of criminal justice to reflect society's moral and practical needs, but we must also recognise its positive side. In particular, we should recognise the liberal, in its own terms progressive, current of thinking which elaborates the virtues of law and, to some extent, punishment. This approach to criminal justice was most influentially expressed by HLA Hart in the 1950s and 1960s (Hart, 1968). It underpins the work of criminal law writers like Glanville Williams (1961), Smith and Hogan (1992) and Andrew Ashworth (1991). It insists that it is a moral strength of the criminal justice system that it is law-based. This is true at the procedural level, at which civil liberties issues are contested (Ashworth, 1994; Sanders and Young, 1994), but also in the substantive law as concerns responsibility and punishment. Liberal theory argues that we ought to punish only those who act freely, either in terms of their capacity or control over their actions. Law respects autonomy and personhood, and this is a value in itself.

The problem comes, however, when we ask just what these liberal ideas mean. What, for example, does it mean to be a free or autonomous criminal given that (processed) crime has always been linked with structurally disadvantaged socio-economic backgrounds? Here we encounter the basic flaw in 'justice model' thinking: the problem of how to achieve 'just deserts in an unjust society' (American Friends Service Committee, 1971; Ashworth, 1989; Murphy, 1979; Norrie, 1993a, 2001b, Chapter 10; Norrie, 1991b, Chapters 3, 9).[4] However, we should not discard lightly the libertarian dimension to liberal justice thinking. This is apparent if we reflect on the practical resonance that responsibility and freedom have for modern society. Consider for example the complaints of prisoners undergoing discretionary,

---

3 Blom Cooper's only real proposal is for a return to the bipartisan political consensus on criminal justice issues which existed in the 1970s.

4 In Norrie, 1991b, I argue for the historical continuity from Hobbes onwards of this problem for liberal retributive theory.

indefinite sentences about the special, additional punishment and injustice in not knowing when they may be released. Consider too the ways the law's categories of responsibility can reflect the moral feelings of those who come before it. For example, in the case of homicide by a battered wife, it is important to many that the accused achieve what they see as the more just, while arguably still inadequate, verdict of voluntary manslaughter through provocation. The alternative of diminished responsibility, in pathologising the woman, does not reflect the moral truth of the accused's position and is therefore experienced as unjust (O'Donovan, 1991; McColgan, 1993; Horder, 1992).

Just and unjust: we should recognise the paradox and ambivalence at the core of criminal justice thinking. The 'penal equation' reflects serious moral distinctions, but at the same time proves a flawed basis for a morally sound (retributive), or even effective (deterrence based), system of social control. We may agree with Stan Cohen, who some years ago described the legal concepts of guilt and justice as old concepts needed by a new criminology, but we should reflect on the limits he found in such an argument. The legal approach, Cohen wrote, makes us 'forget that by the time many offenders get to this wonderful justice system the damage has already been done'. It is obvious, he says, 'to anyone who has spent five minutes in a court or prison that it would be blatantly unjust to return' to an undiluted legal approach (Cohen, 1979, pp 35–41). From one side, the 'penal equation' is part of the solution, from another, very much a part of the problem. The picture is ambiguous. Any adequate theoretical underpinning, even more so practical reforms, must acknowledge this moral ambivalence about criminal justice, and the forms that express it.

This chapter is concerned with understanding this ambivalence and ambiguity in three rather different but related sections. In the next section, I seek to locate ambivalence and ambiguity by considering the theoretical perspectives within which legal justice is understood. Moving from the liberal approach, which essentially endorses the legal conception of justice, to the deconstructive approach, which essentially rejects it (while still seemingly wishing to hold onto it), I outline a critical approach which would seek a standpoint beyond either a more simple endorsement or rejection. Thereafter (third section), I seek to show the moral inadequacy of the legal conception of justice with regard to a central concept of criminal responsibility (recklessness), and to explain this inadequacy in critical terms. I suggest that legal categories both reflect and deny moral issues of judgment and justice, and that there are historical, structural reasons why this should be so. There is a structural splitting of legal and moral judgment which explains what the law lacks in moral terms and which explains conflicts in its discourse which it cannot overcome. In this section, I move from a broad focus on the theory of justice to a narrower consideration of one category, recklessness, which is supposed to do justice in the law. My claim is that the broad critical standpoint developed in the second section can be brought to bear on the intricacies of substantive legal argument, and that exploring these intricacies illuminates the broader moral issues. In a fourth section, I develop the idea of a split between law and morality by contrasting a legal conception of responsibility with a moral conception derived from social psychology. My argument is for the idea that judgment and justice through law occupies a 'space between' the legal and the moral. From these arguments, I conclude on the moral limits of criminal justice and return to the problematic relation between a theory adequate to criminal justice and the possibility of practical reform.

Theorising justice

Liberalism and justice

If we are going to confront criminal law and justice, we need first to consider the traditions within which they are understood. Our starting point has to be liberalism, for the theory of retributive punishment and criminal justice is founded on it. Since I have already sketched this above, I will be very brief. Generalisations always do violence, but there is an identifiable core to the liberal tradition which involves its conception of the individual as an abstract, universal subject endowed with capacities for rational action, autonomy and self-determination (Norrie, 1991b).[5] The individual is a unified, centred being who acts as the basis for legitimating the state, law and punishment. He gives consent to the state, or recognises its rational necessity,[6] participating in its law as a rational legal subject. Punishment unifies political legitimacy and legal sanction. The rational subject receives punishment as 'just deserts' from the state through the law. The 'penal equation' – crime plus responsibility equals punishment – is founded, with many variations, on this kind of liberal bedrock.

Poststructuralism and justice

This liberal subject has been subjected to sustained critique from a variety of perspectives. The poststructuralist approach, influential in recent years, stresses instability and disunity within the individual subject. It points to what is excluded by the construction of the liberal individual and it affirms the moral value of difference over universality (Derrida, 1990; Douzinas and Warrington, 1995; Goodrich, 1995). To the rational will of liberalism, it opposes human needs and sentiments associated with 'the body'. To abstract reason, it opposes embodied being and particularity. It emphasises singularity, an ethics of the contingent, over universality. Most importantly, it calls into question the idea of the individual as a unified, centred being, insisting on the fragmented character of subjectivity. I am not one but several persons, and my central identity is a construction denying the difference within me. In order to be a unified subject, I must repress this otherness (Barron, 1993).

This critique has important consequences in terms of showing how a theory of liberal law, which purports to include, excludes. A theory of what all individuals have in common, liberalism excludes difference: of gender, race, class and

---

5 I discuss the liberal model more fully above in Chapter 4. For a historical survey of the development of the liberal theory of punishment from Hobbes to Hart, see Norrie, 1991b. For discussion of the modern variants of liberal theory including its individualist *and* communitarian forms, see Norrie, 2000, Chapters 5, 6.

6 For the contractarian tradition, see Hobbes, 1968; Beccaria, 1964; for rationalist approaches, see the German idealist tradition: Kant, 1965; Hegel, 1952. For discussion, see Norrie, 1991b, Chapters 2–4.

community. It does so in favour of a single, apparently neutral, standard that is in fact gendered (male), classed and aged (middle) and raced (white). However, there is, I would suggest, a danger of overkill. Liberalism as a locus of exclusion may be a fair argument, but does it lead one to exclude in turn the positive effects of liberalism? A system based on individual rights, on reason and universality surely has some advantages. Poststructuralists who want to argue for legal or human rights surely accept this, but then the question must be, on what basis? On grounds simply of 'strategy', which appears a weak, unthought-out basis, or on more solid theoretical grounds which concern the interplay between legal, personal, ethical and social identity, however these may be conceived in poststructuralist terms?

Notwithstanding attempts to come to terms with this question, there seems to be an unresolved theoretical and methodological tension in poststructuralism. In seeking a critical standpoint in what lies 'beyond', poststructuralism ultimately has a problem in coming to terms with the forms of the social world as they are. Either it insists on the deconstruction of existing forms of subjectivity and reason (including those of the law), and therefore that the criteria for progressive political and moral change exist entirely beyond 'what is', in an unactualised and unactualisable 'other' place; or it illicitly returns to what exists, for example, legal rights, seeing this as strategically necessary for moral and political practice 'in the meantime'. The latter approach is illegitimate in terms of the method of deconstruction, but cries out to be implemented in the face of real, pressing injustice (see above, Chapter 2, below Chapter 8; cf Cornell, 1992; Douzinas and Warrington, 1995, Chapter 5).[7]

These sceptical comments notwithstanding, it is important to hold on to the poststructuralist emphasis on the partiality, the exclusionary and incomplete character, of law and legal justice, and the difference that it masks, in order to probe the paradox and the ambiguity of legal justice I have described. However, we need other theoretical terms with which to understand the Janus-like character of law, both its significance and its problematic character, for justice.

Critical realism, dialectic and justice

My approach is through the critical realist work of Roy Bhaskar and others in the philosophy of social science, and also draws here on the work of Rom Harré in social psychology. I will first say a little about the basic outlook of critical realism and its recent 'dialectical turn' before exploring its relevance to justice thinking.[8] Bhaskar's starting point is that social and historical processes are ontologically real and emergent foundations for human being and that differently situated human beings act to reproduce and (sometimes) transform such foundations. Human

---

7   Compare Douzinas and Warrington's abstraction with the 'practical application' of a Levinasian approach to human rights (Lyotard, 1993). The latter appears indistinguishable in its programmatic conclusions from a liberal approach.

8   What follows is a very limited account of the dialectical and realist argument. In this book, there is a more developed account in Chapter 3, and in Chapters 8 and 9. See further Norrie, 2000, Chapter 4 and more generally Bhaskar, 1975, 1979 and 1989; Collier, 1994; Outhwaite, 1987 (on critical realism) and Bhaskar, 1993 and 1994 (on the 'dialectical turn' in his philosophy). Harré's work (Harré, 1983; Harré, Clarke and de Carlo, 1985) is considered below, where I develop an alternative relational account of responsibility to that of the retributive tradition. The relationship between dialectical critical realism and Harré's social psychology is a controversial one. For my own approach, see Norrie, 2000, pp 199–202.

beings live in society and history, by and through norms, forms and relations that are historically structured and shaped, including those of the law. This is important vis-à-vis poststructuralism. Recognising that we are irreducibly part of an emergent social and historical world, and that we are differentially situated in it, we can hold onto the insights of poststructuralism concerning difference and exclusion without relating these to an abstract, ethical 'beyond'. There is no metaphysical 'other',[9] rather there is real emergent history and developing social structure, and these generate actual difference, conflict, change, sometimes crisis. Difference, 'something new', is emergent in real time, space and history. New perspectives and critical standpoints, new ways of looking at old phenomena, including the phenomena of law and justice, are produced in this process of emerging change and difference.

A crucial aspect, which Bhaskar has recently developed, concerns the use of a dialectical approach. The essence of such an approach is given in the ideas of dialectical connection and contradiction within a developing social totality. Dialectical *connection* exists:

> between entities or aspects of a totality such that they are in principle *distinct* but *inseparable*, in the sense that they are synchronically or conjuncturally *internally* related, ie both ... or one existentially presuppose the other ... (Bhaskar, 1993, p 58)

Dialectical *contradiction* also refers to situations where elements existentially presuppose each other, but in this case, they are also in conflict. Elements are in dialectical contradiction where one premise cannot be satisfied save at the expense of another, to which it is internally related. In this situation, 'a system, agent or structure, S, is blocked from performing with one system, rule or principle, R, because it is performing with another, R1' (Bhaskar, 1993, p 58).

This dialectical development of critical realism highlights both continuity and difference with poststructuralist theory. Continuity: we can use the sense of dialectical connection and contradiction to locate the problems of difference, exclusion and partiality poststructuralism identifies. Difference: we can do so without being drawn onto poststructuralism's metaphysical plane if we recognise that these problems are the effects of social and historical conflicts and contradictions which penetrate and constitute the forms through which we live. If the world is contradictory, then we need to understand phenomena like law, legal justice and subjectivity in their contradictory aspects. Theory must be able to identify and explain the different, opposing and exclusionary propositions that a social and historical phenomenon generates. Thus, a theory that claims that both 'p' and 'not-p' are true may offend against a system of formal logic, but may more truly capture the different aspects of the object of investigation. What kind of theory can hold together for example the arguments, which are both held to be true, that law promotes and obstructs equal opportunities (Lacey, 1993b)? Holding the different and contradictory propositions concerning a phenomenon together as a way of understanding its totality involves thinking dialectically.

The approach to legal justice adopted here is not based on what lies in a metaphysical sense 'beyond', but on the contrasts that we identify between the claims of legal justice and other moral and political claims that emerge historically

---

9   For more on this reading of Derrida, see below, Chapter 8.

within modern social structures. Our critical faculties exist on the same historical terrain as the social forms through which we live. Living in the here and now, thinking dialectically about the forms of justice that emerge, explains both our satisfactions and dissatisfactions with legal justice. Law is constituted by, and constitutes, social practices. As social beings in historical time and place, formed by a multitude of historical and contradictory experiences, we bear witness to the moral and political values in law. We see what they include but also exclude and we have regard to other forms of justice that abut, complement or negate legal forms. We can compare and contrast legal justice with, for example, relational justice, so-called 'popular justice', 'substantive justice', as well as forms of justice in other contexts like the family or the workplace. There is also important scope for comparative, historical and anthropological dimensions, looking at forms of justice in societies different from our own (Abel, 1992; de Sousa Santos, 1992; Merry and Milner, 1993).[10] These provide the real critical standpoints from which to examine the law.

Before I move to develop a dialectical conception of justice, I have one further comment to make concerning the significance of development and change in society. As our experience emerges in a historical period that throws up new views of the world, so we come to re-evaluate our old judgments. In a world in which many of the old certainties and securities are disappearing, we revisit legal justice and what it can deliver with a different eye to that which seemed appropriate earlier. While we remain sceptical and ambivalent about legal justice, we recognise the role its forms play in recording and resisting various forms of tyranny. It is important to be able to say these things today, and the same will be true, probably truer, tomorrow. The question is whether we can develop a theoretical method, adequate to our changing experience, for questions of law.

With these comments about the theory of legal justice, and the relationship between legal and other forms of justice, we can now move to a more concrete analysis of justice in the criminal law. Does law express a viable conception of justice? If legal justice is in its own terms consistently contradictory, why should this be so? What does legal justice *lack*?

Justice and criminal law: the problem of recklessness

The liberal subject lies at the core of the 'penal equation' and therefore at the core of the criminal law. It is expressed, for example, in Ashworth's central idea of individual autonomy and choice as the basis for desert and punishment. From these premises is born the dominant subjective approach to criminal law, and the 'general', 'positive fault requirements' of intention, foresight, knowledge and belief (Ashworth, 1991).[11] Criminal responsibility should be based upon a concept of guilt, which means on actual mental states, hence the term 'subjective'. However, even a defender of the liberal model must recognise its limitations. Ashworth comments 'how individualistic, even atomistic, are the assumptions implicit in the liberal theory which underlies the subjective principles' (Ashworth, 1991, p 132). Liberal

---

10 Discussion of such alternatives is not necessarily easy: it requires substantial conceptual clarification: see above, Chapter 3.

11 This section draws on and develops the fuller argument in Norrie, 1993a, 2001b, Chapter 4.

theories of subjective right and justice need to be supplemented by premises of a more social or communitarian kind, and this would be true, for example, in the law of recklessness. However, the development of these additional premises is not synthesised with the existing subjectivist categories. Rather, they are grafted on, producing an area of law in which there is substantial incoherence. What underlies this process of grafting? In what follows, I shall examine three conceptions of recklessness: the subjective, the objective, and the recently noticed concept of 'practical indifference' proposed by Antony Duff (1990). I will suggest that the last mentioned approach, which occupies a curiously detached position in the law, discloses a deeper problem in its vision, one that takes our analysis beyond law's justice and to its structural conditions of existence.

Subjectivism versus objectivism in the law of recklessness

In the law of recklessness, there are two competing and conflicting approaches based upon either actual foresight (the subjective approach) or the foreseeability (the objective approach) of a criminal risk. The distinction may be explained by thinking of someone lighting a fire in a haystack to keep warm at night (eg, *R v Stephenson* [1979] QB 695). If the haystack is burned down, there may be a charge of criminal damage, but responsibility could be based on whether the person actually foresaw the risk of burning the haystack (the subjective approach), or whether it would have been foreseeable to a reasonable onlooker (the objective approach), even if the person involved did not foresee it. The subjective approach says there must be foresight in fairness to the accused; the objective approach that people ought to come up to a general standard of behaviour, in fairness to the rest of society.

The objectivist case of *R v Caldwell* [1981] 1 All ER 961[12] prompted apoplexy in criminal law scholars (Williams, 1981; Smith, 1987). What was regarded as an established bastion of 'subjectivism', the law of criminal damage, had been hijacked by the judiciary. The old *R v Cunningham* [1957] 2 QB 396 requirement of actual foresight of a risk was supplemented by a new test of foreseeability to a reasonable person (see the later case of *Elliott v C (A Minor)* [1983] 2 All ER 1005). Pouring scorn on subjectivism, Lord Diplock proposed in *R v Caldwell* a double test including subjective and objective variants. An accused was reckless if:

(1) he does an act which in fact creates an obvious risk that property will be destroyed and (2) when he does the act he either has not given any thought to the possibility of there being any such risk or has recognised that there was some risk involved and has none the less gone on to do it. (*R v Caldwell* [1981] 1 All ER 961, p 967)

12 The recent case of *R v G* [2003] 4 All ER 765 has altered the practical criminal law landscape by overruling *R v Caldwell* and reverting to a subjective approach to recklessness in matters of criminal damage. This has rendered the following discussion obsolete as a description of the actual law. *R v G* has not, however, resolved the underlying dilemmas with which the law is faced: dilemmas of moral under- and over-inclusion with regard to culpability for acts that are in some sense 'reckless'. The judgment is indeed a disappointing one in that it reflects none of the academic discussion of the weaknesses of a subjectivist approach, preferring to focus only on its strengths. That these dilemmas remain in the law is witnessed by the move to an objective mental test for serious sexual offences under the Sexual Offences Act 2003 (where the concept of recklessness is subsumed within a general test of 'reasonable belief' as to consent), just as the law of criminal damage moves back to a subjective test. The pre-*R v G* law accordingly remains instructive as to the underlying problems, which, it may be anticipated, will surface in some form or other in the years ahead.

What evoked the scholars' outrage? At one level it was the practical contradictions in the law. Smith and Hogan gave the example of the unthinking defendant who points an air rifle at his victim and pulls the trigger. The pellet breaks the victim's glasses, and destroys his eye. The defendant is responsible for the broken glasses because a foreseeability test works in criminal damage cases, but not for the destruction of the eye, because a foresight test operates for offences against the person. Because of inconsistency, Smith and Hogan castigate the law as 'indefensible' (Smith and Hogan, 1992, p 67). These contradictions, however, also disclose deeper issues.

Subjectivism, objectivism and 'practical indifference'

Williams has a more theoretical criticism of *R v Caldwell* (Williams, 1988). His argument is that the two parts of the Diplock formulation are also inherently contradictory. On a subjective test, all that would be required is foresight of some risk, while part (1) of the test purports to state that the risk must be '*obvious*'. Furthermore, the jumbling of approaches means that the person who foresees a risk, but then rules it out in his own mind, falls foul of neither the subjective nor the objective criteria. This is the so-called *Shimmen* loophole (*Shimmen* (1986) 84 Cr App Rep 7; see also *Reid* [1992] 3 All ER 673). A would-be karate expert boasted of his ability to aim a kick a fraction of an inch away from a plate glass window. He smashed the window and was charged with criminal damage. He claimed that he had calculated and ruled out the risk, so could not be said to have given no thought to it, while having ruled out the risk in his mind meant that he could not be said to have recognised the risk and taken it either. Unfortunately for him, Shimmen was caught because he said that he had eliminated 'as much risk as possible', suggesting he recognised that there was still *some* risk that he had foreseen and taken. He would not have been caught, however, had he slightly changed his story, and that story been believed. It was surely not the judges' intention in *R v Caldwell* to establish a loophole for a defendant such as Shimmen, but the attempt to combine subjective and objective approaches had produced this lacuna in the law.

In short, the law of recklessness is theoretically and practically inconsistent and contradictory. Unable to settle on a middle way, it oscillates between subjective and objective approaches. Why should this be so? According to followers of the subjective view, the judges in *Caldwell* manipulated the law in order to make convictions easier, and in the process betrayed liberal principles of justice based on subjectivism. However the underlying problem is not the 'perfidy of the judges', but the inadequacy of the moral categories, subjectivist and objectivist, for judging criminal responsibility. The liberal principles themselves need to be examined. On the one hand, as Duff (1990, Chapter 7) has argued, subjectivism does not go far enough. While it is appropriate to see awareness of risk as one basis for responsibility, subjectivism cannot recognise the recklessness of he who does not foresee, but is 'practically indifferent' or callous, an attitude of what one might call cruel indifference that is not tied only to matters of foresight or foreseeability. Callousness may be manifested in the *failure* to foresee the risk to which conduct gives rise, so subjectivism is too narrow. On the other hand, objectivism is too broad. While it catches the unthinkingly callous or indifferent person that subjectivism misses, it fails to separate the callous from the stupid or merely thoughtless. It also fails to recognise the special significance of subjective awareness as one form of responsibility. What both subjectivism and objectivism have in common, however, is a failure to reflect a *moral* conception of the substantive quality of actions and attitudes that can be called recklessness. Foresight and foreseeability never penetrate this domain while they remain central to the law. Practical indifference, on the other hand, remains on the outside, a critical standpoint that identifies a lack but one that is admitted only at the margin into the legal analysis.

The problem of inconsistency and contradiction is, then, not the result of judges failing to make up their minds between different approaches, but of the inadequacy of each approach standing by itself. This leads to the desire to combine them, but combining them does not work either. Rather than complementing each other, they only expose their different defects, producing in the process the anomaly of *Shimmen*. They are Siamese twins of judgment, symbiotically linked, yet unable to coexist. Consistency, the hope for a rational rule of law, founders on the rocks of the raw juridical materials, the antinomial subjectivist and objectivist approaches to recklessness in liberal legal theory. It is not wrecked by simple judicial inconstancy. This conclusion, however, only leads to further questions. Why the contradictions? What is so fundamentally awry with the law's categories? Are the judges looking for something that they cannot find in the law, and which threatens to subvert it?

The problem's social and historical roots

There is a clue in the subjectivist case of *R v Cunningham*, which relied on Kenny's turn of the century definition of 'malice'. This old legal term, still used in serious offences against the person, denoted subjective awareness of a risk for Kenny in so far as it concerned recklessness. Kenny argued, however, that this subjective meaning of malice had to be distinguished from an older moral form of recklessness. He wrote that 'in any statutory definition of a crime, "malice" must be taken not in the old vague sense of "wickedness" in general' (Kenny, 1902, p 186; cited in *R v Cunningham*). That 'old vague sense' of wickedness had been discussed by early modern criminal lawyers in relation to the doctrine of implied malice in the law of murder. Foster described malice as 'a heart regardless of social duty and fatally bent upon mischief', as the manifestation of a 'wicked, depraved, and malignant spirit'. These full blooded moral terms are not a million miles away from Duff's callously reckless – practically indifferent – individual that the criminal law ought to recognise, but does not. In pre-modern times, lawyers recognised the need for what one can call *morally substantive* accounts of criminal responsibility. By the time Kenny wrote, however, at the turn of the century, such an approach was disparaged as 'vague'. What lay behind this change?

A crucial pivot was the work of the Victorian Criminal Law Commissioners, who reduced the old moral approach to malice to a question of psychological *wilfulness* (voluntary action with knowledge), and therefore, to a matter of subjective cognition. Wilfulness became the bridge between *moral substance* and *mental form*:

> It is the *wilful exposure* of life to peril that constitutes the crime ... Where the offender does an act with manifest danger to life wilfully, *that is with knowledge of the consequences*, he may properly be said to have the *mens mala*, or heart bent upon mischief. (Criminal Law Commissioners, 1839, xxiv, emphasis added)

The Criminal Law Commissioners also argued that the old morally substantive approach led to 'danger of error and uncertainty in its application'. What should be seen as a matter of fact, and therefore relatively uncontentious, became a 'matter of law' and 'involved in doubt' (Criminal Law Commissioners, 1843, p 23). Translating the old morally substantive conception of recklessness into a question of subjective knowledge was a way of avoiding contention and uncertainty, but it also led to the contradictions in the modern law. Neither subjectivism nor objectivism could reflect the morally substantive aspects that are part of social judgments of recklessness, and which are caught, for example, by Duff's formulation of practical indifference. In exceptional cases where judges seek to reach beyond subjectivism, I think they are, subconsciously, looking for legal categories to reflect moral judgments of responsibility they think the law should embody,[13] but the route is barred by the process of factualisation and demoralisation that went into the making of the modern criminal law. In *R v Caldwell*, they took refuge in an objectivist doctrine that mirrored the subjectivism they rejected. Neither approach, however, could reach the moral parts that a substantive morality might reach, because both were designed to close the door upon a crucial moral dimension of recklessness. Moral arguments that were too much at large would be contentious and political. They would threaten the routine working of a legal code in a time, as today, of disagreement as to what constituted right and wrong in general, and moral recklessness in particular. The apparently 'factual', mentalistic approach seemed to counter this subversion, but it barred the door to morally substantive conceptions of recklessness. It gave the law categories of judgment, but categories which were forever damned in their ability wholly to reflect underlying moral judgments.

Employing legal categories of subjective and objective recklessness to reflect social and moral judgments of responsibility and justice is always therefore a question of fighting with one hand tied behind one's back. Criminal law categories of fault, like recklessness, are presented in liberal theory as informed by a broader moral philosophical conception of responsibility, and they are. However, they are also *doppelgänger*, pale shadows of a moral and political substance that is excluded in the interest of the positivisation of law and depoliticisation of the courtroom. The so-called vagueness of the old approach resulted because old style moral malice was left at large in the community, and was open to the conflicts and gradations of moral judgment that exist there. The foresightful, autonomous individual was linked to moral processes of judgment, because foresight is relevant to judgments of wrongdoing, but it was also a way of *excluding* such judgments taken more broadly. These might disrupt the working of the law, the working of legal justice, and therefore the operation of the 'penal equation' by introducing substantive conflicts into the law.

Relating this to the theory of the previous section, we can understand the subjectivist/objectivist controversy in the law of recklessness dialectically. Subjectivism and objectivism both necessitate and contradict each other as forms of legal justice emergent within a particular historical context. These historical forms

---

13 The formulation of recklessness in cases like *R v Stone and Dobinson* [1977] 2 All ER 341 and *R v Satnam and Kewal* (1984) 78 Cr App Rep 149 can be understood as an imprecise reaching beyond the subjective and objective concepts available within the law towards a morally substantive approach (Norrie, 1993a, 2001b, Chapter 4).

can be critically compared with other views on, or forms of, justice generated by modern social relations, but excluded from the law.[14] Duff's view, rediscovering an original moral account of recklessness, is such a view. There is an historical limit to legal justice which stems from its development out of an engagement with the underlying social and political contradictions present in modern English society, and which the liberal conception of subjective justice (and equally, its objective twin) sought to exclude. In poststructuralist terms, there is an 'other' beyond subjectivism and objectivism, but it is the other of real history and emergent social perceptions, and does not pertain to a metaphysical 'beyond'. It is with us, in the here and now, but it struggles to take its place in a law based on liberal subjectivism (and its objectivist double).

At the same time, it must be remembered that a limited conception of justice is still a conception of justice, so that there is an overlap between the legal conception and broader conceptions glimpsed 'through a glass darkly' by the law and lawyers. It is this overlap that we will eventually consider once we have moved to develop further a dialectical sense of what justice and responsibility mean, this time from the 'inside'.

The sense of justice

We began with a dilemma concerning the 'penal equation'. On the one hand, the liberal model of justice is a source of dissatisfaction. We keep convicting and punishing so-called 'responsible individuals', but the attempt to deter only leads to the need for more deterrence, and we question the moral validity of retributive justice. On the other hand, we recognise the practical ways in which the law resonates with individual moral experience. People hold onto a system that still carries a sense of justice, and this is not a matter of simple 'false consciousness'. This ambivalence is also carried into the heart of criminal law. There, in the example of recklessness, we have a legal subject with foresight, a concept that is reflected in its objectivist mirror, the reasonable person test in *R v Caldwell*. This legal subject/object partially expresses and reflects issues of judgment but also misses those central moral aspects of justice that may be described as 'morally substantive'.

The 'internal' and the 'external'

We are left with a view of liberal legal justice that stresses its paradoxical form. Can we hold onto these ambiguities without appearing plain contradictory? In postmodern terms, we could perhaps simply accept the dilemma, recognising that only a sense of what is strategic can tell us how to view law. The limits of discourse, the finitude of meaning, the need for a supplement, all force us to embrace the conflict. Becoming playful or pragmatic, we acknowledge the way things are 'in a postmodern world'. In critical realist terms, by contrast, we can draw upon a

---

14 It is significant that it was the issue of reckless rape that was instrumental in promoting a more critical perspective on the existing forms of recklessness. This resulted in large part from an emerging feminist consciousness in the 1970s that the existing forms of recklessness did not reflect what many women regarded as acceptable sexual conduct. A similarly critical, and potentially innovative, reflection on the law's justice is being developed out of the experience of women who have endured domestic violence in the law of provocation.

historical and dialectical understanding of liberal law which holds together its contradictory aspects as expressions of a particular social and historical totality. I view law as sited on an edge between abstract, general attributes of individual subjectivity (the person as rational, intentional, foresightful, voluntary) and representations of human agency as contextualised (crime as a product of socially and historically generated moral conditions). This contradictory location has its provenance in the Enlightenment representation of a world of free individuals coming together in civil society. However, crime is a social problem generated in ways that can be statistically correlated. It can be located differentially in different socio-economic classes. This social context is refocused through law into a matter of individual responsibility, justice and deterrence. Each criminal act is relocated from the social sphere, where crime is produced, to the individual criminal agent, who is left, in less than splendid isolation, to 'carry the can'. It is this translation, which is also a repression, a refusal to see the individual as always-already social, that lies behind the dilemmas of legal justice and criminal law. What is suppressed always returns, and I would trace the dilemmas produced as they surface and resurface across the terrain of criminal law's 'general part'.

As we have seen, this argument has an 'external' historical and sociological form, but I now want to develop it to include an 'internal point of view'.[15] We need to understand the social and political functions that legal individualism play, but we also need, as I have indicated, to understand the resonances of the legal individualist conception of justice, reflected, for example, in the struggles of prisoners to have the penal equation restored, or battered women to have their story acknowledged properly in and through legal categories. An 'external', historical and structural approach is insufficient to understand the ambivalence we *feel* towards the legal conception of justice. Questions of judgment and justice are not just politico-historical effects of a particular social structure; they pose real existential and experiential questions for individuals and communities. There is an issue of moral agency 'inside' the historical and structural questions as to how criminal law reflects or fails to reflect moral experience. The split between individual and social context is not only a 'structural decoupling' between law and society. It is also present for individuals as they negotiate the moral effects of their actions with regard to the law.

In short, after the historical and sociological critique of the inadequacies of criminal law and the penal equation, there remains a liberal, in effect Kantian, question to be asked: what does criminal *justice* mean for the individual?[16] However, it cannot be answered in a Kantian way, for that would take us back into the false unity of the liberal subject. We need to explain how it is that our categories of legal judgment give rise to moral ambiguity and paradox.

---

15 I use this phrase, associated as it is with Hart's legal positivism, with a measure of irony. The idea of two standpoints in social theory, one structural and 'external', the other agential or 'internal', is one that is widely deployed. I develop it below, Chapter 8. It is to be distinguished from the liberal legal positivist use, which I have criticised (Norrie, 2000, pp 227–29) insofar as it purports to set up a clear distinction between the realm of law and other forms of knowledge and practice and to identify a specifically legal terrain disconnected from others.

16 I develop this argument further in Norrie, 1998b and especially in Norrie, 2000, Chapter 9.

Selfhood and society

One way to do this is to draw upon the 'new psychology' of Rom Harré (Harré, 1983). Harré's approach can be introduced by a quotation which focuses on the ambiguity present in the psychological experience of personhood. This concerns a sense, stated at its strongest in what follows, of both being and not being in control of ourselves and our actions:

> On the one hand we feel we know all the facts that impinge upon us, and we seem to be in control of the actions we perform. We experience ourselves in one sense as being all-knowing and all-controlling. But at the same time life does not go as we want, and we do not understand why. Perhaps our conscious mind is not after all the strategic controller of the system, but just the middle manager of the mind ... subject to more compelling and longer patterns of authority. (Harré, Clarke and de Carlo, 1985, pp 24–25)

Harré is describing here the balancing of personhood between a sense of self as autonomous, and the pervasive pull and push of social relations which create and maintain that sense. A more common way of experiencing this feeling may be in less black and white terms than Harré employs, but the ambivalence we often feel as to how much we are in control of our lives hinges on the polarity he describes. In his account, the individual self is a project wrought out of social difference. Social and normative 'conversations' constitute the 'primary structure' of human life, since society always exists before the individual, who is delivered into, and develops a sense of being out of, a relationship to the social. Nonetheless, individual, personal being is a real phenomenon, for persons operate within a society that requires them to act as individual selves. The self is then a 'secondary' but necessary structure generated by, but differentiated from, the 'primary' social structure. Social relations are reproduced because persons exist both as role-playing individual agents and, more fundamentally, as selves. They are created out of a language of individual biography, identity and capacity for action. This language creates the sense of being a self 'behind' the social roles that individuals perform, although, in Harré's account, the ability to be 'one's self' is intimately linked to, and generalised from, the ability to perform individual social roles.

Individual selfhood is real, but inherently, dialectically, linked to the primary social structure through the playing of roles. The self is ambiguously sited between a sense of itself as autonomous and its location in social relations which produce and maintain it. This is illustrated, for example, in the uncomfortable sense that while we feel in control of what we say or do, we sometimes appear only to speak the parts bequeathed to us by history and context. Thus, the child who vows never to speak to his children as his parents spoke to him is surprised to find as a parent the very same words coming out of his mouth. The self is always in relation, which amounts to saying that selfhood is a relation, at the same time as it understands itself as autonomous. Being a person involves being in relation to others in time and space, *and* a denial of that relation. The denial is an existential presupposition stemming from the dualistic character of selfhood, for the act of denial (of sociality) is also an act of (individual) self-constitution. Mastering a language of selfhood, we become selves, although not without a sense of ambiguity. We feel in control but, every so often, realise we are not.

Selfhood, society and justice

This ambiguity translates into moral judgments of wrongdoing and a sense of justice. In ordinary moral life, I suggest, we follow a two phase approach in which at first we are angry and seek to blame, and then, later, proceed to judge the person more 'in the round', taking their circumstances and overall situation into account. We interpret what was done as part of a person's history which disposed them to actions of certain kinds regardless of their will. We 'explain' what they have done and, so doing, come to excuse them. In morally judging crime, we do something similar. Even in the most demonised cases, like those of a Rosemary West or Myra Hindley, we come to wonder how they could have done what they did. We do not do this in order to deny the terrible wrong in their acts, but we are led to wonder about their ultimate responsibility for them, no matter what the law's judgment may be. We also come to see the refusal to understand and to contextualise by those who unthinkingly condemn as itself a failure of human being.[17] Thus, our initial reaction of anger and condemnation may be followed by a sense that the criminal was also a victim. In so doing, we move from the sense of the individual as an autonomous agent (the law's view) to that of the person as a being-in-relation.

However, there is then a further third stage that is particularly significant and remarkable with regard to serious crimes. After the initial sense of anger and condemnation, and the second stage of contextual interpretation, we go back to the question of responsibility in a more considered way. How many are really satisfied, for example, with the sense that can be drawn from Myra Hindley's late essay (*The Guardian* (1995) 18 December) that the person who committed her crimes was 'another person' from the one Hindley became? There remains a sense of moral reckoning that corresponds to neither the immediate sense of responsibility (the sense employed by the law), nor the diffuse, contextualising approach to which I have also referred. It is a floating sense of what doing justice means, one that is hard to pin down. It operates in the space between what a person did and the ways in which that person was herself created, a dialectical space between conflicting alternatives, but a sense that is part of our lives as moral individuals and agents.

Part of this sense involves coming to terms with events with which we are directly associated in our pasts, even those that are long past. This deeper sense of responsibility is particularly seen in the case of serious crimes committed many years ago, by someone such as Myra Hindley, and also in the case of prosecuting former Nazi war criminals. The past may be 'another country', occupied by 'other people', yet the sense of injustice that a denial of past responsibility evokes, or the sense of justice that demands the trial of serious crimes done long ago is linked, I suggest, to the complexity in understanding what individual life is as both a socio-historical and a personal, self-based phenomenon. This sense of the need to come to terms with the past and to acknowledge responsibility is a more complex phenomenon than that of individual responsibility within the liberal theory of criminal justice, but it clearly shares common aspects at a superficial level. Both involve a focus upon the individual, but the sense in which I am interested asks

---

17 One must distinguish the reaction of families of homicide victims from the kneejerk reaction of those who follow the tabloid press, although it is unlikely that families are helped to live with their loss by the views of the latter.

more deeply what it means to be a person in a particular time and place (see below, Chapter 6, for further discussion) rather than the momentary conception of personhood accepted by law and legal theory.

It is this sense of agency and selfhood as real yet ambiguous and double-sided that I take from Harré, but we need to add to it if we are to understand the concept of justice with regard to the bulk of ordinary crime. Most crime mercifully lacks the horror of child killing or wartime atrocity, and therefore does not attract the broad and consensual condemnation that these do. Many forms of crime, most notably crimes against property, occupy a contested social space in which conflicting views of right and wrong co-exist. Here, the 'normative conversations' in Harré's 'primary structure' are contradictory and competing. They give rise to different views of what is acceptable with regard to law-breaking. Social consensus about wrongdoing may historically be possible, but it is always a produced, contingent and variable phenomenon, rather than inevitable in a society based upon deep-seated structural tensions (Reiner, 1992). This has a major impact on the sense of justice in a community and its members, and presents a fundamental challenge to any consensual interpretation of Harré's account of the relationship between selfhood and the social. The social conflicts within Harré's primary structure inform persons and their conduct, and are part of the raw material of selfhood. Because modern life is fundamentally inegalitarian and structurally conflicted, the actions of individuals are coloured by inequalities and conflicting moral standpoints. Thus, we act as selves, as agents, as persons in control, but also as people located in structures that are conflictual, and this adds a further layer of complexity into our explanations of the dualism, the contradictions, the paradoxes in our judgments of criminal wrongdoing.

Just deserts from one side is social injustice from another, and we feel the pull of both arguments. There are always two sides to the question of criminal responsibility. It is not that law is wrong to identify individual agency as important to moral responsibility. There is a link which provides law's resonances with the moral lives of persons who act in particular ways. Agency is central to what we are as persons, but it is so in a more complex way than law allows. The problem for law, for criminal justice, for the penal equation, is that it is one-sided in its treatment of people being in control. There is a double, linked exclusion here: of the social conditions of selfhood, and the structural conflicts which inform those conditions. Selfhood is real, but doubly conflicted – existentially and in terms of its location within the historical conditions of modern society. The penal equation does its work, but only by ignoring the moral import of these conflicts with regard to the ways we are constructed and the resulting, more complex and ambiguous, sense of justice this entails.

Conclusion

What, however, could the criminal justice system make of this? This chapter has developed some of the ideas which underlie an ambivalent attitude to the 'penal equation', including some alternatives to it, which can be grouped under the umbrella of 'relational justice'. Whether it be mediation, reparation, reconciliation or diversion, non-custodial or intermediate treatment, there have been a number of attempts to break the 'penal equation' in favour of more 'relational' forms of justice. If we compare relational justice in these senses with criminal justice, the former might be seen as morally more appropriate in the light of the arguments advanced here. Relational justice involves a sense of the particularity of human life, a sense of social engagement, and a sense of responsibility that is contextualised both in terms of looking to the wrongdoer's past acts and their provenance, and to his relationship with a community that includes his victim. It returns the individual to the normative conversations out of which his agency emerged, offering the prospect of a reconciliation and a new beginning.[18]

Criminal justice by contrast remains stuck with a backward-looking and desocialising view of the role of punishment, particularly insofar as it relies on imprisonment. It also has a static conception of individual responsibility, in which the individual is seen as in control, save in tightly circumscribed exceptional situations. That sense of control is not an illusion. It is part of human agency, but it is partial. In a situation like provocation, we see this as battered women push to recognise a contextually sensitive account of how they act when they are provoked. The aim in developing the defence is to push against its abstract boundaries and make it recognise the moral and political context in which provoked women act. The law is being pushed beyond its abstract conception towards an approach which sees the nature and meaning of 'being in control' as more complex and ambivalent, but the movement is limited and hesitant.

Because the sense of being in control involves ambiguity, not simple illusion, the law still touches the subjective understanding of being a person. In situations involving the relationship between the individual and the state, this is extremely important. Laws which confine the liberty of the subject are precisely rules concerning the amount of control that the person has over his life vis-à-vis the police or the prison authorities. There is an irreducible existential basis to the demand for rights, because such a demand is a demand for control of oneself and one's conditions of life. This is not a matter of what is strategic, but a moral demand based upon the sense of being a person, even if we know that that sense is a more ambiguous one than liberal political theory allows. This is why law speaks to those who resist the discretionary powers of state officials, such as the Home Secretary with regard to life sentences.[19]

Can we move from these theoretical views directly to the kind of radical reform of the criminal justice system advocated by Blom Cooper (1995)? An ambivalent view leads to caution. Liberal law gives us a conception of a rights bearing subject at

---

18 Although this may be highly constrained in practice by the political context within which relational forms of justice are introduced (Dignan, 1992). The problem here relates to the danger from the criminal justice system's point of view that an emphasis on relationality would open up the moral and political issues of justice that are closed off by the abstract individualism of the penal equation. On the other hand, and more likely, relationality can become the excuse for increased authoritarianism in the name of a community of which the individual is a 'failing' member. One has to distinguish two senses of 'relational justice', one philosophical, the other practical. One can endorse a relational approach theoretically (as I do: Norrie, 2000), while having serious misgivings as to its likely practical effects under modern political conditions. This is but one illustration of my general thesis: that there is a necessary disjuncture, and therefore an uneasy relation, between theory and practice in modern society.

19 For development of this perspective with regard to the advent of the Human Rights Act 1998 in the United Kingdom, see Norrie, 2001c.

a price. The subject enjoys formal rights, to the extent that he does, in a trade-off. Formal rights exist within existing social and political arrangements. They allow subjects to speak, but in strictly limited terms. There is a political closure that relational forms of justice would begin to set loose, and it is this that I think condemns relational justice to operate in the margins of the social control system, and to act only to ameliorate the main engine of social control, the criminal justice system.

Is this necessarily undesirable? In one way it is. Relational justice is less alienating, more morally expressive and developmental. Against this, however, criminal justice does in principle operate a system of rights, reflecting the idea of being in control of one's actions. If we were to move to a more relational approach, one that went behind the idea of the subject in control, would we not also be in danger of losing the defences relating to individual subjectivity that law in principle embodies? Nor is relational justice as a practical phenomenon in any sense 'politically innocent'. Translated into proposals for action, relational justice is itself a historical and social practice, a form of control in a society in which structural inequality has a profound effect on the criminal justice system. Moving beyond a formal system, it is potentially more invasive than law. In an authoritarian society, what may appear agreeable, relational means of dealing with offenders may in practice turn out to be more far-reaching forms of intervention into people's lives, sugar-coated in an enticing rhetoric.

The picture of reform that emerges is a nuanced one. If radical changes are sought, we need to ask what their consequences will be in the light of a broad understanding of how law operates. We do indeed need a radical theory, one that can get to the roots of law. Such a theory must come to terms with the ambivalences that we experience in thinking about the penal equation. Bearing in mind the overall relationship between legal justice and the structural social injustice within which the equation operates, such a theory must criticise the absences and failures, but also recognise the positive aspects of liberal legality. There are political choices to be made. Such a theory may push for recognition of the needs of disadvantaged groups, where they are barred by the law's decontextualising: this is the import of the battered women and provocation debate. However, it must be conscious that this is a political task, and that, in the absence of the possibility of progressive change in the broader society, liberal legality may itself involve a progressive agenda: this is the import of the critique of arbitrary discretion in life sentences.

The upshot of this conclusion is to argue for a necessary but uneasy relationship between theory and practice. They operate at different, irreducible levels. Theory does not lead immediately to systematic practical conclusions, but that does not mean that it is irrelevant to practice, or that it cannot illuminate it. In truth practice can never escape theory. It is only a question of how adequate and explicit theory is. My argument has been that a contradictory and ambiguous phenomenon like law needs a theory sufficiently sophisticated to capture contradiction and ambiguity within legal forms without simply surrendering to it. Such a theory would treat law dialectically, in two ways. In its 'external', structural aspect, it would see it as a contradictory social phenomenon which both reflects and refracts modern historical conditions. In its 'internal', experiential aspect, it portrays it as a set of categories with some limited purchase on the ways in which moral and political agents live under modern conditions.

Chapter 6
Albert Speer, Guilt and the 'Space Between'

Introduction

This chapter seeks to extend a theme in the last two chapters concerning the nature of individual responsibility. It does so, first, in relation to some reflections by Anthony Giddens (1991) on the nature of guilt in 'late modern' society and, secondly, in relation to the argument of the previous chapter concerning the irreducible relationship between individual agency and social context. It then relates these themes to discussion of one particular case study of the nature of guilt, the case of Albert Speer, as interpreted in an important book by Gitta Sereny (1995). The chapter is of a preliminary and investigative kind, drawing on disparate sources. Its basic aim is to consider the role of 'community' in the formation of selfhood in a way that steers a middle course between positions that would see the question of individual guilt or responsibility for an act as either a discrete question for individuals or for communities. Sereny's biography of Speer reflects the former standpoint, Giddens' argument the latter. What I seek to do is to develop the idea of guilt or responsibility as involving a 'space between' the individual and the community. In speaking of guilt and responsibility, I will use these two terms interchangeably to reflect the sense of responsibility HLA Hart (1968, p 225) describes as being 'morally blameworthy, or morally obliged to make amends for a harm'.[1]

The chapter has three main sections. In the first, I introduce the argument by considering Anthony Giddens's work on the nature of self and community in 'late' modernity. Central to this argument is a sense of the historical development of modernity such that we can identify a period that is qualitatively 'late'. I am sceptical about this terminology, but it is not the categorisation of different phases of modernity that is relevant here. Rather, I am interested in Giddens's argument about the central importance of the idea of community in developing a sense of selfhood and responsibility. With this I agree, although I challenge his claim that such an idea is less important for us today. I argue for the continuing relevance of community to ideas of individual responsibility and guilt. In the second section, I develop this argument by drawing on a theme in my own work concerning the development of selfhood out of community (see above, Chapter 5). That work, drawing on the social psychology of Rom Harré (1983) and the dialectics of Roy Bhaskar (1993), asserts the relationality of the self, its 'in betweenness', or co-mediation by the individuated agent and his or her communities. Individual identity exists within an overall, totalising, context and its nature is radically affected thereby. Philosophically, Bhaskar develops the concept of 'entity

---

1 I take this meaning to be consistent with Giddens's description of guilt in the next section, though he adds a psychological element to the basic moral form. Hart finds this meaning at the core of the criminal law, where issues of guilt and responsibility of course meet. This essay, however, is not so much about the law as about the sense of guilt or responsibility with which it is linked.

relationism' as a means of explaining how individual identity goes beyond the individual:

> To grasp totality is to break with our ordinary notions of identity ... It is to see things *existentially constituted*, and permeated, *by their relations with others*; and to see our ordinary notion of identity as an abstraction not only from [its] existentially constitutive processes of formation (geo-histories), but also from [its] existentially constitutive inter-activity (internal relatedness) ... When is a thing no longer a thing but something else? ... [I]n the domain of totality we need to conceptualise *entity relationism*. (Bhaskar, 1993, p 125)

This position, translated to the level of social psychology, stresses that selfhood always exists 'in relation' but it holds onto the importance of personal agency in social relations. The result is a sense of responsibility-in-relation, a reduction of the moral phenomenon neither to the individual nor to social relations. The impact of relationality (community) on agency and judgment is then explored in the third section through an analysis of Gitta Sereny's work of judgment on Albert Speer. My argument here is that there is a tension in Sereny's account, an ambivalence in her judgment, which stems from an ambiguity in her reading of the character of Speer. At various points in the book, Sereny refers to Speer's attempt in Spandau and beyond to become morally a 'different man'. Some of the difficulties of judging Speer stem from the different meanings that can be given to this idea. Was Speer attempting to become another person in a deep moral sense, or was he, more calculatedly, seeking just to reinvent himself as a person who could evade the condemnation on his head? Sereny takes the first position, while reading Giddens could lead to the second. For Sereny, Speer was working imperfectly towards his own redemption as he wrestled with guilt concerning his Nazi past. This is an essentially liberal conception of the individual's rediscovery of his intrinsic moral values. From Giddens, we could read Speer as switching his 'stories' reflexively in order to accommodate the needs of the moment in a world where universal moral values have been fundamentally eroded.

Is there, however, a third possibility: did the post-war Speer occupy some intermediate position between these two possibilities, and, if so, what was the nature of that position? Was his sense of guilt 'real', or was it cultivated; or, was it both real *and* cultivated? More broadly, what does it mean to be a 'different man' and what is the relationship between attempts at development of the self and a person's existence across time in societies with very different public moralities? These questions are all posed by Sereny's account of Speer, and my suggestion will be that answers to them reside in the sense of the relationality of the self that I will develop. The dilemmas Sereny finds in judging Speer are real dilemmas in the sense that they reflect real issues about what it means to be an individual in modern society.

Guilt, community and the self in late modernity

I begin with certain themes developed by Anthony Giddens, and in particular with his discussion of the erosion of guilt as a moral category in late modernity. For Giddens, guilt is 'anxiety produced by the fear of transgression' where the 'thoughts or activities of the individual do not match up to expectations of a normative sort'

(Giddens, 1991, p 64). Guilt concerns things done or not done, it concerns wrongdoing, and it has as its obverse reparation. It concerns 'discrete elements of behaviour and the modes of retribution that they suggest or entail':

> Guilt carries the connotation of moral transgression: it is anxiety deriving from a failure, or an inability, to satisfy certain forms of moral imperative in the course of a person's conduct. (*Ibid*, p 153)

So far, this sounds like a modern version of Kant, perhaps mediated by Freud, but for Giddens, there is a social link between the expression of particular moral emotions and the nature of historical periods. He relates the experience of feelings of guilt to the periods of 'early', 'mature' and 'late' modernity. In this last phase, he accepts that 'guilt mechanisms persist' (*ibid*, p 153), but their significance is substantially diminished. The reason for this is the erosion of established normative communities in late modernity. The individual lives less 'by extrinsic moral precepts but by means of the reflexive organisation of the self' (*ibid*, p 153), so that the 'characteristic movement of modernity, on the level of individual experience, is away from guilt' (*ibid*, p 155). For Giddens, late modernity marks a further qualitative individualisation of the experience of the self so that its inward reflexivity is at the same time a result (and also a cause) of the erosion of the moral communities that previously held the self in check.

This argument raises three questions. The first is whether Giddens is correct to identify a diminution of issues of guilt in late modernity. The second concerns the relationship he posits between the decline of guilt and the diminution of community. The question here is to what extent it is correct to speak of an *erosion* of community, or to what extent, rather differently, one should speak of an emergent, or just more visible, *fragmentation* of communities. The third question concerns the nature of the self, guilt and responsibility in Giddens's account: can we conceive of the self in Giddens's terms as self reliant and reflexive to the extent that issues of guilt and responsibility concern it less and less?

First question: the diminution of guilt in late modernity?

At certain levels of society, Giddens may be correct to identify a trajectory of the diminution of guilt, but I would question how far this goes. He himself hedges his bets by recognising that 'guilt mechanisms persist'. Nor do I think that such persistence is only a 'throwback' to an earlier period, for 'late modernity' itself continues to generate questions of guilt, and questions of what guilt means. For example, one of the features of 'late modernity', as Giddens (1991, p 4) describes it, is the risk of the 'rise of totalitarian superstates', and this, together with the breakdown of such states, throws up some of the most poignant and important questions about the nature of human responsibility and guilt. Think, for example, of the war crimes trials in the Hague, the 'Commission for Truth and Reconciliation' in South Africa, or the trial of East German border guards after reunification. The issue of guilt remains one of the most compelling questions in a world in which individual and collective atrocities are commonplace and late modernity remains as fascinated by such questions as any earlier period. Beyond violence associated with globalising phenomena, think also of the concern, which includes but goes beyond prurience, with the guilt of individuals such as Rosemary and Fred West, of the two boys who killed James Bulger, of Mary Bell and of Myra Hindley.

However, it might be argued that these cases support Giddens's hypothesis. Perhaps the very fascination with guilt indicates, in Durkheimian fashion, the need to hold on to a moral reaction that is in fact going out of currency. On the other hand, pressing Durkheim into service, perhaps these cases reveal a continuing modern need to create the values of moral community and to mark the boundaries of the unacceptable. The need to know how a person could have transgressed such boundaries is part of understanding how it is that communities exist where most people would not do such things. Of course, in these cases there is often more going on than meets the eye. The demonisation of the two boys in the James Bulger case, or in that of Myra Hindley, suggests that, beyond the horror of the crimes, these cases carry other social and political baggage. However, I believe these cases reveal a continuing focus on moral transgression as a 'late modern' concern and this is so even if we say that it is precisely the breakdown of moral communities in late modernity that leads to an increased focus upon the worst kinds of normative transgression. Guilt mechanisms continue to remain important in modern society, and there is no sign of their diminution.

However one understands this, Giddens does point to the significance in general terms of the existence of moral communities as a crucial factor in the creation of individual guilt. It is impossible to feel guilt without feeling that one has transgressed a norm, and impossible to feel that one has transgressed a norm without some sense of a relationship to a community to which a norm pertains. We need therefore to consider more closely the role of community in modern society.

Second question: the diminution of community in late modernity?

This brings us to the second question concerning whether we are witnessing, as Giddens claims, an absolute erosion of community in 'late modernity' or whether we are seeing, as I prefer, fragmentation and change in patterns of community, together with a greater visibility of this process. There is a difference here. While Giddens suggests that the individual is thrown back on her own reflexive devices by the erosion of community, the alternative suggests the continuing existence of a variety of conflicting, perhaps overlapping and intersecting, communities rather than their overall absence. For example, the rise and fall of super-states brought about by 'globalisation' has often led to a 'balkanisation' of very strong and conflictual communities rather than to a reflexive individualism. In making this point, we pick up continuing themes in sociology about the significance of social, national, class and gender conflict as structural and relational features of late modern societies. Such features are of course present in Giddens's argument, but they are in a way relegated to a subsidiary position by his argument about the modern self and his or her guilt. The problem with community may be not so much that it has gone away, but that conflicts between communities have either become sharpened or more visible or both. It is very important to hold onto this different notion of the nature and persistence of moral community(ies) when we think of the conflict between, for example, a liberal democratic and a fascist community, an issue that underlies many war crimes trials from Nuremberg onwards, and which is directly relevant to thinking about, as we will, Albert Speer. It is not that 'community' in the abstract has qualitatively diminished to the advantage of flourishing individualism, but that the nature and conditions of community are changing. For some, this may lead, it is true, to new opportunities to express their individuality, but for others, it may not. What appears as new forms of individuality may also end up as no more than rather circumscribed ways of being in community.

However matters develop, it seems to me that communities in their changing forms remain crucial to individual social and moral experience, and this situation requires us to think about how modern individuals continue to develop in such contexts.

Third question: the reflexivity of the self in late modernity?

This brings us then to the third question. Giddens writes of the negotiated and changing nature of selfhood in late modernity. Self-identity increasingly is 'reflexively' maintained by individuals apart from moral communities. They maintain a biography about themselves through the 'capacity to keep a particular narrative going' (Giddens, 1991, p 54). This is an essentially fragile activity 'because the biography the individual reflexively holds in mind is only one "story" among many other potential stories that could be told about her development as a self' (*ibid*, p 55). This ability of the individual to shift reflexively from one account to another fits with the idea of the erosion of guilt in late modern conditions. To avoid feelings of guilt, individuals are able simply to reinterpret life events. This account of the self generates a sense of both its fragility and its ambiguity: if Giddens is correct, we might look to pin individual responsibility to a site whence it has already, in structural terms, fled. The agent responsible for a particular act may resist feelings of guilt by reinventing herself as a 'different person' with a different story to tell as to why an action occurred. For example, the move might be from a confession that 'I was to blame for "x"' to 'you (society, my parents, teachers, etc) made me do "x". I was a victim. The person who did those things is now no more for I have overcome what you did to me'.

This idea that selfhood is at the mercy of the different stories we could tell about ourselves seems to me to have an element of truth, but at the same time to be overstated. To be sure, we can all recognise examples of attempts to avoid responsibility by reinterpreting the past. However, we recognise these because they do not usually seem plausible or acceptable practices. It seems to me that reinvention in the face of what we have been is hardly so simple, and that our sense of selfhood is hardly so fragile. Giddens does acknowledge that the self is both fragile *and* robust: fragile for the reason stated, robust because 'a sense of self-identity is often securely enough held to weather major tensions or transitions in the social environments within which the person moves' (*ibid*, p 55). What, however, is the nature of this 'robust' aspect of the self and what is the precise connection between these robust and fragile aspects? Giddens says less about the robust than the fragile side of selfhood. It seems to involve a minimum content permitting continuity of the self, sufficient only to maintain the basic attributes of personhood and fend off serious pathologies such as mental illness. How much continuity *could* Giddens permit it given his thesis about fragility of the self? If the robust side of selfhood underpins the fragile side, does it produce the possibility of a unified 'meta-narrative' of the self? It is hard to see how it could, given Giddens's diagnosis of the late modern condition of reflexivity. It must be sufficiently minimalist to allow the switching of life stories and the conclusion that guilt is under attack in conditions of 'late modernity'. That thesis, as I have said, is qualified, but it remains Giddens's main argument. Selfhood cannot be so robust as to undermine the question about 'late modern' guilt: how would we hold a person responsible where that person has reinvented herself to evade the blame associated with her transgression?

This is Giddens's critical question concerning the reflexive self under the declining conditions of moral community in late modernity. It seems to me to hold a grain of truth: the sense of who a person is can change over time, particularly if the context and conditions of their lives also change. To look back at old acts in different times and places may be to be presented with a sense of a very different person from that of the here and now. A person may indeed tell a very different story of who they are now and were then. However, it seems to me that 'late modern' personhood still involves a more 'robust', 'meta-narratival' quality than Giddens allows. There remains a sense of selfhood across time and space that cannot be evaded simply by telling a different story. 'Late modern' selfhood may be subject to flux, but it is not so fragile as Giddens suggests. Guilt remains alive just because people who reinvent themselves cannot fully push away the acts they were associated with in the past.

To put these three issues together, my suggestions against Giddens are: (1) that questions of guilt are alive and well in late modernity; (2) that this may be linked to the continuing importance of community, in terms perhaps of the fragmentation of communities in conflict rather than a trajectory of absolute community breakdown; and (3) that if the self's 'fragility' leads to the possibility of the evasion of responsibility, this observation has to be reconciled with the continuing need for individuals to come to terms with what they have done even under 'late modern' conditions, and the sense that individuals continue to feel guilty. To put this last point more concretely, the evasion of responsibility by the apparent reinvention of the self may be a strategy that is adopted by a *guilty* individual.

These are points against Giddens's thesis, but I want to end by stating why it remains important. What is significant is the intrinsic connection he posits between selfhood and community. He gives us a start in our exploration of ideas of guilt and community. He points importantly to the relation between selfhood and community in the construction of guilt. More contentiously, he claims that selves are able under 'late modern' conditions to avoid the inner sense of guilt by freeing themselves from the receding claims of community. Giddens's image of 'late modern' individuality has shorn his initial 'Kantian-Freudian' conception of guilt of both its affective and its morally imperatival qualities.[2] However, how far must we follow this thesis and accept that the decline of community and the reflexivity of the self lead to an erosion of the concept of guilt? If the impact of 'late modernity' is less radical than Giddens thinks, we can still hold onto the intrinsic relation between guilt and sociality he posits.

---

2 Although I will argue below that there still remains a close affinity with the Kantian subject in Giddens's position.

Ambiguity about guilt, ambivalence about judgment

In this section I continue to investigate selfhood and community and how the relationship between the two affects notions of responsibility and judgment. I begin with the question of selfhood and relate this to the issue of moral responsibility and how a community (a social audience) comes to blame a person for wrongdoing. My argument is that audiences' reactions to a person who has done wrong reflect an ontological ambiguity in selfhood, which arises from the dialectical relationship between selfhood and community. This argument retains the emphasis found in Giddens on the relationship between self and community, but insists, in a context of the continuing existence of community, on the persistent situatedness and relationality of the self.

In the previous chapter (see also Norrie, 1998b, 2000), I suggested that people often have an *ambivalent* attitude to the attribution of fault stemming from an *ambiguity* in the nature of what it means to be a responsible individual agent. This ambiguity feeds into moral judgments of wrongdoing and the sense of what it means to do justice. In ordinary moral life, ie, in relation to judgments of matters that do not concern crime and punishment, we often follow a two phase approach. At first we may be angry at what has been done and seek to blame the person who has done wrong, but then later we may proceed to judge the person 'in the round', taking the context of their actions into account. We interpret what was done as part of a person's history and situation. We 'explain' what they have done and, in so doing, come to excuse or forgive them.

Consider, for example, in a non-punitive context the ways in which we judge what we regard as the reprehensible conduct of those we like with that of those we do not. In the latter case, we are likely to accuse, to insist on the wrongful agency of a 'bad' person, to condemn. In the former case, perhaps initial irritation or anger at the bad act gives way to empathy, sorrow, explaining and excusing. This illustration depends, I would suggest, not just on the emotional orientation to the individual, but on two possible ways of regarding agency. In one, agency is *personalised* or *individualised* to achieve an immediate sense of responsibility; in the other, agency is *contextualised*, which has the effect of questioning the immediate sense of responsibility that comes from personalisation. Importantly, the 'duality of judgment' observed in this discussion reflects a duality in agency itself: human beings are both acting persons and persons who act in contexts.[3]

To illustrate the link between 'personalising' and 'decontextualising' judgments and the nature of the agency that is judged, this time in a punitive context, take an example I have used elsewhere (Norrie, 1998b). In the United Kingdom in the 1970s, a climate of what was later labelled as corruption developed in local government. Council officials and local developers became involved in relationships that were

---

3 This argument is informed theoretically by Bhaskar's account of the 'duality of structure and agency'. Under his transformative model of social action, agency 'reproduces and/or more or less transforms, for the most part unwittingly, its conditions of possibility', which include 'social structures and their generative mechanisms ... the agent herself and, generally, what was given, the *donné* ... which has now been reproduced or transformed' (Bhaskar, 1993, p 155). This implies a duality of structure and agency, 'dual points of articulation' which are the 'differentiated and changing *positioned-practices*' within structures which agents occupy, reproduce and transform. Structures constitute the system of social relations in which intentional human activity occurs.

too close and involved the acceptance of hospitality and gifts by officials. These were later seen as bribes, but at the time they could be seen as simple emollients or 'just the way things are done'. When these officials were eventually tried and convicted for accepting bribes, they were held to be guilty of corrupt acts, yet for many at the time, it seemed normal activity within a particular culture. At the same time, is it not possible that, at the back of their minds, a part of them also knew that there was 'something wrong' in what they were doing? The point is that individual subjectivity may not be fixed with regard to a moral code, but rather may shift between vocabularies of right and wrong which social contexts provide and agents mediate. Agents do things that can be interpreted in different and contradictory ways. We can either view the convicted councillor as a corrupt agent 'in control of his actions' and operating with a conventional moral vocabulary of right and wrong (a personalising strategy), or as a 'victim of the times' (a contextualising strategy). Most appropriately, we should see *both* sides of the question, but if we do, we recognise not just the *ambiguity* in our sense of individual responsibility, but also the *ambivalence* in judging that goes with it. The important point is that the ambiguity of responsibility and the ambivalence of judgment are dialectically related. They feed off each other in order to resolve what is essentially irresolute, the judgment of individual responsibility in the particular case.

The two-sided character of agency thus gives rise to ambivalence in how an audience judges conduct. Ultimately, ambivalence about judgment is 'resolved' according to the general social, political and moral standpoint of the onlooker. How does the onlooker view the actions of the friend or enemy, the actions of the local government officer? Such questions involve general and particular aspects. A friend's actions are judged as responsible or irresponsible in part on the basis that one is judging a friend, local government officers in part on how one feels about such people. Consider, for example, the likely different judgments of one who believes that local government officers generally 'mean well and try to do their best in difficult circumstances' and one who sees them as a 'drain on local resources'. What comes out is a judgment about individual responsibility for an act, but this is context-driven because personal agency is context-emergent. They cannot be separated.

The guilt of relatively benign council officials is one thing, but surely the example is an easy one. What about the most serious crimes involving horrible violence? Does a similar ambivalence and ambiguity operate there? I would argue that even in the worst cases, such as those of a Rosemary West or Myra Hindley, we do still wonder how they could have done what they did and question the personalising strategy that establishes their guilt. We do not do this in order to deny their wrongdoing, but we ask about their ultimate responsibility for what they did. Nothing makes us excuse or forgive their acts, but we still seek to understand contextually how they could have done them, how they could have become the sort of person who committed such crimes. Thus, our initial reaction of anger and condemnation is followed by a sense that the criminal was also, in a different sense, and one that does not diminish the horror of what he or she did, a victim. In so doing, we move from the sense of the individual as an autonomous responsible agent to that of the person as a social phenomenon. We place the criminal wrongdoer in his or her context.[4]

Which of these two kinds of judgments is the right one? Ultimately, neither. Personalising and contextualising involve contradictory responses, yet both are appropriate, if one-sided, reactions to the phenomenon. Both are evoked by one facet of individual being and agency. Condemnation is relevant for acts over which the individual has control, while empathy and excusing are relevant for acts over which the individual has not. Both standpoints reflect something of what is going on but both are one-sided because they reflect only one aspect of an ambiguous phenomenon, that is, *the individual operating* between agency and context. This is evidenced in a further third stage of moral reflection that is particularly significant and remarkable with regard to serious crimes. After the initial sense of anger and condemnation, and the second stage of contextual interpretation, we go back to the question of responsibility in a more considered way. How many are really satisfied, for example, with the sense that can be drawn from Myra Hindley's late essay (*The Guardian* (1995) 18 December), that the person who committed her crimes was 'another person' from the one Hindley became? There remains a sense of moral reckoning that corresponds to neither the immediate sense of responsibility (the personalising sense described above), nor the diffuse, contextualising approach to which I have also referred. It is a floating sense of what doing justice means, one that is hard to pin down. It operates in the space between what a person did and the ways in which that person was herself created, a dialectical space between conflicting alternatives, but a sense that is central to our lives as moral individuals and agents.

Part of this sense involves living with and coming to terms with events in our pasts, even those that are long past. This deeper sense of responsibility is accordingly particularly seen in the case of serious crimes committed many years ago, by someone such as Myra Hindley, and also in the current interest in prosecuting former Nazi war criminals. The past may be 'another country', occupied by 'other people', yet the sense of injustice that a denial of past responsibility evokes, or the sense of justice that demands the trial of serious crimes done long ago is linked, I suggest, to the complexity in understanding what individual life is as both a socio-historical and a personal phenomenon. However, a crucial mediating factor in 'fixing' responsibility is the role played by the social audience – the community – making judgments. With these considerations in mind, I turn now to consider a case study on the possibility of guilt.

---

4   If retributivist philosophy is the theoretical home of a personalising attitude to guilt, it is instructive to observe a leading modern retributivist's acknowledgment of, and discomfort in relation to, the contextualising strategy. Michael Moore writes that 'Undeniably, many people soften their judgments about responsibility when they know more of the causal story behind a person's bad behaviour', but happily for the retributivist, this is no more than an example of 'philosophically impure common sense [which] should not survive ... insights into its philosophical impurity' (Moore, 1997, p 512). In justifying a personalising strategy on the other hand, Moore is convinced that our feelings about wrongdoing are otherwise 'our main heuristic guide to finding out what is morally right' (*ibid*, p 115). See further Norrie, 2000, Chapter 5.

The two Speers of Gitta Sereny

In her book on Albert Speer, Gitta Sereny sought to understand the 'origin of Hitler's evil' and 'Speer's realisation of – and participation in – it'. Part of Hitler's genius was to corrupt others, and corruption is insidious, so that 'Speer, in the course of his growing relationship with Hitler, inevitably became – although for a long time unwittingly – a part of it' (Sereny, 1995, p 9). This is how Sereny describes Speer at the beginning of her book:

> Speer, I was already convinced, had never killed, stolen, personally benefited from the misery of others or betrayed a friend. And yet, what I felt neither the Nuremberg trial nor his books had really told us was how a man of such quality could become not immoral, not amoral but, somehow infinitely worse, morally extinguished. (*Ibid*, p 10)

If he became 'morally extinguished', then his 'struggle with the truth' (the title of Sereny's book), must have been a struggle to recover that which had been lost. At the very end, Sereny writes as follows:

> I came to understand and value Speer's battle with himself and saw in it the re-emergence of the intrinsic morality he manifested as a boy and youth. It seemed to me it was some kind of victory that this man – just this man – *weighed down by intolerable and unmanageable guilt ... tried to become a different man.* (*Ibid*, p 720, emphasis added)

Sereny summarises the process from moral extinction to awareness. She details Speer's growing recognition of 'Hitler's madness' through two formative war time experiences. The first was at Posen, where in a speech in October 1943 Himmler directly confronted all the top Nazis with what had been done to the Jews. The second concerned his own personal visit in December 1943 to the 'Dora' project, the underground rocket factories built with slave labour, where Speer was again directly confronted with what was happening. After the war, Speer was subject to the 'revelations of Nuremberg' and was confronted 'with the reactions of the civilised world'. He came to realise the 'horror of what had been done' and to experience 'feelings of personal guilt' which were illuminated by, most importantly, a pastor at Spandau, Casalis, and his daughter, Hilde. In the context of the solitude of a 20-year sentence at Spandau, Speer experienced a 'continuing and tormenting awareness of guilt' and 'out of all this, there came to be another Speer'. This is Sereny's summary (with a crucial part of one sentence missed out) of the 'other' Speer, a man who sought with all seriousness to come to terms with his past:

> In this Speer, obsessed with a history he understood perhaps like no other man, I found a great deal to like over the four years I knew him. This, I feel, had become the real Speer ... This was a very serious man who knew more about that bane of our century, Hitler, than anyone else. This was an erudite and solitary man who, recognising his deficiencies in human relations, had read five thousand books in prison to try to understand the universe and human beings, an effort he succeeded in with his mind but failed in with his heart. Empathy is finally a gift, and cannot be learned, so, essentially, returning into the world after twenty years, he remained alone.

> Unforgiven by so many for having served Hitler, he elected to spend the rest of his life in confrontation with this past, unforgiving of himself for having so nearly loved a monster. (*Ibid*, p 719)

In this account, Speer sought resolution with his guilt, but remained essentially solitary. He could not ultimately get there, but his effort in seeking to do so was what Sereny admired. In a newspaper interview, she states that 'to me, there was one extraordinarily redeeming thing, that his sense of personal guilt was so deep' and that through this guilt, he regained 'some of his morality' (*The Guardian*, September 1995). This is a compelling and sympathetic account of Speer, a man whom Sereny admits she 'grew to like' (Sereny, 1995, p 3).

It rests, however, alongside another story she tells. In the long passage I quoted above, I missed out part of one sentence. Just after Sereny has spoken of the 'real' Speer, there is a line in which she notes that for a brief period before he died, Speer discarded his 'moral seriousness', and started boasting about his past. She states that she is convinced that he would have rediscovered his new moral self 'after the euphoria of his late-life passion had passed'.[5] Sereny refers here to an affair Speer conducted in his final years with a woman much younger than himself. In Sereny's estimation, this affair jolted Speer into a different moral outlook. The woman with whom he became involved bestowed upon him 'unlimited and uncritical acceptance' which was to 'free him from the questioning self he had been for so long' (*ibid*, p 715). The fruit of this was observed in a phone call Sereny took from Speer shortly before his death in which he reflected self-satisfactorily on his life. She quotes him:

> 'What I wanted to tell you,' Speer said happily, 'was that after all I think I haven't done so badly. After all, I was Hitler's architect; I was his Minister of Armaments and Production; I did serve twenty years in Spandau and, coming out did make another good career. Not bad after all, was it?' (*Ibid*, p 781)

Was this just a final deflection from contrition, as Sereny has it, or did it reflect another side to Speer that Sereny's positive moral image of him downplayed? Compare her account of the end of his life with her assessment of its beginning. We have already seen Sereny comment on 'the re-emergence of the intrinsic morality [Speer] manifested *as a boy and youth*' (emphasis added) but this can be contrasted with what she says, only on the previous page, that Speer 'felt nothing' for the Nazi slaughter:

> There was a dimension missing in him, a capacity to feel *which his childhood had blotted out*, allowing him to experience not love but only romanticised substitutes for love. Pity, compassion, sympathy and empathy were not part of his emotional vocabulary. (*Ibid*, p 719, emphasis added)

These are two deeply opposed accounts of Speer's youth, which offer crucially different lenses for the interpretation of his later moral behaviour. At varying points in the book, this 'other' Speer, lacking in what Sereny would call significant moral experience, makes himself felt. Speer could write letters from Spandau that acknowledged something of his moral responsibility, but these were ultimately evasive. He could acknowledge feelings of guilt, but also consider his position in coldly calculating and strategic ways. In addition, it should not be forgotten that Sereny's whole interrogation with Speer had to negotiate his continuing *denial* of

---

5   The full passage omitted, which belongs where I have placed the square brackets in the quote, is as follows: 'the one I am convinced – after the euphoria of his late life passion had passed – he would have become again, had he lived on.'

direct knowledge of what was happening to the Jews under the Nazis, so that his entire post Nazi life involved a lie. Even his final apparent acknowledgment of a form of direct complicity he challenged later himself.

Sereny encountered this 'other' Speer during her conversations with him, when she would occasionally trip a circuit in Speer's mind which would replace sympathy and urbanity with something threatening and violent:

> Here was not the reasoning Speer, my urbane host. Here was Hitler's great Minister who had ruled Germany's economy and the lives of millions ... I was suddenly keenly and somewhat frighteningly aware ... of the authority coiled inside this man, which manifestly suppressed with constant deliberate effort, only burst out at moments of disappointment, intense irritation or weary anger. (*Ibid*, p 222)

Again, at the very end of the book, Sereny counterposes the guilt-feeling Speer to the pragmatic Speer who gave up every consideration to satisfy his own ambition, and who 'manipulated, cajoled, intrigued against and threatened those who interfered with his power and his aims' (*ibid*, p 718). In her interview with *The Guardian*, counterposed to the image of Speer's deep sense of personal guilt was Sereny's acknowledgment that 'Speer was a man of such multi-personalities and if you didn't understand that, you could not deal with him'. Thus at one level, Sereny was forced to recognise Speer's morally schizophrenic character, but the picture that dominates her analysis is of a man who once was lost but now is found, one 'weighed down by intolerable and unmanageable guilt' who 'tried to become a different man'. It is that figure, whom she admires, who dominates her biography.

Guilt: the space between

In the light of Sereny on Speer, let us now return to our consideration of the nature of guilt and community in the first two parts of this chapter. As regards the self, Giddens suggested that an increasing individual reflexivity erodes normative boundaries and leads to a diminution of the sense of transgression that underlies guilt. The self is able more and more to create and recreate itself through the fashioning of changeable narratives that position and reposition it according to the needs of the moment. Reflexivity undermines transgression, which undermines guilt. The reflexive self reinterprets its biography to suit the context, so that a sense of a unified self becomes increasingly problematic. There is a minimal level at which this self remains robust, able to weather major transitions or tensions, but otherwise selfhood has become fragile.

If we consider Speer in this light, one could interpret his conduct during and after the Second World War in terms of the 'fragile' aspect of Giddens's self. Relying on the minimal 'robust' side of selfhood to get him through the transition from Nazism to liberal democracy, Speer would be a person who reinvented himself to suit the changing times. Many people see Speer in such terms: as an amoral opportunist out to promote himself. However, what then of the sense of guilt, on which Sereny focuses? As we have seen, Sereny's image of a 'morally continuous' Speer, seeking to come to terms with his past, is undercut by the 'other' Speer who irrupted into her narrative and consciousness from time to time. We might be inclined, therefore, to dismiss Sereny's view and say that Speer was just manipulating her and anyone else prepared to listen to him. Perhaps, then, we would say that Giddens is right: Speer is an early example of the reinvention of self in the absence of guilt and responsibility that is the hallmark of 'late modernity'. However, I think we have to grasp the post war Speer in a more complex way than saying *either* that he was an inherently moral being (albeit incomplete: Sereny) *or* that he was a cynic and manipulator (flipping stories of his life at will: Giddens). The truth seems to involve capturing a sense in which both aspects could be true, and so doing, to move beyond both.

A way into this complexity comes from considering the role of community in establishing guilt. Recall the second aspect of Giddens's account, the idea of the erosion of community in 'late modernity'. I suggested that another interpretation of 'late modernity' might involve us looking as much at the fragmentation, conflict and change between communities as at the absolute erosion of their moral influence. This seems to me particularly important in thinking about Speer. The post war process from Nuremberg onwards represented a confrontation between the moral values of two quite different communities, the fascist and the liberal democratic. When Speer was charged with crimes against humanity, when he was confronted by the pastor Casalis at Spandau, when he was asked by his daughter what he had known and done, when he was interrogated by Sereny herself, when he wrote explaining for a post war society what Nazism had meant, he was confronting in each case a condemnatory moral outlook different from the one of which he had been a part.

What we get from Sereny's analysis of Speer is the sense of a moral dialogue not just between two people but between two political communities in which an individual, who passed historically from one to the other, was confronted with and was engaged by the condemnation of his past. From this, he developed, at one level of his being, feelings of guilt. It seems to me that Sereny is not wrong to recognise his feelings of guilt, but these always coexisted with careerist calculation. He both felt guilt and was 'a man of such multi-personalities' so that he could set guilt aside and revert to an underlying Nazi persona. This sets up an ambiguity in her analysis. While recognising both sides of Speer, Sereny cannot bring them together. She gets drawn too close to the Speer she liked, while remaining both too acute not to note his other, deeply unattractive, side *and* unable to reconcile this with her account of his moral qualities. Hence her two accounts of the boyhood Speer: as both youthful moral individual and psychopath. The ultimate problem she faces is how to judge this level of conflict and complexity in one man. It is this that causes the tension in her book.

This problem of complexity takes me to my own argument about the ambiguity of the self and the ambivalence of judgment in modern society. Post war liberal democracy established, at one level at least,[6] different public norms and judgments to those of fascism. Nuremberg, Pastor Casalis, Speer's daughter and Sereny all approach Speer from the judgment of the utter wrongs of the Nazis, so that they impose a judgmental context upon Speer with which he became engaged. Post-Nuremberg involved a process of dialogue between one who had been a fascist and a liberal democratic community, and whatever feelings of moral guilt occurred

---

6 Any full assessment of the gap between post war morality and that of the Nazis would have to absorb the lesson of the ways in which, as Tom Bower puts it, a blind eye was turned to murder in the post war denazification of Germany (Bower, 1997).

within Speer were invoked by that dialogue. The point seems an obvious one, but its impact on Speer is significant. Recall the two images Sereny provides: one of his intrinsic morality, the other of his cynicism. My suggestion is that both currents ran through Speer in the post-war period. Speer was both the calculating careerist who knowingly turned his back on the consequences of his actions and endorsed Nazism, and one who evolved moral responses to what he had done in his later years. The transition, however, was never such that the later Speer completely subsumed the earlier. Speer's life spanned two different socio-political periods, and accordingly so too did his personality and his morality.

After the war Speer was really two Speers spread out across two historical contexts. Dialogue with Sereny, Casalis and his daughter contextualised his subjectivity in the liberal democratic context, setting up a profound conflict with what he had been. This led to genuine feelings of guilt, but feelings that were not strong enough to lead him to draw a clear line against what he had been. The escape into a romantic and sexual affair in his last years can thus be seen not, as Sereny sees it, as a moral 'blip', but as the creation, as it were, of a 'moral micro-community' with his girlfriend sealing Speer off from the broader liberal democratic context. In this situation, his guilt could be set aside and his earlier amoral egotism and pride in his fascist achievements resurface. Similarly, the occasional irruption of his violent Nazi persona through the urbane liberal democratic self was an indication of the different selves coexisting in the later Speer.

Where does all this take us in relation to the questions of guilt and responsibility? I have been trying to get at the relationship between the individual and the community as a nexus within which responsibility and guilt are established. Individuals shift between registers of self-accounting, so that it is socio-political contexts that 'fix' responsibility. War criminals provide a particularly vivid illustration of this process because they move historically between quite different moral contexts of judgment. In the process their responsibility for their crimes, as a matter of individual guilt, is something that they ambiguously and ambivalently negotiate with their interrogators. Individual guilt and responsibility are thus real categories which we need to understand, but contextually and dialectically, as processes, by individuals, of symbiotic engagement within different socio-political communities.

They do not as a result, however, possess a complete fluidity, so that no judgment becomes possible. Recall that in my reference to Myra Hindley, I suggested that beyond an immediate finding of guilt and a contextualisation of personhood, there was a further third step. At this point, it was possible to ask whether, taking into account what was done and the context within which it was done, there could be an acknowledgment by a person that it was he or she who had done the wrong, even taking into account a context that was different and distancing from the here and now. Such an acknowledgment, in dialogue with a community, is possible and necessary; it is the price of agency, even under conditions not of our own making. The evidence of Sereny's account is that Speer had such a dialogue – with his daughter and with Casalis – but that he never took the third, morally totalising, step of fully acknowledging for himself guilt for what had occurred. The ultimate problem was that he lacked the character fully to acknowledge and condemn what he had done and been and therefore lacked a full sense of his own guilt as an agent in another time and place.

Beyond 'individual' and 'community' in the philosophy of punishment

I want to end by locating the foregoing in the context of problems within the philosophy of punishment. The dominant tradition here is broadly Kantian in the sense of a reliance on 'notions of personal agency, responsibility, and the moral law' (Bird, 1995, p 439; cf Gardner, 1998). Such a sense of individual responsibility informs in different ways the analysis of guilt in both Giddens's and Sereny's work. With Sereny, the idea of a man coming to terms with his guilt is plainly Kantian in this broad sense; but the same is true in a rather more refracted way with Giddens's emphasis on the isolated, reflexive individual of late modernity. Indeed, one might say that Giddens's individual, freed of the norms of a community, is living out the solipsistic quality that Hannah Arendt finds in Kant's failed moral law, the categorical imperative. The categorical imperative requires the rational individual to agree with himself because it 'is based upon the necessity for rational thought to agree with itself' (Arendt, 1961, p 220). Such an unconnected individualism is not so far from the 'reflexive organisation of the self', but it clearly misses the continuing linkages I have sought to demonstrate between individual morality and the historic community(ies) of which it is a part.

If much modern philosophy of punishment proceeds in this broadly Kantian mode (eg, von Hirsch, 1993; Moore, 1997), there have been attempts to link issues of responsibility to questions of community, and a sense of dialogue between individual and community. For example, Antony Duff (1986, 1996) has written of punishment as a process of communication between individual and community. However, I have argued elsewhere (Norrie, 1998b, 2000, Chapter 6) that Duff retains an essentially Kantian notion of the responsible subject which he himself undermines by his attempt to locate that subject within a broader community. At the same time, he fails to recognise fully the moral effect on issues of guilt and blame of acknowledging what community means in modern Western societies with their structural social conflicts. In this regard, Duff's move is not a new one, bearing a strong resemblance (though there are important differences) to the work of the late 19th century English Hegelians, TH Green and Bernard Bosanquet (Norrie, 1991b, Chapter 5) who were earlier initiators of a communitarian political philosophy.

Green and Bosanquet were Victorian inheritors of the idealist tradition of Kant and Hegel, and their work was designed to relocate what they saw as the too ideal individualism of the Germans in a more realistic sense of the nature of modern capitalist society. Viewed in this perspective, the past and present concerns of communitarian writers are really the other side of the Kantian heritage against which they frequently rail; they are still dancing to a Kantian tune. Indeed, if we follow Arendt's interpretation, Kant was himself an enthusiastic participant in the individualist-communitarian *pas de deux*. She describes a striking philosophical contrast between Kant's critique of moral reason and his critique of aesthetic judgment. In the latter, she identifies a different relationship between the individual and the community in which, contrary to the categorical imperative, 'it would not be enough to be in agreement with one's own self', but rather there would be a relationship which involved 'being able to "think in the place of everybody else"'. Under what Kant called an 'enlarged mentality', the power of judgment:

> rests on a potential agreement with others, and the thinking process which is active in judging something is not, like the thought process of pure reasoning, a dialogue between me and myself, but finds itself always and primarily, even if I am quite alone in making up my mind, *in an anticipated communication with others with whom I know I must finally come to some agreement.* (Arendt, 1961, p 220, emphasis added)

To be sure, Kant's target in the critique of aesthetic judgment is quite different from moral wrongdoing, but there are parallels. Arendt continues that aesthetic judgment is both impossible without, and limited by, the nature of community. As regards the necessity of community, judgment:

> cannot function in strict isolation or solitude; it needs the presence of others 'in whose place' it must think, whose perspectives it must take into consideration, and without whom it never has the opportunity to operate at all. As logic, to be sound, depends on the presence of the self, so judgment, to be valid, *depends on the presence of others. (Ibid,* emphasis added)

As regards the limitation of judgment by virtue of its place in community, Arendt observes that it:

> is endowed with a certain specific validity but is never universally valid. Its claims to validity can never extend further than the others in whose place the judging person has put himself for his considerations. *(Ibid,* p 221)

She concludes that judgment 'is a specifically political ability', the ability 'to see things ... in the perspective of all those who happen to be present'. As such, it is 'one of the fundamental abilities of man as a political being'.

I suggest that Kant, on Arendt's rendition, got at least as close to issues of guilt and responsibility in his discussion of aesthetics as he did in his moral philosophy. His emphasis on the role of community and its relationship with the individual, far from the solipsist bar of the categorical imperative, identifies the place where judgment occurs, and which generates the complexity, ambivalence and ambiguity I have sought to identify here. Community, as I hope I have made clear, is not the whole story, but it is an integral part of it. It is only in a community that the floating stories of the self that Giddens identifies *theoretically,* and Sereny identifies *biographically* can be 'fixed'. My approach locates a 'site' of judgment that is both within a community and a means of bringing to bear judgment on individuals for whom guilt is a possible moral sentiment. This involves a more complex, dialectical, understanding of individuals and communities than individualistic or communitarian approaches have been able to provide.

I want finally to anticipate one serious possible objection to the foregoing and at least to indicate how it might be met. The objection would be that in moving our debate beyond Kantianism and into an area where morality operates *between* an individual and a community, the force of an absolute morality is lost. Kant's categorical imperative might have proved empty in practice, but at least it marked a site where deontological issues were discussed as real moral possibilities. In locating guilt and judgment somewhere between individuals and communities, one may be committing oneself to the dangerously relativist view that all that exists morally is the morality of communities.

To do no more than identify one possible response to this objection, let us consider briefly Roy Bhaskar's discussion of an example provided by Isaiah Berlin (Bhaskar, 1994, p 110). Berlin contrasted four descriptions of what happened under Nazi rule in Germany: 'the country was depopulated'; 'millions of people died'; 'millions of people were killed'; 'millions of people were murdered'. Language is the place where communities in conflict can seem to agree on 'the facts', while disagreeing fundamentally on their moral import: think of 'ethnic cleansing'. However, what Berlin's example shows is that, while all four of his statements are true, it is the last that is 'not only most evaluative, [but] also the best (ie, the most precise and accurate) description of what actually happened' (Bhaskar, 1994, p 110). Bhaskar's moral realism relates the description of social phenomena to their truth content, and their truth as adequate descriptions, where relevant, to their truth as moral descriptions. The fourth statement's factual and moral truth 'turns not on the subject's interest in the subject matter, but on the nature of the subject matter itself and criteria for its adequate description and explanation' (*ibid*, p 110). In the last sentence we could talk just as easily of the 'community's interest' as the 'subject's interest'.

This reference to a moral realist underpinning to the discussion of the historical and community mediation of individual responsibility requires to be developed, but I will conclude on the main themes of my argument. The issue of legal or moral guilt is a complex one that defies the easy answers of those who assume the existence of a fixed, responsible individual subject, or argue for the 'late modern' erosion or reflexivity of all subject positions. Central to the establishment of guilt is the dialectical relationship between a subject and his or her historically evolving communities. Speer's ambivalence concerning his guilt, reflected on but not fully understood by Gitta Sereny, illustrates such a relationship. When all was said and done, Speer had not decisively moved to acknowledge his guilt, and it is on that basis that he is ultimately judged: as a person who confronted with the evils of Nazism remained at heart a Nazi. However, he had felt guilt, and it is the phenomenal texture and possibility of this ambiguous subject position I have sought to explain, by a relational theory of responsibility.

Chapter 7
From Criminal Law to Legal Theory: The Mysterious Case of the Reasonable Glue Sniffer

The qualitative moment is preserved in all quantification, as the substrate of that which is to be quantified. (Adorno, 1973, p 43)

Criminal law: problems and approaches

Criminal law theorists live in times that could be described, relatively speaking, as 'interesting'. At the core of modern argument is an ongoing conflict, explicit or implicit, between the dominant 'orthodox subjectivist' tradition of the textbooks and law, and a host of critical perspectives which can be broadly described as 'morally contextual' or 'substantive'.[1] The dominant tradition relies upon a formal model of individual responsibility resting on psychological traits which reveal a person to be in control of her acts (intention, foresight, voluntariness, rationality). The critical opposition insists that the moral context or substance, for example, of an intention are as important if not more so in gauging responsibility (Norrie, 2001b, Chapter 3). Thus, under the law of murder the contract and the mercy killer may both be equally responsible, both possessing the intention to kill, but the contextualist would say there is a world of moral difference between the two which the law ought to reflect. This chapter will try to highlight and explain the significance of this conflict. My immediate target will be one consequence of it, the 'reasonable glue sniffer' in the law of provocation (Norrie, 2001a), but the argument then moves from the particular to the more general conflict between 'orthodox subjectivism' and 'moral contextualism' in the law.

As regards the law of provocation, it is in a bad state at present after a string of Court of Appeal and House of Lords decisions. In these cases, the courts wrestle with precedent, but they also engage with the underlying moral problems reflected in legal concepts. The question that emerges is how to establish a general standard for judging provocation while attending to the individual particularity of the accused. Hence the idea of the 'reasonable glue sniffer' (*R v Morhall* [1995] 3 All ER 658), the 'reasonable immature person' (*R v Humphreys* [1995] 4 All ER 100), the 'reasonable obsessive' (*R v Dryden* [1995] 4 All ER 987), or even, if the case of an Australian stalker were transposed to this country, the 'reasonable erotomaniac' (*Stingel v R* (1990) 171 CLR 312), an oxymoron if ever there was one. The underlying issue concerns how we examine and explain this tension between the general and the particular in the law. Some might see it as an inevitable

---

1   For general discussion, see Duff, 1990; Dennis, 1997; Gardner, 1998; Norrie, 2000, Chapters 2, 5 and 6. I use these terms to express dualities in the law that can variously be described as involving a 'formal' versus a 'substantive' morality, or an abstract formalism in opposition to a contextualised understanding of legal concepts.

consequence of submitting human actions to the governance of rules. I will present four arguments that suggest a more complex problematic. These concern: first, the tension between moral judgment and legal form; secondly, the relation between individual justice 'internal' to law and an 'external' social justice; thirdly, the 19th century foundation of the criminal law in abstract individualist categories; and, fourthly, law's involvement in an historically specific dialectic of the universal and the particular. Let us look at these in turn.

Criminal law antinomies

Questions about the relationship between law and morality are central to discussions of legal responsibility. My own view is that criminal law is as much a moral as a technical legal business, and criminal lawyers, though they may try to, cannot avoid this conclusion. If they try to, the moral issues have a habit of biting back, and this is evidenced by legal confusions going to the law's very heart. In the present or immediate past, the law has entertained at least three different and conflicting meanings of intention[2] and four of recklessness.[3] This is clearly unsatisfactory, and my first argument is that the underlying problem is that criminal law seeks to be both a set of technical legal rules and a means in an important, but not necessarily obvious, moral sense of 'doing justice'. There is a duality of law which involves an uneasy and unstable relation between legal forms and moral values.

If there are moral problems within the criminal law relating to what it means to do justice, why should this occur? Any argument about what is 'within' the criminal law must reckon with how a sense of what is internal to law is constructed, and what then lies 'outside' it. My second argument concerns the relationship between individual justice within the criminal law and a broader sense of social justice, which is seen as lying beyond it. My argument will be that what lawyers essentially think of as a commonsensical separation between two distinct domains and sets of questions does not work. The problems which haunt criminal law can be traced finally to a false but primal separation between individual justice and social justice, such that the latter is taken to involve issues extraneous to legal justice. My claim is that it is this ultimately unsustainable separation between two concepts of justice which constitutes the deep structure underlying the problems of law, be it in relation to provocation, or any other of a range of problematic criminal law concepts. It also informs the unsatisfactory intellectual split between the orthodox

---

2   Intention as purpose (*R v Steane* [1947] 1 All ER 813), intention as purpose plus foresight of virtually certain side-effect (*R v Woollin* [1998] 3 WLR 382), intention as purpose plus foresight of (highly) probable consequence (*Hyam v DPP* [1974] 2 All ER 41). While *R v Moloney* ([1985] 1 All ER 1025) first formulated the *Woollin* approach, it also refers favourably to *Steane*, and opens the door to the *Hyam*-style guidelines developed in *R v Hancock and Shankland* ([1986] 2 WLR 357) and *R v Nedrick* ([1986] 1 WLR 1025). *Woollin* arguably has not entirely shut the door on the *Hyam* approach (Norrie, 1999), which is independently endorsed in the case of the accessory to murder (*R v Powell and Daniels; R v English* [1999] AC 1). For general discussion of motive and the law of intention, see Norrie, 2001b, Chapter 3.

3   Advertent recklessness (*R v Cunningham* [1957] 2 QB 396), advertent or inadvertent recklessness (*R v Caldwell* [1981] 1 All ER 961), recklessness as practical indifference (*R v Satnam and Kewal* (1983) 78 Cr App R 149), recklessness as committing a crime of 'basic intent' while intoxicated (*DPP v Majewski* [1976] 2 All ER 142). See now *R v G* [2003] 4 All ER 765, discussed above at p 82.

subjectivists and the moral contextualists described above. Note that I do not say that questions of individual justice within the law are immediately reducible to questions of social justice. That would be to deny the real, practical and intellectual substance of legal forms and their relative autonomy. I do, however, insist that a fuller understanding of how these forms work involves appreciating the porous boundaries of law, and how it nests in a broader social and historical 'dialectic of justice'.[4] This is both its context and what it enacts, an absent presence that it both denies and embodies in the act of separation.

Invoking the social history of modern law brings me to my third main argument about the nature of legal justice. The reason for these splits and problems in law concerns the nature of the legal individualism that informs discussions of criminal law and justice. Our modern law begins in the early 19th century with a separation of the individual from her social and moral context. This allows the law to find the individual responsible for her acts in isolation from questions of the social causes of action, and of social responsibilities for what occurs (Norrie, 2001b, Chapter 2). This separation of the individual from the social is carried into legal categories by virtue of a model of individual responsibility that emphasises the person's 'factual', psychological control of her actions, through her intentions, foresight, voluntariness and so on. This is how a technical understanding of criminal responsibility is built up through doctrines of *mens rea*, in opposition to conceptions of what is substantively morally significant about mental states. Thus, the law separates off, for example, questions of intention, which are central to culpability, from questions of motive which are said to be irrelevant (Williams, 1961, p 31; Smith and Hogan, 1999, pp 77–79). However, it is the question of motive, the 'why' question, which carries the moral punch, and ultimately, the law cannot do without it.[5] What has been left out therefore has to be allowed back in, even though the legal concepts had ordained its exclusion. Modern criminal law comes thus to be founded on a series of false splits, or antinomies, between motive and intention, direct and indirect intention, subjective and objective forms of recklessness, issues of offence and defence, justification and excuse, and so on. Ultimately, these can be traced to deeper splits between 'factual' and 'normative' accounts of basic legal categories, between 'internal' and 'external' accounts of criminal law, and between questions of individual and social justice.[6] These splits derive from the abstract concept of the

---

4 This is a stronger claim than to say that criminal law simply presents opposing and conflicting views. For example, as regards the split between orthodox subjectivists and moral contextualists, it entails the view that moral contextualism is invoked by the limits of the orthodox subjectivist approach and possesses an intrinsic connection in the form of a shared focus on individual justice and responsibility to the exclusion, marginalisation, and/or false separation of issues of social justice and responsibility. This is one of the central claims in Norrie, 2000 and is argued briefly below, in the conclusion to this chapter. The prefatory quote from Adorno describes a dialectical relationship involving antinomy. The law has its own correlates in the ideas of 'technical' or 'factual' forms of responsibility (matters of 'quantity') and opposing 'morally substantive' ('quality') approaches.

5 Thus, the point is not that the law as a whole is uninterested in motive, but that it organises its interest in a particular way. Motive is excluded from the central categories of the 'definition of the offence' (*mens rea* and *actus reus*) but there are inclusions elsewhere, such as in the defences. However, the search for a motive-free law of intention fails, as does the effort to distinguish 'offence' and 'defence'. These are false but necessary separations (Norrie, 2000, Chapters 7 and 8).

6 For more on these oppositions, see Norrie, 2000. For debate on a distinction between a realm of retributive legal justice and one of distributive social and political justice, see Duff, 1998; Horder, 2000; Norrie, 2000, pp 22–30.

individual at the law's core. Relating this back to my first two arguments, it is this historically achieved abstract individualism which engineers the primal separation between legal and social justice, and which enjoins a split between legal and moral judgment.

Universals and particulars

If disjuncture, split and separation constitute the province of legal justice, how do these constitute a pattern or logic of the law? Here I want to develop a fourth argument concerning the idea that law embodies a dialectic of justice. This involves the relationship between the 'universal' and the 'particular' in the law. When we hold someone up to legal judgment, we bring that person under rules and categories that derive their legitimacy from the fact that they appear to transcend the immediate context and the interests of the judgers. For example, in the move to set up international tribunals of criminal justice to adjudicate war crimes, the aim is to establish neutral and impartial organs according to universally acceptable codes of law. A similar claim is made for domestic criminal law, particularly through categories of responsibility which are relevant to individuals of every class and creed. One can call this an 'Enlightenment' view of responsibility for its commitment to universal criteria of justice.

Against this, there are a number of criticisms of universal justice. At one level, there is the kind of deconstructive criticism that says that seeking the universal is a means of denying the particular. The universal in fact involves a series of partial standards masquerading as a universal. At another level, it is the kind of criticism that says that the claim to do universal justice does no more than provide a legitimating cover for history's winners, either as a class, a nation, or a religion. Thus, the charge is laid that so-called universal justice is the partial justice of the powerful. Here is a quote from the feminist legal writer Margaret Davies, which focuses on the relationship between the universal and the particular:

> On the whole, jurisprudence is about universals. It is about distilling general principles and discerning what is essential and what marginal. Jurisprudence takes the central case as the universal ... The whole liberal tradition has been one in which the central case of the human being has corresponded to the central case of the man ... The practice of thinking solely in terms of universals, rather than in terms of the specificity of particular situations and relationships, casts everything as a variation on the same set of standards, and perpetuates hierarchy in our modes of being and knowing. (Davies, 1996, p 91)[7]

Could what Davies says of jurisprudence not equally be said of criminal law: that its universal categories occlude and repress? The difficulty with the charge is that it seems to involve both truth and overstatement. On the one hand, it seems wrong to think that the idea of a universal basis for criminal justice is an unimportant aspiration and requirement in doing justice. We *should* all be treated according to universal rules. On the other, it is no doubt true that in the name of legal justice,

---

7 Davies's analysis is directed primarily at the false universalisation implicit in the notion of 'man'. There are, however, clear convergences between her approach and that adopted here. For a brief attempt to describe the theoretical links, see below, Chapter 9, fn 1. The links between a feminist approach to criminal law and that adopted here are discussed in Lacey, 1998b, 197–201. I have used feminist perspectives in discussing the impact of insanity and diminished responsibility laws in the criminal law (Norrie, 2001b, pp 188–93).

many unjust things pass, and that the abstract universals of legal responsibility are implicated in this. The model of the responsible individual looks, from Davies's standpoint, to be a way of avoiding central truths about the particular situations of individuals who come before the criminal courts. In the main it is the poor, the poorly educated, those with the lowest life chances who get constructed as 'responsible' individuals under the law's universal categories. Thus, we are pushed both to endorse and to reject universalism.

Is there any way of understanding the conflicting demands for both a universal standard and to 'attend to the particular'? I am going to suggest a dialectical way of looking at this that helps us to hold these two aspects together in our thought, and, I believe, to explain the law's own intrinsic dynamic. I will suggest that we can build an understanding of legal justice that enables us to discern a systematic dialectical pattern in how law handles the splits, oppositions and separations (the antinomies) described above. We live, I shall argue, in a legal world that embodies and lives a dilemmatic or antinomial structure of justice issues. I will explain this as a 'dialectic of the universal and the particular', in a slightly more developed form below. I will argue that, whether we like it or not, this dialectic underlies and informs central debates in the criminal law. This is so both in relation to provocation, and to the battle between orthodox subjectivists and moral contextualists, the two illustrative foci for my discussion here. Criminal law lives this dialectic.

To conclude this introduction, let me outline how the chapter proceeds in its two main sections. In the first of these, I develop the idea of a dialectic of the universal and the particular in two ways. First, I examine some decisions of Lord Edmund-Davies in the area of duress and necessity. These embody the plight of what I call the humanitarian judge, that is the judge who is required to do justice through law, but appreciates the limits of what this means. I will then side-step to consider how the greatest philosophers of modern times, Kant and Hegel, spoke about criminal justice. From the House of Lords to German idealism: these are, deliberately, two very different discussions. I want to show the connections between Enlightenment philosophy and modern legal practice, and how they reflect the same kind of thought pattern. In both discussions, I will be focusing on the idea of criminal justice as involving a universalisation of individual justice, but I will be identifying also the limits of that universalisation. This entails recognising the way in which the law's universalising strategy is undercut by a 're-particularisation' associated with questions of social justice. These two discussions are grouped together under the general heading of exploring the relationship between the universal and the particular in legal and moral judgment.

In the second main section, there is a gearshift in the chapter as we move to look in greater detail at a specific legal artefact, the 'reasonable glue sniffer' in the law of provocation. This is presented as an example of the broader conflict in the law between 'orthodox subjectivism' and 'moral contextualism'. These two topics are grouped under the heading of the relationship between the 'formal' and the 'substantive' in legal judgment. I will discuss the ways in which the modern law operates an uneasy balance between formal, orthodox subjectivist ways of stating culpability and the substantive critique of the moral contextualists. I will then conclude in a final section by linking the argument of the two main sections together. Legal conflicts between form and substance will be related to questions of individual and social justice and the dialectic of the universal and the particular. I will conclude that to live under the criminal law is to live this dialectic and to do so through the experience of antinomy. In this way, the two main sections, on the universal and the particular and the formal and the substantive, are brought together. The relationship between formalism and substantivism (or contextualism) in criminal law expresses an underlying conflict between universalism and particularism, and both sets of oppositions are set in motion by the law's historically constituted abstract individualism. The antinomy that underlies all this, but whose name dare not be spoken, is that between individual and social justice.

Criminal justice: the universal and the particular

Criminal justice and the humanitarian judge

As a judge in the Court of Appeal and the House of Lords in the 1970s and 1980s, the late Lord Edmund-Davies delivered judgments in many important cases. As a result of dialogue with textbook writers in the orthodox subjectivist tradition, this was a period of intellectual ferment in the criminal law and judgments by Lord Edmund-Davies often captured the pulse of the legal moment.[8] The following sample does not purport to reflect Lord Edmund-Davies's overall contribution to criminal law, which was substantial, but to highlight important issues within it.

One area of the criminal law that has always caused problems is that occupied by the twin defences of duress and necessity.[9] When a person acts under either defence, she acts under a threat to life or serious injury from another person (duress), or from an impersonal situation (necessity). In the case of *DPP for Northern Ireland v Lynch* [1975] AC 653, the House of Lords had to decide whether a man involved, under threat to his own life, as the driver to a murder in Northern Ireland could claim duress. One argument was that he should be convicted, and that the proper place to reflect the duress involved was not through a formal legal defence but through mitigation of his sentence. Rejecting this on the ground of doing individual justice to the defendant, Lord Edmund-Davies had this to say. Mitigation:

> at least makes for neatness. No matter how terrifying the circumstances which have impelled a man (and, indeed, which might have impelled most men) to transgress the criminal law, he must be convicted ... The trouble about such neatness is that it may work intolerable injustice in individual cases. (*Ibid*, p 707)

---

8 Relevant cases in this period were *Hyam v DPP* [1974] 2 All ER 41, *DPP v Morgan* [1976] AC 182, *DPP v Majewski* [1976] 2 All ER 142, *DPP for Northern Ireland v Lynch* [1975] AC 653, *Abbott v R* [1977] AC 755, *R v Caldwell* [1981] 1 All ER 961. For a full biographical and analytical essay on Lord Edmund-Davies, see Hall, 1985, p 18.

9 This continues to be the case in light of the emergence of a recent necessity defence of 'duress of circumstances' and the recognition of necessity as a defence to murder in the case of *Re A (Children)* [2000] 4 All ER 961 (see Norrie, 2001b, Chapter 8).

This strongly moral argument won the day. Lynch, however, was the driver to the killing, the aider and abettor rather than the actual perpetrator. He was a 'principal in the second degree'. In the slightly later Privy Council case of *Abbott* [1977] AC 755, the question, following *Lynch*, was whether the defence was also available to a 'principal in the first degree'. To distinguish between degrees of involvement in a crime is often hard, sometimes impossible. However, the majority in *Abbott* held that the defence of duress was not available to the defendant as the actual perpetrator. Abbott was on a capital charge in Trinidad and Tobago, so this was no minor matter, and Lord Edmund-Davies caustically scorned the argument put forward by the majority:

> It has to be said with all respect that the majority opinion of their Lordships amounts, in effect, to side-stepping the decision in *Lynch* and, even were that constitutionally appropriate, to do it without advancing cogent grounds. (*Ibid*, p 772)

The commitment here is still to doing individual justice. Justice involves a commitment to the rational interpretation of the precedent case. It involves treating like cases alike, which in turn entails a commitment to a proper logical universalisation of decisions. Doing justice involves treating like cases alike. It locates the individual decision within an over-arching set of rules so that the particular case is decided by how it falls within the generally applicable categories. If *Lynch* goes one way, then *Abbott* must be treated under the same rule unless his case can be properly distinguished.

However, matters are not always so clearcut from a judicial point of view. Let me take as a third illustration one further case on which Lord Edmund-Davies sat, this time in the Court of Appeal. This was a necessity case called *London Borough of Southwark v Williams* [1971] 2 All ER 175. A homeless family with a five year old child and a five month old baby had illegally entered a derelict property, and the borough wanted to evict them. The question before the court was whether the couple could use necessity as a defence to trespass. The court held that they could not for the defence was unavailable in English law. considering the situation, Lord Edmund-Davies lamented the plight of the families but could see nothing the law could do to help. He spoke of the 'deep depression' that anyone of 'even ordinary sympathy' (*ibid*, p 80) would feel for the family's plight. The defence of necessity was not, however, available to them. Lord Denning in the leading judgment explained why not:

> If homelessness were once admitted as a defence to trespass, no-one's house could be safe. Necessity would open a door which no man could shut ... The plea would be an excuse for all sorts of wrongdoing. So the courts must for the sake of law and order take a stand. They must refuse to admit the plea of necessity to the hungry and the homeless; and trust that their distress will be relieved by the charitable and the good. (*Ibid*, p 179)

This case is one of the few in which the issue of individual justice is directly counterposed to a deeper sense of social justice and injustice. Doing individual legal justice to Williams would have involved granting him the defence of necessity, but to do so would have meant looking four square at the plight of the homeless, and therefore at the social dispensation of public and private property at the time. It would have meant aligning the criminal law's view of individual justice with the needs of the homeless family. The law, however, could not, or would not, go there. This was not because individual justice did not require it, for there was a clear matter of necessity in play on which the decision might have rested. The problem was that giving Williams a defence would mean recognising not just an individual's need but a systematic social problem with consequences far beyond the individual case. Individual justice through the law was therefore partitioned off from the broader questions of social justice, despite the recognition that such partitioning occasioned 'deep depression' for one required to do it.[10]

Note also that this decision points up the problem of legal individualism. Who is 'the individual' that legal justice recognises? This is not a straightforward question. We can think of the individual in abstract terms as the intending, acting, voluntary subject, or as the socially and morally located person, in this case the homeless parent acting under necessity. The law declines to accept the second, more rounded, image of the person in his or her context, opting for an abstract individualism. This serves to draw a line between what can be done within the law and what must be done outwith it, by the 'charitable and the good', if it is to be done at all.

The point to take from this concerns the limits of legal universalisation. Law's categories of responsibility are cast in a set of rules which insist on doing individual justice, but the individual to whom justice is to be done is not to be understood as the homeless person. He can be the individual under personal threat (duress), but not the individual under environmental or social threat (necessity). The law's universal categories accept certain aspects of the individual's situation, but draw a line against the social particularity of homelessness. Justice, such as it is in *London Borough of Southwark v Williams*, is maintained by refusing to particularise, and remaining at the level of abstract universality.

The philosophical idea of criminal justice: Kant and Hegel

It is a long way from the Court of Appeal sitting in 1971 to the Enlightenment theories of punishment of Kant and Hegel (Norrie, 1991b, Chapters 3 and 4). However, as I will now suggest, there are similar dilemmas in their philosophies concerning the universal and the particular, and the link between individual criminal and social justice. The idea of individual justice under general law is not a new one, and nor is the problem as to what individual justice means. The model of modern law is one derived from liberal Enlightenment thinking, so how did the liberal Enlightenment itself confront the problems of the universal and the particular, and of individual and social justice? .

The key point to note is that Kant and Hegel both see criminal justice as a matter of universalising the moral law in the name of the freedom of the individual subject. In Kant, reason and the moral law universalise individual responsibility so that it transcends the particularities of actual life. Just punishment is a result of this universalisation:

---

10 At this point, an argument can be advanced concerning the different institutional roles of different parts of the state, in particular, the courts and the welfare agencies. A delimitation of the defence is possible if it can be shown that the problem of homelessness is dealt with by another state agency. For discussion of this issue, see Duff, 1998; Horder, 2000; Norrie, 2000, pp 22–30.

> When ... I enact a penal law against myself as a criminal it is the pure juridical legislative reason (*homo noumenon*) in me that submits myself to the penal law as a person capable of committing a crime ... (Kant, 1965, p 105)

Contrast this universal, rational individual with the person committing the actual crime. This is the individual located in his or her particular context who is in a strong sense different from the rational individual. He or she is:

> another person (*homo phaenomenon*) along with all the others in the civil union who submit themselves to this law. (*Ibid*)

The subject who justifies the norm and supports just punishment is thus an abstractly rational person who stands apart from the actual person. It is abstract rational thinking (*noumenality*) which grounds universal law in the form of the 'pure juridical legislative reason'. Thus criminal justice is achieved by abstractly universalising (the *noumenal*) from the particular person (the *phaenomenal*) in favour of a rational abstraction of the individual.

This 'universalised particular', however, immediately runs into philosophical trouble, and breaks down in problem cases. The image of a universally free subject cannot deal with cases such as those of the mother who kills her illegitimate child, or the soldier who kills in a duel. In these cases, social conceptions of honour and shame force the soldier and the mother to do the criminal acts. Kant acknowledges that society itself, not the individual:

> is responsible for the fact that incentives of honour among the people do not accord (subjectively) with the standards that are (objectively) appropriate. (*Ibid*, p 107)

By 'subjective', Kant means 'particular' (or, his word, 'phaenomenal'); by 'objective', he means 'universal' (or 'noumenal'). Justice, which is achieved by 'universalising the particular', is undercut by the need in a society that is, in Kant's words, 'barbaric and underdeveloped' (*ibid*) to acknowledge the particular situation of the actual criminal. We cannot hold the woman or the soldier responsible in the normal way, for we must recognise the circumstances in which they acted. The result is that, again in Kant's words, 'public legal justice as administered by the state is injustice from the point of view of the people' (*ibid*). Justice according to the universal moral law and relating to the abstract universal subject is undermined by the actual state of society and the social identities of particular persons. Society, which is 'barbaric and underdeveloped', is in short to blame for what has happened. In this way, individual right (justice according to universal law) is undermined by social wrong (injustice according to the nature of society). Logically, this happens because what began as a philosophical move to universalise away from the particular is put into reverse as the universal is 're-particularised' in the face of killing for honour.

Moving from Kant to Hegel, we see a similar dialectic at play. Crime and its rightful punishment is understood as a discovery of the universal within the particular. Punishment is 'a right established within the criminal himself' for:

> his action is the action of a rational being and this implies that it is something universal and that by doing it the criminal has laid down a law which he has explicitly recognised in his action ... (Hegel, 1952, p 170)

Kant and Hegel are very similar on this point. They both see justice as a matter of a universal principle derived from individual freedom and reason. However, just as

Kant had problems with the particular contexts of the unmarried mother and the duelling soldier, so Hegel has a problem, this time with the broader issue of poverty. Against the universalism of rational being, poverty asserts the needs of the particular. It demands 'subjective aid ... arising from the special circumstances of the particular case' (*ibid*, p 149). It also leads to a 'loss of the sense of right and wrong' and even to repudiation of the possibility of universal order:

> Against nature, man can claim no right, but once society is established, poverty immediately takes the form of a wrong done to one class by another. (*Ibid*, p 277)

Thus in Hegel, as with Kant, there is a crisis of universal justice resulting from particular social conditions. The universalised abstract individual is contrasted with particular individual conditions in contemporary society. In Hegel, the problem of individual right and social wrong, what, in modern terms, we call the problem of 'just deserts in an unjust society' (Hudson, 1998; Ashworth, 2000, pp 214–15; Norrie, 2001b, pp 209–12), is like an open wound. Universalising the individual away from her particular context is reversed by this pervasive social problem. We are returned from the universal to actual conditions, particularity, with a bump. From the move to vindicate individual justice (universalising the individual), we are returned to the actual individual's location in an unjust society. In Hegel's own terms, we could say that we have a new, inconclusive, dialectic in operation, one of the 'universalised particular' being returned to the 're-particularised universal'. There is no transcendence here of the kind for which Hegel is famous, rather the reverse. Hegel's account is left unresolved, a great dialectical movement subjected to stasis by an unrelenting social condition.[11]

For non-Hegelians, this dialectical formulation is an intellectual mouthful. However, I think it is a way of explaining the underlying dynamic of the criminal law. It links together not only Kant and Hegel, but also both philosophers with modern judgments on the law of necessity in the English appeal courts. There we saw how the universalistic justice of the law hit a limit when it confronted the problem of homelessness. The law was not prepared to make the concession Kant and Hegel made in terms of re-particularising away from the universal, but not without regret, with 'deep depression' for the humanitarian judge. The need to re-particularise was felt, even if it was not acted upon. I want therefore to carry this idea of a dialectic of universalising the particular and re-particularising the universal forward. Once we have looked in more detail at the development of law around ideas of orthodox subjectivism and moral contextualism, we will return to it to see how it informs this development.

---

11 What is universalised is an abstract image of a free individual, which is then opposed by the need to see individuals in the particularity of their social conditions, their needs and so on. Of course, if poverty were a truly general condition pertaining to crime, then it and its relation to need would have the greater claim to be seen as 'the universal'. This then highlights the *contingency* in the abstract universal model of the free individual which classical retributive thinking (and *mutatis mutandis* the law) is based upon. It is because of this element of contingency (falseness) in juridical univeralisation that I describe the dialectic of law as the 'universalisation *of the particular*', which then must be followed by the 're-particularisation of the universal', rather than a simple 'dialectic of the universal and the particular'.

Criminal justice: form and substance

I am now going to undertake the gear change I described at the beginning of this chapter. I am going temporarily to leave the universal and the particular and proceed to general problems of the criminal law today, beginning with the prosaic and somewhat improbable case of the reasonable glue sniffer. My argument will be that the problems associated with this character stem from the dominance of the orthodox subjectivist standpoint in this area of the law. Analysing provocation in some detail permits us to see how orthodox subjectivism works, and how its failures invoke a need for a morally substantivist response. From this platform, I will then describe more generally the conflict between orthodox subjectivism and moral substantivism as two different theoretical approaches in the law. These are the two main themes of this section. I will then return in a concluding section to the theme of the universal and the particular, linking it to the clash between formalism and substantivism in the law. In that section, I will bring together my accounts of the plight of the humanitarian judge and of Kant and Hegel with the problems of criminal law theory today. It is however now to the law's more immediate problems that I turn.

Provocation: the problem of the reasonable glue sniffer

In 1991, Alan Morhall got involved in a fight with a friend who had nagged and chided him over the fact that he was addicted to glue sniffing (*R v Morhall* [1995] 3 All ER 658). Morhall beat his friend over the head with a hammer and eventually stabbed him with a dagger. The friend died and Morhall was convicted for his murder. Morhall appealed on the ground that he had been provoked and that in considering the provocation, the jury should have been able to take into account the fact of his addiction to glue sniffing. It is Morhall's case that gives rise to the second part of this chapter's title.

The English law on provocation has both a factual and a regulative aspect. The factual aspect concerns whether the accused in fact lost his self-control such that he could be said to have been provoked by things said or done by his victim. The regulative aspect is the requirement that what was said or done should have been enough to make the reasonable person do as the accused did (s 2 of the Homicide Act 1957). Who is the reasonable person in this situation? The question can be put in terms of the old case of *R v Bedder* [1954] 2 All ER 801. If an impotent man is taunted by a woman with whom he tries to have sex so that he is provoked into killing her, is the fact that he was impotent to be taken into account in determining whether the reasonable person would have lost self control in such circumstances? Is the reasonable person to be read as the reasonable impotent person? If not, how can one make sense of his losing his self-control?

Under the then existing law, Bedder's characteristic was not taken into account. In the later leading case of *R v Camplin* [1978] 2 All ER 168, however, the House of Lords held that the reasonable person is one:

having the power of self control to be expected of an ordinary person of the sex and age of the accused, but in other respects sharing such of the accused's characteristics as they think would affect the gravity of the provocation to him. (*Ibid*, p 174)

On this basis, the fact that Bedder was impotent should be relevant as a characteristic going to the gravity of the provocation, and should be taken into account in considering the reaction of the reasonable person. Should Morhall's characteristic of addiction to glue sniffing then be taken into account in considering whether he was provoked to lose self-control? The Court of Appeal thought not, because the concept of self-addicted glue sniffing was inconsistent with the concept of a reasonable man. The House of Lords rejected this view, holding that the mere fact that a characteristic was discreditable did not make it irrelevant to the reasonable person test.

It seems then that one can depict the law as licensing the idea of the 'reasonable glue sniffer', just like the reasonable impotent man in *Bedder*. There are two problems here. The first concerns the question whether there should not be some moral cap on the characteristics that can be taken into account. In Australia, a recent case involved an obsessive person stalking a young woman who then became provoked into killing her boyfriend (*Stingel v R* (1990) 171 CLR 312). It seems that in this country, the stalker could use his characteristic obsessiveness (his erotomania) to help explain why he was provoked. Is there then no end to the horribleness of a characteristic that the law is prepared to recognise as being relevant to the test of provocation? It appears not. Although Stingel's characteristic has been discussed as one the law should not admit (*R v Smith* [2000] 4 All ER 289, pp 308–09, 311, *per* Lord Hoffmann), it is not clear that there is a real reason for disallowing it.

The second problem concerns the very idea of the 'reasonable glue sniffer'. According to Lord Goff in *R v Morhall*, talking thus is to caricature the law because all that 'reasonable' means is 'ordinary'. We should therefore speak of the standard of self control expected of the 'ordinary' rather than 'reasonable' glue sniffer (*R v Morhall* [1995] 3 All ER 658, p 665). However, to talk of the standard of self control to be expected of an 'ordinary' glue sniffer is no more helpful than to talk of a 'reasonable' glue sniffer. How is the jury to gauge how an ordinary person with such a characteristic would react? An 'ordinary' person with an obsessive character or addiction acts like an obsessive or addicted person acts. If the law ceases to say 'reasonable', we get out of the difficulties of talking about such odd creatures as the 'reasonable obsessive', but the underlying problem still exists. Opening law up to the characteristics of the accused subjectivises the regulative test beyond recognition. From being a form of control upon the use of the defence, it is in danger of becoming an open invitation to it.

This second problem is even more developed than *R v Morhall* suggests. *R v Camplin* [1978] 2 All ER 168, p 174 talks about the relevance of sex and age together with such other 'characteristics as they think would affect the gravity of the provocation to [the defendant]'. This suggests a limit on admissible characteristics (other than sex and age) to those directly linked to the provocation. It suggests that one can distinguish characteristics which bear on the gravity of the provocation from those bearing on the person's general level of self-control (Ashworth, 1976, p 300), admitting only the former as relevant to whether the reasonable person is provoked. It suggests that we can draw a line between matters that are 'provocative' and persons who are 'provocable' (Smith, 1995). However, this is not necessarily the case. For someone like the impotent man in *R v Bedder*, the taunt concerning his impotence is more provocative, and therefore he is more provocable, because of his impotence. We cannot appreciate his 'provocability' without knowing of the gravity, the particular 'provocativeness', of the taunt to him. If the law is to do justice to his particular situation, it has to recognise that he is more provocable than the average person precisely because of the characteristic at which the provocation is aimed – precisely because it is more provocative to him. Once this is conceded, however, there is no logical reason why any characteristic which would make him more provocable should not equally be taken into account. In short, if provocativeness depends upon provocability, then provocability is the issue.[12] However, if the subjective provocability of the accused is ultimately what is at stake, then it becomes harder to deny the relevance of any characteristic, whether it is the direct subject of provocation or not. This conclusion was accepted by Lord Diplock in *R v Camplin*, who agreed that:

> in strict logic there is a transition between … a characteristic that may be taken into account in assessing the gravity of the provocation … and … a characteristic to be taken into account in determining … the degree of self-control to be expected of the ordinary person … ([1978] 2 All ER 168, p 174)

However, he held that the distinction was 'of too great nicety' to be upheld. The result of this 'transition' has been an opening of the gates to a wide variety of characteristics. In various English cases, we have encountered alongside the reasonable (or ordinary) glue sniffer figures like the reasonable obsessive (*R v Dryden* [1995] 4 All ER 987), the reasonable depressive (*R v Smith* [2000] 4 All ER 289), and even the reasonable immature and attention seeking individual (*R v Humphreys* [1995] 4 All ER 1008).

Thus, the law's plight on the defence of provocation is, first, that there is no moral cap on the characteristics which can lead to provocation, and, secondly, that there is no control on the characteristics which can be said to increase general provocability. 'Reasonableness' or 'ordinariness' hardly check the standard of conduct to be expected of the obsessive, the depressive or the immature and attention seeking. Of course, the law is not happy with this outcome and recent cases in the Privy Council and the House of Lords have sought to restrict the defence. *Luc v R* [1996] 2 All ER 1033 sought to limit characteristics by requiring a

---

12 The contrary argument, that 'provocativeness' and 'provocability' can be satisfactorily distinguished, lies behind the judgments in cases such as *R v Morhall* [1995] 3 All ER 658 and *Luc v R* [1996] 2 All ER 1033. It is supported by Ashworth (1976, p 300); for a fuller argument in favour of the position taken here, see Norrie, 2001a, pp 321–22. For other recent commentary on the English law, see Gardner and Macklem, 2001a, 2001b.

direct link between the provocation offered and the accused's characteristics, but it failed to address the intrinsic logical link between the provocativeness of the victim's deeds and the resultant rising provocability of the defendant such that provocability is the underlying issue. It failed to address Lord Diplock's point that the distinction between provocativeness and provocability is of 'too great nicety'. It was properly not followed in the latest House of Lords case of *Smith*, which maintains *Camplin's* open door to subjective characteristics. *Smith* is therefore both correct in its elucidation of the law and inadequate in its ability to provide any control on the characteristics that are to be taken into account in determining the result of a provocation plea.[13] All that is of real interest in *Smith* is whether the individual was in psychological control; all the moral issues about which characteristics should be taken into account and how their admission should be regulated are lost.[14]

What is the underlying problem in the law of provocation? If we dig down a level, we find that the issue can be understood in terms of matters of 'justification' and 'excuse' (Ashworth, 1976; Horder, 1992). The law has moved from a position where provocation was regarded as a question of the right response, a (partial) justification for killing, to one in which it is regarded as a matter of wrongdoing, but excused. Under the pre-modern law, provocation existed as vindicated anger and rightful retaliation. An insult had been made and honour was at stake. The accused acted in a state of righteous, and even controlled, anger, with no need for him to lose his self-control. Killing was in short a rightful and justified reaction. The modern law is quite different. In the 19th century, it moved away from the idea of controlled righteous anger to a vision of provocation as resulting from wrongful but partially forgivable loss of self-control in the face of the provoking conduct. Whereas rage and loss of self-control had previously not been of the essence of the law, the Victorians moved it to the centre of the picture. The issue now became not that the accused had done something rightful, but rather that he had done something wrong for which he could be partly excused. Provocation, reducing murder to manslaughter, was seen as a 'concession to human frailty' rather than a reflection of morally justified anger.

What does this tell us? The core of the law has shifted from the question of how morally provocative the provocation was to how psychologically provocable the

---

13 The Australian approach is to establish two questions where the English approach has one. Where there is a loss of self-control, the first question is whether the provocation was capable of causing an ordinary person to lose self-control, and the ordinary person is attributed any relevant subjective characteristic of the accused. The second question is: where the ordinary person would have lost self-control, was the provocation such as could cause the ordinary person to act as the accused did? Here, the ordinary person involves an objective test, admitting only the characteristic of age (Bronitt and McSherry, 2001, pp 265–73). The two questions seem to be focused on much the same issue; perhaps this is why different decisions to reflect or reject individual circumstances are inconsistent, serving only to 'function as a distorting echo of contemporary fears and concerns' (Wells, 2000, p 99).

14 In Canada and the US, this problem has led to calls to address openly the normative content of the ordinary person test: what are the *morally acceptable* 'ordinary standards' of reaction to particular forms of provocation? (Boyle, 2000 (Canada); Nourse, 1997 (US)). My argument is that the modern law has evolved precisely to avoid addressing openly normative questions, which leaves a dilemma. On one hand, there is a problem in moving to a terrain of openly contestable moral judgments; on the other, it is the case that the law must reach *sotto voce* for just such moral judgments under the cover of supposedly neutral formal categories (Norrie, 2001a, pp 322–30, 335–44).

accused was, and ought to be, in the circumstances of the provocation. In moving from justification to excuse, provocation has moved from a matter of moral judgment to a question of psychological fact. The question of what level of self-control is reasonable is tacked onto the factual question, while questions of moral right and wrong, or a broader moral, contextual judgment of what we should expect from the accused are, in formal terms at least, cut out of the reckoning.[15] The law is accordingly unable to impose any moral cap on the defence, for moral issues have been literally ruled out of court. The problems of provocation stem from the adoption of an orthodox subjectivist standpoint stressing factual mental states such as cognition, foresight and, in this case, loss of psychological self-control. The 'reasonable glue sniffer' is a consequence of this modern evacuation of moral substance from the law of criminal responsibility.

The problem with the law of provocation lies with its adoption of an orthodox subjectivist approach to criminal responsibility. In this regard, it represents but one instance of a general tension in the law between orthodox subjectivism and morally substantive approaches to responsibility. I will now explore this tension between form and substance more generally in the law before moving to a concluding section in which I link these problems to the idea of a dialectic of the universal and the particular.

'Orthodox subjectivism' versus 'moral contextualism'

Central to the formulation of the modern criminal law has been the 'orthodox subjectivist' approach which first emerged in the nineteenth century with the Victorian Criminal Law Commissioners, but which was given post-war significance by the work of Glanville Williams and Smith and Hogan (Williams, 1961; Smith and Hogan, 1999; see Lacey, 1998a for discussion). Their works have been extremely influential in today's criminal law. In the 'orthodox subjectivist' approach, subjective *mens rea* is part of a package of ideas that emphasises that the individual is in control of his or her actions. Thus, proof of intention or foresight, of voluntariness of agency and of rationality, are all signs that the person was in control when the criminal act was committed. Provocation leads to a partial excuse precisely because the accused was not in control when the crime was committed. This idea of a self in control is the 'orthodox subjectivist' agent in the form of an autonomous subject, responsible for her fate.

Since around 1980, this approach has been subjected to a certain kind of criticism. First, it was noted that, despite incessant and sometimes quite polemical argument from leading academics, the law stubbornly refused to be completely persuaded by the orthodox subjectivist line (Lacey, 1985). For all that judges seemed generally interested in 'subjectivist principle', so-called 'policy arguments' kept intruding in

---

15 As noted above, this is not a claim that moral issues are in fact avoided; rather, they come into play indirectly. Thus in England the process of opening up the reasonable person to particular characteristics was largely driven by the moral figure of the battered woman who kills her partner (*Thornton* [1992] 1 All ER 306; *Thornton (No 2)* [1996] 2 All ER 1023; *Ahluwalia* [1992] 4 All ER 889). In other countries, other figures animate the debate: in Australia, male panic at homosexual advance and questions of ethnicity have also been significant (Bronitt and McSherry, 2001). In the US, Nourse's account (Nourse, 1997) reflects concern about the availability of the defence to the male when a female partner leaves home.

judicial thinking. One view was that such happenings simply revealed the compromise that principle had to make in a less than perfect world; another view, however, was that subjectivist principle was *rightly* rejected in certain cases. For example, in rape, the argument was made that it was wrong to rest the defendant's liability on whether he knew his victim was not consenting to sex, or on whether he was aware that there was a risk she was not (Wells, 1982). That placed too much emphasis on safeguarding the defendant and not enough on protecting the victim in circumstances where it would both be easy to enquire about consent, and self-serving not to do so. There was an element of moral complaint against the defendant who didn't respect his partner sufficiently even to consider if she was consenting to sex.

To make this argument was, however, to enter into a discussion of the *moral context* in which agency occurred. Increasingly academics began to argue that considerations of moral context or substance were significant to determining liability alongside questions of the accused's subjective mental state. Subjective control might be a necessary, but it was not a sufficient condition. Thus, Andrew Ashworth began to argue that the principle of subjective fault had to be balanced with a general social welfare principle (Ashworth, 1999, pp 27–32), and Antony Duff argued that judging wrongdoing went beyond the question whether the accused was in subjective control of his actions (Duff, 1990). For Duff, it was the ill will manifested in a person's actions, whether he intended or foresaw a particular result, that was important (*ibid*, pp 113–14, 177). Criminal lawyers now began to resurrect ideas that up to this point had been regarded as only of historical interest. The idea of a killing being accompanied by 'indiscriminate malice', an old yet persisting Scots law notion, regarded as essentially void for vagueness in the English debate, began to re-feature in the law of murder alongside the debate whether death or serious injury had to be foreseen as a virtual certainty or a (high) probability (Goff, 1988; cf *R v Woollin* [1998] 3 WLR 382, remarks of Lord Hope). In the law of recklessness, Duff suggested a form of 'practical indifference' (callousness) which did not necessarily involve foresight, but equally did not include all those who would come within an objective reasonable person test. The judges appeared to agree, identifying a form of reckless rape where the defendant was indifferent or 'could not care less' whether his victim consented, whether or not he had foreseen the risk she did not consent (*R v Satnam and Kewal* (1983) 78 Cr App R 14).

Moral contextualism or substantivism is not just seen in cases exhibiting a moral ill will. It is also seen in cases where a defendant possessed a morally good will, yet at the same time had the necessary technical *mens rea* for a crime. Here, the judges are torn between acknowledging that the crime is constituted (*mens rea* is present) and trying to avoid that conclusion. A number of cases in this area concern the medical profession. A doctor who drugs a terminally ill patient knowing that it is virtually certain this will hasten death possesses in principle the *mens rea* for murder, yet the conclusion is morally counter-intuitive. A jury may therefore be directed, as one was recently, that only *purpose* to kill will satisfy the *mens rea* for murder, despite the fact that foresight of virtual certainty is an alternative form of intentional liability (Arlidge, 2000). In another case involving doctors, it was held that a doctor who supplied contraceptives to an underage girl did not aid and abet unlawful sexual intercourse, even if he knows that to be the consequence of supply (*Gillick v West Norfolk and Wisbech Area Health Authority* [1986] AC 112).

Per contra, this narrowing of the law of intention to exclude its indirect form (foresight of the criminal result as a virtual certainty) was recently rejected in a case involving conjoined twins (*Re A (Children)* [2000] 4 All ER 961, pp 1012, 1029). There it was held that doctors separating Mary and Jodie knowing that Mary would die would intend to kill Mary, their only refuge against a charge of murder being a defence of necessity, or perhaps self defence. However, when it came to dealing with the Human Rights Act 1998, under which everyone has the right (European Convention, Article 2) not to be intentionally deprived of life, the judges held that no doctor could be said to kill intentionally in the circumstances of *Re A (Children)* (*ibid*, pp 1050, 1068). The intention to kill under the Human Rights Act 1998 was given precisely the meaning they had rejected when considering intention under the law of murder (Norrie, 2001b, pp 56–58). In this case, one can say that the judges first reject, then accept, the existence of a contextual moral threshold concerning how intention is to be judged. They alternate their definition of intention to achieve the desired moral result, that the doctors can operate to save Jodie. The underlying problem is that the legal concept of intention in its technical, de-moralised form is out of phase with the intuitively desired moral result. In consequence, there is a need to manipulate the category to achieve the right conclusion. One is tempted to say here that the road to legal hell is, quite literally, paved with good intentions.

In a different kind of case, a defendant broadcast for the Nazis to save his family from the concentration camp (*R v Steane* [1947] 1 All ER 813). He was held not to intend to assist the enemy but only to intend to save his family, despite the fact that only by assisting the enemy could he save his family. In modern parlance, it was virtually certain that broadcasting would assist the enemy. This case predates by 30 years the intellectual challenge to orthodox subjectivism posed by the moral contextualists, but it reveals the intrinsic structural problem for the law. There is something missing in terms of moral judgment from the factual, psychological forms of cognitive responsibility the law deploys. The law misses the underlying contextual and substantive moral concerns that alone permit a sense of justice.

To summarise, we see a law that is orthodox subjectivist in its fundamental forms being challenged by the kinds of arguments that reflect an interest in the substantive moral context, where this manifests either a morally good or a morally ill will. The existence of a factual psychological state (the core orthodox subjectivist demand) is not morally sufficient to determine culpability, yet the law remains essentially orthodox subjectivist. It insists that we need to know about intention, foresight and the rest, but such knowledge is not enough to attain the proper judgment. This general problem of the inadequacy of mental states parallels the problem encountered in the previous section of the 'reasonable glue sniffer'. There, too, the factual issue whether the accused was in control was insufficient to answer the moral question within legal judgment: is the accused culpable for an offence and, if so, which one?

In all these areas, orthodox subjectivist forms have to be manipulated to meet the morally contextualised need for judgment. It is this conflict between form and substance, between orthodox subjectivism and moral contextualism, that underlies the law's problems. What remains to be seen is how this relates to the broader issue of a dialectic between the universal and the particular outlined in the first half of the chapter. To that matter, I now turn.

Living with antinomy

I now want to link the idea of a dialectic of the universal and the particular and of individual and social justice on the one hand with the dilemmas of form and substance, of 'factual' provocation and its moral regulation, and of orthodox subjectivism and moral contextualism in the criminal law, on the other.

Abstract individualism and legal universalisation

The key idea which links all this together, the judgments of Lord Edmund-Davies, the thought of Kant and Hegel, the mysterious case of the reasonable glue sniffer and the conflicts and problems around orthodox subjectivism, is the concept of the abstract individual discussed in my introductory comments. It is the abstract individual, separated from the social problems that underlie crime, that is the basis for legal universalisation, and which leads to the threat of a return to the particular. In *London Borough of Southwark v Williams*, a humane and compassionate judge confessed the 'deep depression' which accompanied denial of the necessity defence to Williams. To deny the defence was to stay with the universal, abstract legal individual and so doing to exclude the social particularity of the homeless. For Kant and Hegel, doyens of Enlightenment thinking, the metaphysical instinct is to present justice as a universal elaboration of individual freedom and reason. However, their abstract rational individual is re-particularised as the shamed mother and soldier, or more generally under conditions of poverty, which transform universal justice into the wrong done by one class to another.

What about provocation and the dilemmas around orthodox subjectivism? Here again, it is the abstract individual that is, as it were, responsible. Legal individualism is couched in terms of supposedly neutral, universal, factual and psychological mental states so that legal principles appear to be of general application. They are to assume none of the particular moral features of the actual, social individual. The provoked person under the modern law is just a person who loses control, not one with a particular moral claim as to why he lost control. That person is then regulated by a reasonable person test which sets a universal standard for measuring loss of control. However, the test will not work because it needs to know something about the particularity of the accused if it is to get any kind of handle on judgment. Just as Kant needs to know what to do with the re-particularised mother or soldier, killing out of shame, so provocation needs to re-particularise the reasonable person as the reasonable person who is impotent, addicted to glue sniffing and the like. However, once the process of re-particularisation of the universal individual is underway, it is very hard to stop it. The insistence on 'value-neutral' universalism around an abstract model of the individual from the very beginning means that the process of moral contextualisation is one that possesses no clearly articulated moral boundaries. Provocation of necessity involves moral categorisation, but this occurs in a legal environment where all the substantive moral categories have been neutralised in advance by an orthodox subjectivist standpoint.

Finally, what of the problems of orthodox subjectivism more generally? I have already said that legal individualism entails a seemingly neutral, factual, psychological set of categories. It therefore lacks the substantive or contextual moral information that can make criminal law judgments align with the moral judgments that are necessary. The 'moral contextualists' recognise this, and seek to supplement the legal categories with the additional moral information that is necessary. This is a particularising supplement to the universal mental states of intention, recklessness and the like.

Abstract universalisation and re-particularisation

In conclusion, I want to represent all the moves we have discussed in terms of the law's claim to universal justice around an abstract model of the individual, and an ensuing, necessary 'return of the particular'. In *London Borough of Southwark v Williams*, the particular is there but it is rejected, at emotional cost to the humane judge. In Kant and Hegel, it is there, and it undermines their grand theory of a universal criminal justice. In provocation, the particular is introduced to make the universal reasonable person test work, and it ends up by overrunning it. In the debate around orthodox subjectivism, the particular is the moral contextualisation that says that this intention or piece of recklessness is a good one, while this one is bad.

Why does this happen? My argument is that the problem for law is that it is founded on an abstract, and therefore false or partial, universal, in the form of the abstract legal subject, removed from the social context of actions. The problem of legal universals and the return of the particular is the product of the primal separation between legal individual and social context. This was a historically engineered separation relating to the need to extricate individual legal (and moral) responsibility from social responsibility and arguments about what was socially just. It is for this reason that the separation between individual and social justice represents the 'deep structure' of criminal law debates, even if they rarely mention it, or see it as 'external' to an 'internal' conception of law. It lurks as a ghostly trace, an absent presence, in the law.

I shall finish with my rather cumbersome and opaque dialectic, of 'the universalised particular and re-particularised universal', linking it with a well known aphorism of Oscar Wilde. It seems to me that demands for legal justice always face us with a quandary. We are urged to 'reach for the stars' of a universal justice that can transcend the partial and particular and set worldly matters to right. At the same time, we know enough of the ways of the criminal law, at both domestic and international levels, to acknowledge that its practices are already too much of this world to resolve our need for a transcendental justice. At the domestic level, we know that crime is a social problem associated with poverty, deprivation and poor life chances, and that criminal justice is in reality a prosaic and profane means of social control. At the international level we are also only too familiar with the claim that criminal justice is the justice of the powerful, 'victor's justice'. We seem, in contrast to the universalising ideal's urge to reach for the stars, to be wallowing in the gutter of some very unpleasant particularities. We seem to be caught in a dilemma between law's claims and its realities. However, it might also be said that these claims represent a genuine need and aspiration for the law. It might be suggested that they indicate a moment of real utopian possibility (Adorno, 1973, p 150). They provide a glimpse of a judgment we should like to be able to make in a world that would be better than ours and for which we could strive. In that sense, legal debate and practice leave us, like Wilde, in the gutter, but looking at the stars.

Part 3
Law, History and Ethics:
The Nature of Critique

Chapter 8

From Critical to Socio-Legal Studies: Three Dialectics in Search of a Subject

My argument, however, is that the most vigorous forms of Hegelianism in the twentieth century have been thoroughly unconscious of the fact. (Barnett, 1998, p 296)

It is important to understand that when logical contradictions are committed, they are real constituents of the *Lebenswelt*. (Bhaskar, 1993, p 58)

The gap between critical and socio-legal studies

This chapter is concerned with the relationship between broadly sociological approaches to law, with an emphasis on social and historical processes, and critical or 'cultural' approaches with an emphasis on ethical interpretation. Nicola Lacey (1996, p 143) has suggested that there is a 'seemingly unbridgeable gap' between critical legal theory and socio-legal studies, which she attributes to the narrow and pragmatic horizons of the latter. There is a question, however, as to whether the relationship is not imperilled on the other side, by the way in which critical legal theory deals with sociological issues. The question is starkly raised in Jacques Derrida's influential essay 'Force of law' (Derrida, 1990), where he describes a 'critique of law' that is 'possible and always useful'. This is 'a critique of juridical ideology, a desedimentation of the superstructures of law that both hide and reflect the economic and political interests of the dominant forms of society' (Derrida, 1990, p 941). Useful it may be, but Derrida leaves this 'sociological' critique well alone in favour of his pursuit of a 'more intrinsic structure'. This involves the 'very emergence of justice and law' in a 'performative and therefore interpretive violence' (*ibid*). This deeper critique is ethical rather than socio-historical in its form.

The distinction represents a clear and, given the importance of its author, emblematic break for critical legal studies. This is not just because Derrida says so little about the first (sociological) critique, but because the elaboration of the second ethical critique proves perfectly possible without reference to it. As a consequence the ethical critique operates not *with* the 'desedimentation of the superstructures of law' but, whatever the underlying intention, against it: the sociological critique is marginalised in 'Force of law'. It could be that this is just a matter of the content of one essay, and certainly it is not the case that all those who have been influenced by deconstruction have as a result renounced the examination of the social and historical forces which inform the law. However, it can neither be denied that deconstruction has licensed work of an abstract ethical kind, nor that Derrida's work has been extremely influential in critical legal studies (Cornell, 1992; Douzinas and Warrington, 1995).[1] I would suggest that there is a theoretical issue within the deconstructive enterprise that ought to be analysed so that we can better understand the gap between the 'social' and the 'cultural' or 'ethical' critique of law.

---

1 My discussion is of Derrida's essay 'Force of law', which I have sought to read in the light of general commentaries on Derrida's work (Norris, 1991; Lechte, 1994; Barnett, 1998). Nor is my aim to address the range of responses in law to Derrida. Compare for example the work of Cornell and Douzinas and Warrington (1995) with that of Schlag (1990, 1991 and 1997). [contd]

This chapter accordingly reflects upon the bifurcation of critical routes in critical and socio-legal studies. It examines 'Force of law' from the point of view of an interest in what deconstruction means and does and a concern as to where it leads. Why not simply discard Derrida? For reasons that will become clear, Derrida's 'foundational act of violence' seems to me problematic, yet I believe that deconstruction remains important for critical analysis. This may seem a paradoxical position because foundational violence is at the core of his critique of law. If we could anatomise the different aspects of his essay, however, we could perhaps identify just what is of importance in deconstruction as well as what is problematic. We might thereby find a way of relating it more closely to the sociological themes 'force of law' marginalises and of addressing what is gained and lost in the 'ethical turn' in critical legal studies. Perhaps we could then synthesise the critical power of deconstruction with the socio-political questions that are invoked by the 'desedimentation' of law and power. In short, my questions are these: can we relate deconstruction to the long-established commitment of the sociology of law to understand law as a site of structured social power, conflict and struggle? Can we find a theoretical way of bridging the gap between critical and socio-legal theory?

Three dialectics and the legal subject

I shall argue, controversially for some, that the key to understanding Derrida's deconstructive critique of law lies in locating it in the dialectical tradition, and in particular in Derrida's ambivalent attitude to Hegel. I will also argue that in order to unite what is important in deconstruction with issues of social structure and power, it is necessary to locate the Derrida/Hegel relationship within the further development of the dialectical tradition inaugurated by Roy Bhaskar, dialectical critical realism (Bhaskar, 1993, 1994). The paper therefore has three main sections on (in order) the dialectics of Hegel, Derrida and Bhaskar. In comparing and contrasting these three, I will have recourse to their differing views of law throughout the chapter. My aim will be to link dialectical ways of thinking about law to ways of seeing it as a site and source of socio-historical power. My aim will be to anatomise the deconstructive method in a way that shows what is important within it, and where it falls down, in furthering this project.

[contd] The profound influence of Derrida and poststructuralism generally on feminist legal studies should be noted. There is an important nexus here concerning the legal subject. Nicola Lacey has suggested that there is a 'striking affinity between the feminist argument about the contours of the legal subject and that developed within critical legal theory such as that in the criminal law sphere' (Lacey, 1998b, p 198). I also see strong connections more broadly between feminist theory and the approach developed here. What Ralph Sandland (1998) discusses in deconstructive vein as 'double movement feminism' describes an approach whose emphasis on 'being and not-being' can be understood as dialectical, and it is significant to recognise the Hegelian inheritance in the theorists Drucilla Cornell (1992) and Judith Butler (1987) he discusses. Where there is a difference relates to the terms in which a Derrida-influenced philosophical programme deals with the problems it identifies. Thus, as Sandland points out, recent divergent work in double movement feminism by theorists like Cornell (1995) and Luce Irigaray (1993) seems 'simply, as a pair, to repeat the liberalism/determinism (or radicalism) opposition ... of much "modernist" feminism' so that 'we seem to be back where we started' (Sandland, 1998, p 330). The resulting antinomy in feminist legal theory between equality and difference shadows Derrida's own antinomial approach to law, as outlined below. Sandland suggests that 'this is precisely where double movement feminism would expect us to be' (ibid) but he still feels the need to identify a 'third way'. This seeks to achieve resolution of the problems he has identified either 'in practice', which is never a solution, or in 'pointing, again, to the beyond' (ibid, pp 334–35), Derrida's own ineffable conclusion, discussed below.

Shortly, we shall come to the three main sections of the chapter. Before we do, I identify in the next section some common ground for relating Hegel, Derrida and Bhaskar to each other, and for understanding law within the dialectical tradition. The common ground is provided by the critique of 'identity thinking'. As will be explained, this is the (contested) idea that objects have a fixed and stable identity, which forms the basis for logical-analytical modes of thought. Law in particular requires to be able to organise itself around such stable ways of thinking, and legal subjectivity constitutes one source of such fixity. Identity thinking will operate as the key focus as we move through the three dialectics of Hegel, Derrida and Bhaskar.

Some common ground: identity thinking

At the core of modern Western law is a nexus between (ontological) questions concerning being – about the nature of subjectivity and responsibility – and (epistemological) questions concerning the nature of legal thought. In the latter, a logical-analytical mode of reasoning possesses a virtually unassailable position. This analytical paradigm supposedly systematises law, but oddly, it keeps breaking down (see, eg, Norrie, 1993a, 2001b). Why does this happen? One answer is that it is destabilised – literally – by its subject matter: its conception of the responsible legal subject. It is conflicts within that conception that undermine the analytical paradigm.

The need for a stable, fixed legal subject reflects a broad problem in western philosophy and society that Theodor Adorno, writing in the dialectical tradition, calls 'identity thinking' (1973, 1993; cf Jarvis, 1998, Chapters 6 and 7).[2] Such thinking is central to modern analytical philosophy. Bertrand Russell, for example, wrote that there are a 'certain number of self-evident logical principles' which 'must be granted before any argument or proof becomes possible' (Russell, 1973, p 40). They include:

(1) *The law of identity*: 'Whatever is, is.'

(2) *The law of contradiction*: 'Nothing can be and not be.'

(3) *The law of excluded middle*: 'Everything must either be or not be' (*ibid*, p 40).

If one considers these 'self-evident' laws, there is a clear connection between the epistemic principles of logic contained in (2) and (3) and the ontic principle of identity contained in (1). Logic, a characteristic of thought, depends on the possibility of a fixed identity or point of origin, a characteristic of being, such that 'whatever is, is' (law 1). Similarly, analytical logic requires that 'whatever is not cannot at the same time be' (law 2) and that 'everything must either be or not be' (law 3). Logic is tied to a certain view of the way things are, and this gives it its characteristics. An entity must in essence be, as John Lechte puts it, 'simple (ie, free of contradiction), homogeneous (of the same substance, or order), present to, or the same as, itself (ie, separate and distinct from any mediation)'. It must exclude

---

2   This chapter does not discuss Adorno's critique of identity thinking. It will become clear that such a critique is shared by thinkers in the dialectical tradition as diverse as Adorno, Bhaskar, Derrida (as I argue) and Hegel. How their different dialectics handle the critique varies significantly. On Adorno, see below, Chapter 9.

certain features: 'complexity, mediation, and difference – in short, features invoking "impurity" or complexity' (Lechte, 1994, p 106). Yet such features constantly return to disrupt analytical thought.

Lechte's comments usefully flesh out the dialectical critique of identity thinking, but they are interesting for another reason. Significantly, they form part of an exposition of the work of the deconstructionist Derrida rather than a dialectician such as Adorno or Bhaskar. This brings us to our common ground. In Derrida's essay on law, a critique of identity thinking – although not in that name – is a key element. Law is a natural target for deconstruction because of the pervasiveness there of 'logico-formal paradox' (Derrida, 1990, p 959). This can be demonstrated, he writes, around ideas of 'the proper and of property', and, most significantly for my focus, 'of the subject ... of the responsible subject, of the subject of law (*droit*) and the subject of morality, of the juridical or moral person, of intentionality ... and of all that follows from these' (1990, p 931). Such ideas about the legal subject are the source of 'complexity, mediation and difference' in Lechte's phrase, for they generate 'logico-formal paradox' in law. I return to this passage below, for it is at the nub of my interest in Derrida. For the moment, however, it is important only to see that the perspective it embraces reveals common ground with the dialectical tradition of which Adorno and Bhaskar are a part.

As with deconstruction, dialectics views the denial of the inherent complexity of basic entities as wrong. As Bhaskar puts it, analytical reason involves exclusion, an illicit 'contra-position of the logical norms of identity and non-contradiction' and a false 'presupposition of fixed subjects' (Bhaskar, 1993, p 394). Dialectical thought by contrast is 'the art of thinking the coincidence of distinctions and connections'. The so-called law of identity at the heart of analytical reason is challenged because 'identity presupposes non-identity, and non-contradiction [implies] incompleteness and change', so that 'identity is always an abstraction from a process or set of processes of formation' (Bhaskar, 1993, p 190). For Bhaskar, questions of non-identity, incompleteness and change are encapsulated in his concept of 'entity relationism', a concept which offers a direct challenge to identity thinking and which shares important common ground with deconstruction.

To recapitulate, these different but overlapping critiques of identity thinking lie at the heart of this chapter. The critique of identity thinking brings together the deconstructive and dialectical approaches, and is also central to the critique of law. My aim is to develop a dialectical critique of identity thinking as it relates to the concept of the legal subject. That is the source of my interest in Derrida, but I want through that interest to consider the nature of the gap between critical and socio-legal studies identified by Lacey. Linking these two concerns, I wish to consider the structure of modern classical dialectics and, in so doing, to relate deconstruction to it. Thus, the paper's 'three dialectics in search of a subject' are, in progressive order, those of Hegel, Derrida and Bhaskar. The subject in question is that of the law, its object, the nature of identity thinking in law. I turn now to our three dialectics and their treatment of identity thinking.

Beyond identity thinking? Hegel's non-dialectical dialectic

In this section, I consider the critical and conservative elements in Hegel's original dialectical scheme in order to establish a basis for examining later approaches like those of Derrida and Bhaskar.

Three moments in dialectical thinking

To understand Derrida's views on the deconstruction of law, it is necessary to relate them to the modern dialectical tradition. It is necessary therefore briefly to start at the beginning of modern debate, with Hegel's reaction to the antinomies in modern Western philosophy identified by Kant (Kant, 1993; Hegel, 1975, pp 76–79, 116–19). Hegel's solution to Kantian antinomialism was to acknowledge contradiction and seek to resolve it within a progressively developing dialectical system of thought. Such thought was conceived as part of a real evolving natural, social and historical totality, groping its way towards a rational unity. The seeming contradictions of thought could be recognised and 'sublated' (preserved and transcended) in a process of development that was both philosophical and practical. Dialectic involved a movement between three moments: from what Hegel called the Understanding (U), to negative (critical) Dialectical reason (D), and from there to positive speculative Reason (R). The movement is represented in Figure 1:[3]

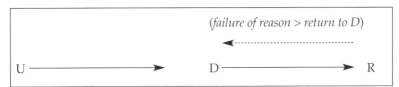

Figure 1: Hegel: the separate moments in the dialectical process

U = Understanding
D = negative Dialectical Critique
R = positive speculative Reason

The first of these moments, Understanding, is the place of analytical or identity thinking in Hegel's schema. In Understanding, Hegel says that knowledge 'begins by apprehending existing objects in their specific differences' producing a 'stereotype of each in [its] isolation'. Thought acts here 'in its analytic capacity, where its canon is identity, a simple reference of each attribute to itself' (Hegel, 1975, p 114), so that, as Michael Inwood (1992, p 81) puts it, 'concepts or categories are taken as fixed, sharply defined and distinct from each other'.

---

3 The U–D–R designation of the three moments of the Hegelian system is drawn from Bhaskar, and will be used below to discuss deconstruction and dialectical critical realism. This figure is a variant on Bhaskar (1993, p 22).

In the second stage, of negative Dialectical Critique (D), contradictions appear. Fixity, definition and distinctiveness, the 'finite characterisations' of the object, 'pass into their opposites' (Hegel, 1975, p 116). Dialectic is 'the indwelling tendency outwards by which the one-sidedness and limitation of the predicates of understanding is seen in its true light, and shown to be the negation of them' (Hegel, 1975, p 117). More simply, Inwood (1992, p 81) writes that when we reflect on the seemingly simple analytical categories of the Understanding, 'one or more contradictions emerge in them'. These are not just contradictions in our subjective concepts or ideas, but also reflect conflict and change in the objective world which ideas reflect. Of this objective world, of which thought is a part, Hegel writes that:

> We are aware that everything finite, instead of being stable and ultimate, is rather changeable and transient; and this is exactly what we mean by that Dialectic of the finite, by which the finite, as implicitly other than what it is, is forced beyond its own immediate or natural being to turn suddenly into its opposite. (Hegel, 1975, p 118)

Dialectic involves the 'grasping of opposites in their unity or of the positive in the negative'. Recalling Russell's 'self-evident' laws of logic, Hegel's view is that formal contradictions, expressed in split and fragmentation, antinomy and aporia, are to be expected within analytical thought. The mutual exclusion of opposites – the analytical watchword of the Understanding – must give way to the dialectical principle of the identity of exclusive opposites, as Bhaskar (1993, p 20) puts it. Formal-logical or analytical reasoning is accordingly a necessary but limited knowledge form sufficient for the Understanding (knowledge at the level of common sense or empirical science), but it needs to be subjected to a negative moment of dialectical critique. This is the first movement of the Dialectic (the identification of split, contradiction and antinomy), before a further moment of sublation of the contradiction through the work of dialectical reason occurs.

From the stage of negative Dialectical Critique (D), we thus move to the third moment of positive speculative Reason (R), which 'apprehends the unity of terms (propositions) in their opposition' (Hegel, 1975, p 119). This involves, to quote Inwood again, 'a new, higher category, which embraces the earlier categories and resolves the contradiction involved in them'. Dialectical Critique identifies the ways in which analytical categories, when pressed, reveal how they presuppose their opposites, 'radically develop[ing] the flaws that they contain and mak[ing] them "pass over" ... into another concept or category' (Inwood, 1992, p 82). Speculative reason then repairs the contradiction by revealing how a new richer, more complete, unity can be forged out of seeming conflict.

How, then, does this theoretical structure operate in relation to a phenomenon like law? In considering this question, we will identify a problem in Hegel's dialectical method.

Hegel's philosophy of law: a genuinely dialectical account?

The movement from the position of the Understanding to a moment of negative Dialectical critique, and then to a further moment of positive speculative Reason is seen in Hegel's account of law. As regards legal Understanding, he writes that logical deduction 'is certainly an essential characteristic of the study of positive law', but he adds that such analytical reasoning 'has nothing whatever to do with the satisfaction of the demands of reason or with philosophical science' (Hegel, 1952, p 20). Legal categories, far from having the fixity that analytical reasoning presupposes, 'pass over into their opposites as a result of their finitude and their dialectical character', a process that is observed by negative dialectical critique (*ibid*, p 32). However, the *Philosophy of Right* restores rationality to law through the positive work of speculative reason. Right and ethics, 'the actual world of justice and ethical life', are comprehended in thought and thereby 'invested with a rational form, ie, with universality and determinacy' (*ibid*, p 7). That form depicts 'the rich inward articulation of ethical life' and 'the architectonic of that life's rationality' (*ibid*, p 6).

The negative and positive aspects of dialectical reason thus lie at the heart of Hegel's account of law. Yet there is a possible tension between Hegel's negative dialectical critique of concepts and his subsequent employment of a positive speculative method. His insistence that philosophy is the 'apprehension of the present and the actual, not the erection of a beyond' does not necessarily sit comfortably with his insistence that 'philosophy is the exploration of the rational'. The former statement is compatible with his negative dialectical method (D), the latter expresses the positive speculative method (R). The two only combine, however, if we are persuaded by the claim of positive speculative thought genuinely to have synthesised thought and reality: that indeed 'What is rational is actual and what is actual is rational' (*ibid*, p 10). Viewing the world and its categories before us, the negative dialectical critique may in fact pull us away from the positive speculative conclusion. It may lead us to the view that reason and the modern world in fact stand against, rather than complete, each other.

In my study of Hegel's philosophy of punishment (Norrie, 1991b, Chapter 4), I argued that this was indeed the case. Reason was used to reconcile social contradictions in the modern institution of punishment, but it only did so by excluding such contradictions from the philosophical understanding of the institution. As a result, issues of social conflict, which threatened to tear apart ideas of responsible subjectivity, of the just measure of punishment, and of the impartiality of the criminal justice system, can be identified lurking unreconciled at the margins of his philosophy (Norrie, 1991b, pp 77–85; also see above, pp 119–20). They occupy such a position not because they are marginal issues, but because the speculative philosophical method makes them so. Thus, Hegel managed to unite theory (reason) and practice (actuality) by being highly selective in the actualities that he permitted his theory to reflect. He only united them on theory's terms, shutting out those aspects that did not fit. This is a particular way of making a general point about Hegel. For all his insistence on the philosophical comprehension of the actual world, an ontologically realist demand, his practice was governed by an idealist philosophy in which thought was always in the driving seat.

The price of Hegel's failure to synthesise theory and practice is a theory which seeks to deny or ignore the conflicts it is supposed to rationalise. The effect is to return the analysis to the contradictions with which it started, and so doing to reinstate them. Since they have not been resolved, they become part of the accepted ontological furniture of the world. This leads, as Bhaskar (1993, p 27) puts it, to the 're-appearance of a Kant-like rift' in Hegel's representation of reality. In effectively establishing reason as the arbiter of reality, Hegel gives it a fixity and certitude it does not deserve and is untrue to dialectical method. Reason is used to 'fix' reality, and is in the process itself given a certain fixity, undermining its dialectical character. Down this path, Hegel's idealism is guilty of the same crimes of which it accuses the Understanding. It sees things in a one-sided, detotalised way, so that Hegel's idealist dialectic itself needs to be exposed to dialectical critique.

One can see this in Hegel's discussion of legal reasoning. In the *Philosophy of Right*, Hegel writes, as we have seen, that logical deduction is an 'essential characteristic of the study of positive law'. However, this 'deductive method of the Understanding ... has nothing to do with ... reason or with philosophical science' (Hegel, 1952, p 20). The latter starts from the *failure* of such concepts, and their inherent tendency to 'pass over into their opposites as a result of their finitude and their dialectical character' (Hegel, 1952, p 32). For Hegel, however, this bold statement of the inadequacy of the Understanding for grasping law ultimately seems hardly to matter for legal practitioners can, it transpires, carry on pretty much as before. Thus, in his Logic, Hegel presents the Understanding of law as 'always an element in thorough training' which consists in 'grasp[ing] the objects in their fixed character'. Such training then flows into legal practice: 'the judge must stick to the law, and give his verdict in accordance with it, undeterred by one motive or another, allowing no excuses, and looking neither left or right.' He must 'fix his eye on the definite point in question' (Hegel, 1952, p 114). But if the negative dialectical critique of law is valid, how can the practical judge find things so easy? When pressed *dialectically*, would not a verdict 'in accordance with law' pass over into its opposite? How *could* one 'stick to the point in question' if it turns out that the point in question contains its own dialectical negation? Where categories necessarily break apart in theory and in practice, it is impossible to maintain what in effect is a theory-practice split between the philosophy of law and the theory of legal practice. However, this is what Hegel calls for: a 'Kant-like rift' appears in his argument between theory and practice.

A world safe for the Understanding

It is as if the speculative method of Reason (R) can restore the disruption caused by the negative Dialectical critique (D) and reinstate the categories of the Understanding (U). For Hegel, as Bhaskar puts it, 'Positivity and self(-identity), the very characteristics of the understanding, are always restored at the end of reason' (Bhaskar, 1993, p 27), so that one might say that Hegelian dialectic ends up making the world safe for the Understanding, against the radical implications of its own negative critical moment. Because of this (ultimately) undialectical character of Hegelian dialectic, it makes a bad starting-point for doing what Hegel said it should: apprehend the present and the actual, comprehend what is. Always there is the rider that such apprehension is the exploration of the rational, because comprehension of what is 'is reason' (Hegel, 1952, pp 10–11). This rationalisation of the real turns a critical analysis into a buttress for the Understanding, while failing to resolve, and thereby surreptitiously maintaining, the underlying contradictions contained within its categories. There is a failed engagement between reason and reality which undermines the U–D–R progression. Marked in Figure 1 above as the broken arrowed line back from R to D, it effectively delivers Hegel back to the contradictions at D that R was supposed to transcend. The failure of R leads to a fall back to an uncritical antinomialism at D.

If we now turn from Hegel to Derrida and deconstruction, we shall see how this U–D–R movement, with a fallback from R to D, is shadowed by Derrida, leading to a different but parallel impasse.

Beyond identity thinking I: deconstruction as dialectic

The previous section has set out Hegel's critique of identity thinking, explored its significance to law, and exposed the problematic character of its rational resolution (at R in Figure 1) of the conflicts (at D) that Hegel's negative dialectical critique had established. In this section, I examine Derrida's deconstruction of law in the light of the foregoing, in order to consider its limits as a critical form of knowledge. To do so, I will invert the order of the previous section. I will begin by outlining the contribution of deconstruction to the critique of law, and then consider some problems with it. I will then argue that the limits of deconstruction stem from its character as a form of dialectics within the Hegelian tradition. As dialectical theory, deconstruction differs significantly from that of Hegel, but also has much in common with it. It shares a moment of negative Dialectical critique (D), which is seen in deconstruction's persistent search for 'logico-formal paradox' (Derrida, 1990, p 959). It also possesses an inverted counterpart to Hegel's rationalising strategy (R) in the shape of deconstruction's 'mad', 'mystical' moment. In what follows, I have termed this moment, which is the foundational act of violence Derrida finds before the law and reason, 'unReason' (uR). This characterisation reflects both the idea that we are dealing with a 'madness' before reason, and also indicates the parallel place of this moment in Derrida's thought to that of speculative reason in Hegel's. Derrida's parallel movement is described in Figure 2:

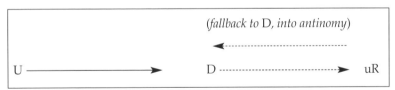

Figure 2: Derrida: the separate moments in the deconstructive process

U = Understanding
D = negative (Dialectical/Deconstructive) Critique (of 'logico-formal paradox')
uR = unReason: deconstruction as ethical 'madness' before reason

Note that, as with Hegel, there is a fallback into antinomy, a rediscovery of 'Kant-like rifts' in Derrida. These he calls aporias, as we will see below. I begin, however, by outlining how deconstruction produces what I argue is Derrida's negative dialectical/deconstructive critique of law (D). While supporting this critique, I recall the two approaches to law which Derrida identifies in 'Force of law', the socio-political and the ethical, and the marginalisation of the socio-political that ensues. How and why does this marginalisation occur? I argue that it is enabled by Derrida's use of the inverted counterpart to Hegelian reason (uR) just described. I employ this analysis to compare and contrast Hegel and Derrida, and to show how Derrida's location within the Hegelian tradition leads him to reinstate antinomy uncritically as the core of his account of law, while the social and the historical is excluded from consideration.

Deconstruction as negative dialectical critique of law

In Derrida's essay on law, he writes that deconstruction 'is generally practised in two ways or styles, although it most often grafts one on to the other'. One way takes the 'apparently ahistorical allure of logico-formal paradoxes' while the other, 'more historical or more anamnesic [recollective], seems to proceed through readings of texts, meticulous interpretations and genealogies' (Derrida, 1990, p 959). Historical genealogy and the demonstration of *logico-formal paradox* are eminently suited, Derrida suggests (*ibid*, p 931), to legal analysis because law's emphasis on formal logic is also a statement of its own ahistory, and both invite deconstruction. Deconstruction starts by 'destabilising or complicating the opposition between ... law, convention, the institution ... and nature ... with all the oppositions that they condition' (*ibid*, p 929). A central concept in Derrida's thought is that of *différance*, a term which signifies the constant slippage of meaning from sign to sign. Meaning is never complete, and the consequent identification of 'differences' within concepts is always 'deferred' within analytical thought (cf Norris, 1991, p 32). Linked to *différance* is the idea of *supplementarity*, the idea of an additional element introduced to buttress an argument which proceeds to undermine its main premises. There is always surplus meaning, a supplement that is both necessary to the concept and too much, going beyond it (cf Fitzpatrick, 1991b, p 2).

Deconstruction also brings out, as we saw in our discussion of identity thinking, the paradoxes of values contained in the ideas of the proper and property, the subject, the responsible subject, the subject of law and morality, the juridical and moral person, and mental states such as intentionality (Derrida, 1990, p 931). Derrida does not develop these ideas but they are clearly suggestive for legal analysis. I have argued indeed in previous chapters that problems associated with the opposition between legal and moral responsibility do engender conflicts and contradictions around the idea of the responsible legal subject. Legal categories, expressed in 'technical' juridical terms, exclude and repress broader moral and political meanings through a conception of legal subjectivity. Although deconstruction has not been my approach, I find common ground with Derrida. These problems can be related to the undecidability of categories, their invocation of supplementarity and *différance*. Such problems are indeed, as Derrida says, problems of the legal subject qua responsible subject, and problems of the juridical individual.

To relate this to what has been said already, the common ground around these concepts exists by virtue of the critique of identity thinking with which we started, and which we pursued through Hegel. It is the nature of the legal subject and its 'identity' that generates the dialectical/deconstructive conflicts in legal thought. Thus Derrida's work can be seen to involve a negative Dialectical critique (D in both Figures 1 and 2 above) of the completeness of legal subjectivity and any logic based upon it. The point is that there is a real rapprochement between dialectical and deconstructive approaches around this moment of negative dialectical critique in the probing of 'logico-formal paradox', but that this is not enough. We must also bear in mind what I said in Chapter 1 about the gap between the ethical and the sociological in Derrida's thought. Consequently, we need to consider more fully the nature of deconstruction and its nature as dialectical theory. If deconstruction relates Derrida to the negative critical side of Hegel, and thence to the possibility of a critique of legal categories, I shall now argue that there is another side to his thought which links him – albeit in an inverted way – to Hegel's ethical rationalism. Here we need to compare Derrida as the purveyor of 'mad', 'mystical' unReason (uR) with Hegel as the philosopher of positive speculative Reason (R). I begin by recalling the two critiques of law described in the introductory section.

Two critiques of law and deconstruction

We saw in the introduction to this chapter that Derrida identifies two critiques of law, but only pursues one. The first, which he sees as useful but puts aside, is 'a critique of juridical ideology, a desedimentation of the superstructures of law that both hide and reflect the economic and political interests of the dominant forms of society' (Derrida, 1990, p 941). Such a critique is 'possible and always useful', but Derrida is more interested in a second critique of a 'more intrinsic structure', which involves the 'very emergence of justice and law' and which consists in a *'coup de force ... a performative and therefore interpretive violence'*. Such violence is a foundational act and as such is 'neither just nor unjust', neither 'legal nor illegal', a foundation that is 'mystical' (Derrida, 1990, pp 941–43). This fundamental *coup de force* gives rise to the main problematic of 'force of law'. This problematic is founded on oppositions between legal justice as regular and calculable, and a deeper sense of justice that goes beyond law, that is singular and incalculable, and which ultimately evades description.

This second critique entails a seemingly deeper sense of deconstruction than that which we have already discussed. It goes beyond exploring logical paradox or historical genealogy into a more complex ethical project that links deconstruction to a quest for the meaning of justice. At this deeper level, deconstruction of a present legal justice resorts to an 'infinite "idea of justice"', infinite because it is irreducible, ... owed to the other ... before any contract ... without calculation and without rules, without reason and ... rationality'. This infinite justice involves a 'madness' and 'perhaps another sort of mystique', and deconstruction 'is mad about this kind of justice' which 'isn't law, [and] is the very movement of deconstruction at work in law and the history of law' (Derrida, 1990, p 965). Justice in this sense is elusive and ineffable. On the one hand it appears to be an absolute and infinite moment that is uncapturable in language or form, on the other it seems to be the space of movement between the finite and the infinite, a restless and unsettled space of critique. Whichever reading is correct,[4] it is important to see that in Derrida's

---

4 There is an ambiguity between justice and deconstruction as dynamic, restless and processual, that exists in an intermediate place, an 'interval' and a more static and absolute – if ineffable – conception of justice, caught in the idea of justice as undeconstructible: 'Justice in itself, if such a thing exists, outside or beyond law, is not deconstructible. Deconstruction ... takes place in the interval that separates the undeconstructability of justice from the deconstructibility of *droit* [law] ...' (Derrida, 1990, p 945).

account, deconstruction stands for *both* a moment of critique, of history and of formal logical paradox, and for a broader ethical critique that invokes a move beyond history and paradox, to a moment of foundational 'violence'. This second critique leads Derrida to marginalise the social and historical dimension in his account of law and this seems to me fundamentally problematic for the limit it imposes upon a critical project. It appears to present a metaphysical barrier to a social and political critique of law. The reason it does so, I will now argue, is that in it, Derrida reveals the problematic side of his allegiance to the Hegelian tradition.

Derrida as Hegelian

At first sight, this linking of Derrida and Hegel may seem unlikely. For Christopher Norris, Derrida's deconstructive critique exposes Hegel 'to a dislocating movement beyond all grasp of dialectic', while dialectic is seen as but 'one chapter in the Western tradition of logo-centric discourse pushed up against its limits' (Norris, 1991, pp 76, 87). Hegelian dialectic is then surely a part of the problem rather than the solution for deconstruction. Recent work, however, depicts a more ambiguous view of Hegel's relationship to Derrida. Stuart Barnett sees Hegel as embodying 'both the culmination of the Western philosophical tradition and the beginning of its dissolution'. Compared with deconstruction, Hegel represents not only the 'most complete manifestation of that which deconstruction seeks to undo' but *also* an opening up of 'the possibility of the task of thinking difference' (Barnett, 1998, pp 26–27). The ambiguity is in Derrida himself, who can write both that a 'definition of *différance* ... would be precisely the limit, the interruption, the destruction of the Hegelian *relève wherever* it operates' (Derrida, cited in Barnett, 1998, p 26) and that Hegel is himself 'the thinker of irreducible *différance*' (Derrida, 1977, p 26).[5] Why does Hegel occupy so ambiguous a place in Derrida's thought?

The answer lies in recalling the distinction between the two dialectical movements in Hegel: of negative Dialectical critique (D) and positive speculative Reason (R) (see Figure 1 above). The first is the intellectual labour involved in finding 'that everything finite, instead of being stable and ultimate, is rather changeable and transient' so that 'the finite, as implicitly other than what it is, is forced beyond its own immediate or natural being to turn suddenly into its opposite' (Hegel, 1975, p 118). The second is the work of resolution (at R) of the conflicts identified at D by the unifying power of speculative reason, the recognition that 'What is rational is actual and what is actual is rational' (Hegel, 1952, p 10).

Compare this with Derrida. We saw how deconstruction initially reflects Hegel's idea of pushing concepts to their limits, of displaying within them their paradoxical and contradictory character. In terms of the U–D–R movement, deconstruction in this sense is a (D) moment of dialectical negation. What of the latter, further, mode of deconstructive critique – as the movement between the finite and the infinite, or as the moment of a mystical infinitude (madness)? Here lies a significant difference between Hegel and Derrida, though ultimately it is insufficient to take Derrida beyond Hegel. Derrida refuses the second dialectical move of reconciliative Reason (R), declining to repair the dialectical contradiction that deconstruction has brought

---

5 For discussions of Hegel, see Derrida (1977, 1978 and 1986). This ambiguity gives rise to a parallel ambivalence in Derrida's understanding of his own position vis-à-vis the modern classical tradition in philosophy: see Derrida (1990, p 966).

out. To the contrary, the aporias of the finite and the infinite are sustained so that the refusal to move from D to R holds onto a level of critical negativity in the deconstructive enterprise. At this point, the further move he makes to what I have called unReason (uR) distinguishes him from Hegel, but by how much? My suggestion is that there remains a close parallel in the overall pattern of Hegel and Derrida's thought. Both possess an abstract metaphysical moment (R in Hegel, uR in Derrida).[6] Further, it is this shared metaphysical patterning that leads Derrida, like Hegel, to marginalise social power and historical structure in his philosophy. This returns Derrida ultimately, like Hegel, to an uncritical acceptance of the most basic antinomies of modern society.

Derrida's 'Kant-like rifts' and his limit

'Madness', or unReason (uR), acts for Derrida as a pseudo-free moment which serves ultimately to return his philosophy to the antinomies identified by the negative deconstructive/dialectical critique at D. The significant discussion of law in 'force of law' is taken up with the recitation of a series of 'aporias' of justice and *droit* which remain the unresolved terrain of the law (Derrida, 1990, pp 959–73). In fact, says Derrida, there is only one aporia that takes many forms, that between finite law and infinite justice (*ibid*, p 959). His elaboration of the aporias which entrain this basic form is acute, but what exactly is he telling us about the nature of law that is not already known? The distinction between the finite and the infinite could be dutifully re-rendered as the general opposition between the particular and the universal, while justice versus law echoes the tired opposition between natural and positive law. This representation of well-known oppositions in new language is accompanied by an indication that legal justice should both be transcended and not transcended (*ibid*, pp 947, 971), which is just to repeat the aporia in Derrida's own philosophy. Thus his powerful insistence on negative dialectical critique ends up marching us back into the arms of the law and its existing antinomies. The old oppositions are simply repeated in modern forms, producing no great flurry in the jurisprudential dovecotes.

At the same time, there is another price to be paid with Derrida in terms of the marginalisation of the social, the political and the historical in the critique he sets aside. Like Hegel, he has a negative dialectical critique accompanied by a further metaphysical position. What Hegel sought to resolve through speculative reason, Derrida refers to as the 'mad' and the 'mystical', to the messianic tradition associated with Levinas, to provide a moment beyond, that is always-still 'to come' (Derrida, 1990, p 959). Deconstruction in this 'deeper' metaphysical form is still in the orbit of Kant and Hegel,[7] and, as a result, steers critical thought in an immediate

---

6 Derrida (1999, p 249) denies that he is guilty of metaphysical abstraction, for deconstruction in pursuit of 'messianicity' refers in 'every here-now to the coming of an eminently real, concrete event'. The problem is that what he calls the 'real' and the 'concrete' involves 'the most irreducibly heterogeneous otherness', which is always coming, and never arrives. In other words, this is a metaphysical and abstract conception of the real and the concrete.

7 At one level, but only one, Derrida would accept this. As Christopher Norris notes, mostly, Derrida acknowledges that he has to 'bore from within', so that his own work is 'inseparably tied to Western philosophy' (Norris, 1991, p 49). But Norris also notes that there is what he describes as a 'theme of Utopian longing for the textual "free play" which would finally break with the instituted wisdom of language' which 'emerges to anarchic effect in some of his later texts', and which by implication is Derrida's 'way out'. My argument is precisely that this is not a way out.

ethical direction. Recall the critique of law that Derrida sets aside, the one that deals with 'juridical ideology' and the 'desedimentation of the superstructures of law that both hide and reflect the economic and political interests of the dominant forms of society' (*ibid*, p 941). It remains at the margin of the essay, silenced by the seemingly deeper critique of violence associated with his ineffable metaphysical ethics of law and justice.

We should have learned enough from Derrida himself about centres and margins to remark upon the significance of this silent critique on the margins of 'force of law'. Equally, if deconstruction, in its negative critical moment is concerned with revealing and recalling the forgotten history of concepts, should not this socio-political critique be an intrinsic and necessary aspect of deconstruction, not something to be politely acknowledged then ignored? While Derrida may reject the work of positive speculative Reason after his negative Dialectical critique, it is nonetheless a metaphysical critique as the negative mirror of Hegel – positive speculative unReason, we might say – that is Derrida's refuge. Such a critique takes us to a place of empty transcendence which in fact marginalises the recourse to history and politics that deconstruction in its negative dialectical form had invited. With Derrida, the issues are short-circuited by a reference to a metaphysical violence which is ahistorical and can only tell us that every law in every time is derived from a justice that lies beyond its particularity.

Derrida and the socio-legal

In my introductory comments to this chapter, I asked if there was not some basis in modern critical legal theory for the failure of dialogue with socio-legal theory. This, I argue, is it: that work deriving from Derrida, in moving from the negative deconstructive (dialectical) critique of concepts to a conception of the ethical, bypasses the terrain of the social and the political. It ends up with a reflection on existing social forms and practices which embraces their actuality in the name of general categorical oppositions such as that between the finite and the infinite. This is not to say that much good work is not done in the name of deconstruction in the manner of its genealogical style, or through its negative critical approach which causes tall concepts to tremble. However, because of its insistence on an abstract ethical moment of transcendence, deconstruction has an inbuilt counter-tendency to marginalise the historical and the genealogical and, once the concepts have trembled, they tend to be restored to their previous positions in the world. This happens because the route has been blocked that would link such concepts to historical structures and social power.

The question then is whether it is possible, after Hegel and Derrida, to understand dialectical method or deconstructive critique in a way that avoids immediate and empty ethical conclusions and reconnects it with the social and the historical. To provide a partial answer to this question, I now turn to dialectical critical realism.

Beyond identity thinking II: dialectic and socio-historical critique

I say a 'partial' answer because there is an initial problem to mention. Dialectical critical realism involves a developing and potentially far-reaching theoretical project, but it is one that is both incomplete and contested.[8] It is indebted to the work of Roy Bhaskar, but this has undergone several developments, and there is substantial debate within critical realism both as to how consistent the different phases in his thought are, and as to whether his dialectical philosophy is internally consistent. This issue is particularly problematic here, for precisely what is contested with regard to Bhaskar's dialectics is the relationship between the social and historical critique of identity he develops and the nature of the ethics that should accompany it. I do not think that dialectical critical realism, as currently formulated, has got this right (Hostettler and Norrie, 2003).

Thus, at the very point where I wish to find a way in dialectics beyond Hegelian and Derridean metaphysical abstraction, dialectical critical realism fails to provide a full answer. Nonetheless, this approach does offer a way forward in that it places a strong emphasis on reinstating a level of socio-political critique within the dialectical process as a *sine qua non* of ethical judgment and practice. It therefore provides a counterpoint to the dialectical theories we have considered by making Derrida's first, marginalised, question central to the critique of identity. I propose therefore to focus narrowly on the relevance of the level of socio-political critique to the questions of identity and logical thought which were examined in the Introduction, while acknowledging the incompleteness of the argument as a whole. In so doing, I want to preserve the negative Dialectical moment (D) in both Hegel and Derrida, but to relocate it away from the direct ethical or metaphysical nexus that they give it (either as R or uR). I do this by insisting on social and historical contextualisation as the necessary prelude to ethical and practical questions. Dialectical critical realism enables this without having resolved some of the further questions it necessarily prompts.

Compared to the dialectical schemata examined thus far, Bhaskar's dialectic conceives of four dialectical moments where Hegel and Derrida see three. Located between the world of social phenomena and their ethical judgment is the level of socio-political structure and history. Negative critical work at D is further related to the critique Derrida mentions but sidelines, the 'desedimentation of the superstructures ... that both hide and reflect the economic and political interests of the dominant forms of society' (1990, p 941). It is only on the basis of a grounded social and historical critique of the structural foundations of the forms of identity that a dialectical ethics and practice should be erected. To the U–D–R movement of the Hegelian dialectic (and its Derridean counterpart, U–D–uR), Bhaskar establishes a richer movement from U to D (this remains constant in all three thinkers) to Socio-Historic Critique (SHC), and thence to ethics and practice (E+P), as set out in Figure 3:

---

8 Bhaskar and Norrie, 1998 provides a brief overview, but one that does not bring out sufficiently the problems in the field. What follows is in part my own interpretation of how the dialectical critical realist schema should be presented.

Figure 3: Bhaskar: moments in the dialectical critical process

U   = Understanding
D   = negative Dialectical Critique
SHC = Socio-Historic Critique
E+P = Ethics and Praxis

In terms of this schema and the comments above about the limits of dialectical critical realism, my focus will thus be upon the movement from the critique of identity (at D) to the level of Socio-Historic Critique (SHC). I will not seek to clarify the further move to ethics and practice (E+P). The essential concept I wish to develop is that of 'entity relationism' as the dialectical critical realist opponent of identity thinking. Entity relationism posits the socio-historical relationality of phenomena and the consequent failures of identity to which this gives rise. One could approach it in a variety of ways. I will introduce the concept through a discussion of Bhaskar's treatment of the relationship between structure and agency as a meta-problem in social science. This leads to a view of agency, subjectivity and identity in a relational field that is intrinsically social, historical and dialectical. In the field of law, this can be related to Derrida's 'logico-formal paradoxes', which are seen directly as the site of issues of the 'desedimentation' of power. It is therefore an appropriate way into thinking about the dialectical critique of law.

Dialectical critical realism and the critique of identity thinking

Before its dialectical turn, critical realism evolved the key idea of 'ontological depth' as a way of explaining how phenomena are related to and explained by structures underlying them. This concept lies at the core of dialectical critical realism's insistence on the importance of the socio-historical critique of identity. I begin by explaining the idea of ontological depth and then move to see how it grounds the structure/ agency problematic in social science. Thereafter, I move to the idea of 'entity relationism' which lies at the core of dialectical critical realism.

Ontological depth

Critical realism evolved out of an orientation to the natural sciences, in which it maintained a central distinction between questions of ontology (what the world is like) and of epistemology (what we know of the world). For science to be possible, it is necessary to posit a world that contains ontological depth, that is a view of the world as made up of natural kinds, emergent properties, and causal structures, all existing within a stratified whole. Scientific investigation consists in the exploration and explanation of the world's phenomena in terms of their location in such a whole (Bhaskar, 1975, 1997). From that starting-point, Bhaskar went on to develop a parallel account of the social sciences which acknowledged both the similarities and the intrinsic differences between the subject matters of natural and social science (Bhaskar, 1979, 1998; cf Benton, 1977; Outhwaite, 1987; Sayer, 1992; Collier, 1994). As with the natural sciences, the social sciences deal with emergent properties, causal structures and a stratified world, but unlike them, the ontological depth of the social world is mediated by human agency. While social structures are a social scientific analogue of causal structures in nature, 'unlike natural mechanisms, they exist only in virtue of the activities they govern and cannot be identified independently of them' (Bhaskar, 1979, p 48). Such activities are the product of human beings *qua* intentional agents, so that social structures do not exist independently of their intentional actions, or their conceptions of what they are doing when they act. Yet social structures are ontologically real entities in social life, underpinning, enabling and conditioning activities and identities.

The structure/agency problem

This ontological relationship between social and historical structure and intentional agency and subjectivity in the social sciences brings us to the point at which critical realism addresses the agency-structure problem. Here, Bhaskar seeks to overcome a longstanding dichotomy in sociology between the voluntaristic tendencies of the Weberian tradition and the reificatory tendencies of the Durkheimian. He develops a 'Transformative Model of Social Action' in which 'social structure is a necessary condition for, and medium of, intentional agency' but intentional agency is also 'in turn a necessary condition for the reproduction or transformation of social forms' (Bhaskar, 1993, p 154).[9] In the connectedness of social structure and individual identity and agency, there is a two-way relationship. From the viewpoint of identity and agency, 'intentional causality would be impossible without material causes which pre-existed it' and, from the viewpoint of structure, 'social material causes exist only in virtue of the embodied intentional agency which reproduces and/or transforms them' (Bhaskar, 1993, p 155). This ontological relation of structure and agency involves both mediation of agency by structure and the reproduction and transformation of structure by agency. It entails 'dual points of articulation' of structure and agency which are the 'differentiated and changing positioned-practices' which human agents occupy but also act to reproduce or transform. It is these which constitute the structural systems of social relations in which intentional human activity occurs. Under this model, transformative activity 'reproduces and/or more or less transforms, for the most part unwittingly, its conditions of possibility', which include 'social structures and their generative mechanisms ... the agent herself and, generally, what was given, the *donné* ... which has now been reproduced or transformed' (Bhaskar, 1993, p 155).

---

9 Lurking behind these apparently simple statements lies a large debate in the social sciences between a variety of theories that have sought to understand the relationship between structure and agency. To the fore in this has been the work of Antony Giddens (1979), with which Bhaskar at one time found substantial agreement. However, Margaret Archer (1995) has shown, and developed, the important implicit differences between the two approaches. Describing Giddens's structuration theory as conflating structure and agency, and as eliding their differences, she argues that the transformational model can sustain, as Bhaskar claims, a 'genuine concept of *change*, and hence of *history*', while the weakness in Giddens's approach is seen in his inability to account for 'stability and change in social systems' (both quotes in Archer, 1995).

Entity relationism

This approach to the structure/agency problem was evolved in Bhaskar's pre-dialectical work (Bhaskar, 1979, 1998). However, his work of the early 1990s argues that this analysis provides a basis for, indeed necessitates, a dialectical reinterpretation. Here we come to the idea of entity relationism, where the lines between structure and agency blur. The dialectical quality of being-in-structure means that human life should be seen as a social and relational 'flow, differentiated into analytically discrete moments' with each moment seen as 'subject to multiple and conflicting determinations and mediations' (Bhaskar, 1993, p 160). The primary category in this social flow of individual being is that of dialectical connection. This describes a situation in which 'entities or aspects of a totality ... are in principle *distinct* but *inseparable*, in the sense that they are ... internally related, ie both ... existentially presuppose the other' (Bhaskar, 1993, p 58). The domain of dialectical connection is one in which there is the existential constitution, or permeation, of one social entity by another.

This sociological idea of both the distinctiveness and the inseparability of different social entities invokes ideas of the ways in which concepts or identities are both expressed as complete and remain essentially incomplete. It invites comparison with a Derridean concept such as supplementarity or the limit, but there is nothing mystical or metaphysical in this real dialectical relationship between different entities. Bhaskar makes dialectic emerge out of a social terrain, at a level at which socio-historical critique is engaged (SHC in Figure 3). He invites us to ponder the extent to which emergent social entities such as people, institutions, traditions, identities and activities not only presuppose their particular geo-histories, in the sense of being dependent on them for their meaning, but also 'are existentially constituted by [them] as a crucial part of their essence'. For this reason, such entities 'contain their relations, connections and interdependencies with other social (and natural) things' (Bhaskar, 1993, p 54). Crucial to dialectical thought is to see identity in its connectedness with the totality of which it is a part, so that it is intrinsically *relational*:

> To grasp totality is to break with our ordinary notions of identity ... It is to see things *existentially constituted*, and permeated, *by their relations with others*; and to see our ordinary notion of identity as an abstraction not only from [its] existentially constitutive processes of formation (geo-histories), but also from [its] existentially constitutive inter-activity (internal relatedness) ... When is a thing no longer a thing but something else? ... [I]n the domain of totality we need to conceptualise *entity relationism*. (Bhaskar, 1993, p 125)

This 'entity relationism' involves a radical development and correction of the 'law of identity' in identity thinking, with which we began this chapter (see above, p 135). Now 'whatever is' is intrinsically at the same time *not* itself, but something else. A fluid, dialectical sense of identity requires us to see 'our ordinary notion of identity' as an abstraction not only from geo- and socio-historical process, but also from the internal relationality of entities which initially appear separate and distinct. On an 'entity relational' understanding of identity, any posited identity will always entail an exclusion of some thing or things that seemingly lie behind or beyond it. Identity presupposes non-identity so that any sense of identity presupposes incompleteness and change. Identity is an abstraction from a process or set of processes of formation so that it is always 'under threat' from what appears as *different*, but is in fact part of it, and from *change*, which leads an entity to become something other than it is. Thus, to identity thinking, Bhaskar opposes entity relationism as a conceptual grounding for the existence of fluidity, supplementarity and the limit. But note that entity relationism is forged out of a meta-problem in the social sciences, not at an edge between what exists and what lies in a purportedly metaphysical 'beyond', viewed either as a positive speculative reason (Hegel), or a mad, mystical unreason (Derrida).

Entity relationism and legal subjectivity

In this last section, I will consider briefly the implications of dialecticising the structure/agency problem for law in terms of the identity of the legal subject and the nature of legal reasoning. Once one sees that questions of identity are fluid, and that that fluidity can be located directly within a social scientific framework, it becomes possible to explain the dynamics of a social institution like law dialectically and sociologically at the same time. The structure-agency meta-problem becomes the basis for seeing how legal subjectivity is both constructed and deconstructed historically and politically within given social relations and structures. One must, however, examine subjectivity from the two intersecting standpoints donated by the structure-agency meta-problem, that is from the standpoints of both structure and agency. Having done so, I conclude by locating legal reasoning in an entity relational view.

Legal subjectivity from the standpoint of structure

From the standpoint of structure, conceptions of legal subjectivity (identity) act as modes of selection – of exclusion and inclusion – of the relations that inform entities. The seemingly universal legal subject is in fact a social and historical figure, whose abstract characteristics function to instantiate a political and moral order, and to exclude alternative and competing voices and claims (see above, Chapters 3 and 4). The legal categories that Derrida (1990, p 131) identifies as ripe for deconstruction, such as the 'responsible subject of law and morality', the 'juridical or moral person', and the 'intentional agent', invite the identification of what prove to be their false limits, their contradictions and meaning-slides, and their necessary but disruptive supplements. This is not *pace* Derrida because they are formed on the site of an inaugural violence but because they instantiate a particular moral, social and political order, with its own violence. In excluding alternatives to this order, they render opaque the broader social relations through and in which moral and legal subjects live.

From this standpoint, law is a structuring system which, with its individualistic emphasis, hypostasises the individual and thereby lays responsibility at her door. Invoking individual responsibility is a process of individualisation of social and relational problems, and a means of evacuating difficult moral problems and political conflicts by the claim of a realm of seeming consent as to the 'basic principles of social life' (Norrie, 1998b, pp 106–14, 119–23). It is this sense of the structural effects of legal responsibility that is caught in Roland Barthes's view (1973, p 45) that law's universal language lends a 'new strength to the psychology of the masters' by taking 'other men as objects, to describe and to condemn at one stroke'. However, while the law may seek, as Barthes continues, to be 'ignorant of everything about the actions themselves, save the guilty category into which they are forced to fit', it cannot do so, for the real practicality of law's categories assures their disruption at every turn. Such disruption, as I argue below in discussing legal reasoning, is the basis for law's continued analytical failures. Identity thinking, as the constitution of an analytical logic based upon the existence of a responsible subject, is pulled 'every which way' – and loose.

The problem is that individualist legal categories deny the social, political and moral relationality with which the subject is suffused, but this relationality forces itself back into the legal picture wherever possible. The subject is constructed through legal-moral concepts which are understood in a 'technical', 'formal' or 'factual' way, which obscures their essential ('substantive') moral qualities. It is these moral qualities that embody the relational aspects of subjective experience, and lead to a set of 'shadow' concepts and theories which operate as oppositional *doppelgänger*. The result is a field of legal and philosophical theories in which antinomial views of the legal subject and legal responsibility abound.

Legal subjectivity from the standpoint of agency

There is a second way of looking at this. The Transformative Model of Social Action insists that communities, structures and discourses (ie, structural figures) are themselves produced and reproduced, varied and transformed, by agents. Agency is real and significant, and not just an effect of structure (Archer, 1995). Maintaining this duality entails the theorisation of a 'perspectival shift' (Bhaskar, 1993, pp 115–16, 401), wherein causal explanations at the level of the structural also necessitate accounts from the point of view of agents in terms of their substantive reasons, intentions, motives and so on for acting.

What does it mean to be an individual agent? Bhaskar sees it as a 'powerful particular', a psychic and physical source of action in the world. It is 'embodied intentionality which earths social life', and in turn 'real reasons for action', based upon 'informed or misinformed desire', 'comprise the existential agent's intentional causality'. Forms such as intentionality and the giving of reasons for action render agency accountable, according to Bhaskar, even where its forms are 'routinised or habitual' (*ibid*, p 164). These comments about the individual must be read in the light of Bhaskar's discussion of the dialecticised subject. This involves relationising the subject so that its acts, intentions, reasons are seen in the context of the 'centrification, fragmentation or alienation of the subject', and of 'conscious and unconscious' aspects of subjectivity. The subject must be understood in the context of 'the open systemic, multiply and conflictually determined nature of the aspects at play in our internal pluriverses' (*ibid*, p 167). This gives rise to a relational conception of the agential subject, in which agency becomes a synthetic practice achieved out of difference. Such a conception can be linked with the most sophisticated work in social psychology which insists on the significance of agency as a real achievement, but one that always remains part of a process of construction of agential categories within and by social relations. The subject is both itself and something else, something that lies beyond itself. Subjectivity involves living in a 'space between' what one is and is not (Harré, 1983; 1998; Norrie, 2000, Chapter 9; also see above, Chapters 5 and 6).

What does this mean in terms of responsibility in, and beyond, law? When people act, they act in a social and moral context, and in a community or set of communities, however these may be established or identified. Subjectivity involves being-in-relation, and therefore responsibility is shared with others in communities in a skein of mutual and structured complicities. In a relational model of subjective responsibility, justice embraces the subject and her context, blurring the boundaries. Judgment is complex and 'distributive', rather than simplistically individual and retributive. This gives rise to an ambivalent sense of judgment in which it is recognised that responsibility extends beyond the subject to the community of which the subject is a part.

Entity relationism and legal reasoning

Between the outreach of a relational conception of responsibility and the suppression of that outreach in law lie the problems of legal analytics. Identity thinking involves a deep interconnection between a conception of being and a conception of thinking about being. An exclusionary sense of identity (Russell's law 1, above, p 135) licenses analytical reasoning (his laws 2 and 3). Placing entity relationism at the core of an alternative account of identity radically affects our understanding of reasoning. Thinking dialectically involves thinking the coincidence of distinctions and connections, as well as the contradictions within basic entities. Thinking analytically involves the thinking of distinctions separately from connections and in the absence of internal contradictions. Dialectic therefore becomes 'the great "loosener"' of the hold of analytic thought, permitting 'empirical "open-texture" ... structural fluidity and interconnectedness' (Bhaskar, 1993, p 44) in place of the formal definitions and logic associated with identity theory. Dialectical thinking threatens the analytical moment because in 'thinking the *constellational unity of identity* ... and *change*', we are required to see it as 'a case when we want to say that a thing both is and is not itself' (Bhaskar, 1993, p 183). This challenges Russell's 'self-evident logical principles' based on the 'law of identity' (1973, p 40). It is a 'blow at the heart of analytic reason where ... everything is what it is and not another thing' (Bhaskar, 1993, p 183).

The precise nature of this threat to legal categories stems from the ways in which categories of legal judgment reflect in a distanced and mismatched way broader relational categories of judgment. Legal categories are cut against the broader, shared sense of responsibility outlined above. Moral judgments beyond the law, based on locating the individual within a broader context, jar with legal conceptions that deny that context. It must be remembered, however, that legal conceptions have been engineered socially, politically and historically precisely to deny context (Norrie, 1993a, 2001b, Chapter 2; see above, Chapters 3 and 4). There is a dysphasia here, and judges who consider the moral issues before them in individual cases are faced with a tension between two standpoints of judgment. On the one hand, they are faced with the legal categories that have been elaborated on the basis of concepts that are understood as 'factual', 'technical' and 'substantively amoral'. On the other hand, they must have regard for the position of real human agents and the social, moral and political dilemmas they face. Sometimes the political issues involved lead to an immediate closure of the legal issues, and the judges hold strongly to the juridical categories of responsibility. They use, indeed, the exclusionary structural conceptions of legal responsibility to shut out the political issues. On other occasions, however, the moral issues that lurk beyond the legal concepts provoke sympathy amongst judges, and they are forced into a dialogue between them and the pre-existing legal categories. In such situations, they are forced to recognise the limits of the legal concepts, and to push against them.[10]

This pushing and pulling of the concepts between the subject and her context cannot leave legal reasoning untouched. Where an underlying moral issue is accommodated, legal reasoning must find ways of controlling its impact on the new development of the legal concept. The innovation has to be controlled lest it admit too much. Legal judgment is often therefore on a dialectical edge between what legal concepts were designed to exclude, and what, in appropriate circumstances, they are desired to admit. In this play between two essentially connected yet conflicting orders of judgment and responsibility, morality-in-, and morality-beyond-, law, the primary victim is analytical legal reasoning.

The underlying point to note here, however, is that analytical modes of thought are power-invested, so that their ideological shape must be maintained and buttressed against the ravages of the relational conflicts and contradictions they traverse (cf Bhaskar, 1993, p 116). If a power-invested analytic is to be maintained in the face of the disruption it itself invokes, it requires a variety of discursive and practical techniques to manage it. In law, ideological 'truth' is maintained by a variety of meaning-slides and fictive constructions, by 'fixes' and 'fudges', exceptions and exemptions, and unrationalised inclusions and exclusions which supplement (Derrida's word) analytical reasoning. These 'techniques of legal reasoning' (that are never named as such) stand alongside the accepted legal architectonics: of the general and special parts, *mens rea*, *actus reus*, justification and excuse, and so on. These go to establish the identity of the legal subject, and need to be protected from their own incoherence in the face of the relationality law denies.

Analytical reasoning *qua* legal reasoning is a way of exercising social and political power and is informed by power relations, it is a means of crystallising and expressing those relations. Analytical reasoning is not in itself innocent.[11] Analytics set up concepts and identities that embody, and legitimate by embodying, powerful and conflicted social practices. Just as, in the case of General Pinochet, the question

---

10 See the plight of the 'humanitarian judge' discussed in Chapter 7. Compare for example the cases of *R v Steane* [1947] 1 All ER 813 (admission of relational context through manipulation of legal category of intention, leading to acquittal for man who broadcast for the Nazis) and *R v Chandler* [1964] AC 763 (denial of relational context by holding to legal categories distinguishing 'motive' and 'intention', leading to conviction of anti-nuclear protestors). See Norrie, 1993a, 2001b, Chapter 3 for discussion of these and other relevant cases.

11 According to Bhaskar (1993, p 176), it assumes 'the shape of an *unself-conscious ideology of the normalisation of past changes and freedoms, and the denegation of present and future ones*'. Here it is necessary to develop Bhaskar's point, and to recognise the double-sided nature of the analytical tradition with regard to power. It normalises past changes and freedoms, but also past repressions, as the history of criminal justice makes clear (Thompson, 1975; 1991; Hay *et al*, 1977).

whether a brutal dictator should be called to account can become a legal matter of 'sovereign immunity', so can the social, political and historical problems of crime become translated into a legal architectonic establishing individual culpability. Social practices are interventions in the conflicts that power relations engender, but, as mediated by law and legal reasoning, they seek to lose the latter's smell in the name of neutrality and formal logic.

Conclusion

One of Derrida's signal achievements has been to permit critical thinkers the use of a dialectical language that helps us to understand the nature of phenomena in a conflictual and contradictory social and political world. There are two paradoxes in this conclusion. First, many attracted to Derrida would not see deconstruction as falling within dialectics. As Barnett says, however, postmodern thought is 'caught in a Hegelian labyrinth' wherein one 'need never mention the name of Hegel' (Barnett, 1998, p 25). Secondly, the whole emphasis of Derrida's essay on law is away from the 'desedimentation' of social and political power, as we have seen. Hence my aim has been to show how the forms of deconstruction can be located within a dialectical theory that can make them relevant to power and conflict. In so doing, I have sought to show a way of bridging the 'seemingly unbridgeable gap' identified by Lacey between critical and socio-legal theory. This involves holding onto what is valid in Derrida and making it available to a sociology of law interested in issues of social and political power, structure and history, a 'post-poststructuralist' sociology of law.

The argument developed here leaves important questions unanswered. If the negative Dialectical critique deployed by both Hegel and Derrida needs to be steered away from the abstract metaphysics and directly ethical standpoints that govern their philosophies (either as positive speculative Reason, or as 'mad', 'mystical' unReason); if there is a need to embed the negative critique in the social, political and historical conditions of a given period, this leaves open the ultimate question where the ethical and the metaphysical fit into the overall picture. Neither Derrida nor Hegel is wrong to insist on the ethical dimension to human living, their error lies in directly founding critique upon it in a way that by-passes the socio-historical conditions which predicate conflict, contradiction and antinomy. This chapter does not answer this question, but it has sought to provide a foundation on which it may be properly raised. The two following chapters seek to bring together the ethical and socio-historical dimensions through engagement, first, with Adorno's negative dialectics and, secondly, with Hegel's treatment of the Beautiful Soul.

Chapter 9
How Does Freedom Lie?
Adorno, Negative Dialectics and Law

As if real history were not stored up in the core of each possible object of cognition; as if every cognition that seriously resists reification did not bring the petrified things in flux and precisely thus make us aware of history. (Adorno, 1973, p 130)

A radical is one who cannot ... believe ... that what we see now is pretty much all we will ever get ... (Eagleton, 2001, p 101)

Introduction

Bill Bowring (2002) has objected to what he sees as too gentle a critique of law in my work, one that leaves too much of it, morally and politically, in credit. In contrast to my kindliness, he suggests an alternative starting point in the work of Theodor Adorno. Adorno's *Negative Dialectics* has much to say about law that has remained unnoticed, and that is in his view more radical. There is some truth in this, Adorno could be extremely critical of law. A close reading of *Negative Dialectics* reveals, however, that alongside the negative things Adorno had to say, some were surprisingly positive. It is hard to reconcile two rather different sides to his argument. To add to the problem, his view of law is linked to an account of human freedom, but that account is neither clear nor univocal. In fact, it too is contradictory, so that a first reaction to Adorno's views on law is to find them deeply confusing. However, Adorno had some extremely penetrating things to say about law and its relation to freedom, and more generally to the Kantian philosophy that underlay it. The first and main task of this chapter is therefore to retrieve and explicate Adorno's account of law, and to seek to make best sense of it. To do so, it is necessary to bring the different aspects of his account into alignment lest his overall argument is lost in a number of competing, one-sided statements of his position.

The chapter also has a second task, which is undertaken in order to achieve the first. It concerns what Adorno means by 'negative dialectics', and this entails, so I will argue, bringing his theory into dialogue with 'dialectical critical realism', which is the philosophical basis for my own view of law. Dialectical critical realism is a philosophical system developed by Roy Bhaskar which has much in common with negative dialectics. In some ways, negative dialectics is a forerunner of dialectical critical realism, but it also contains important differences, and these, I shall argue, contribute to its imperfect and conflicted quality. They also feed into the problems with Adorno's view of law. Thus, I shall contend that to give the best statement of what Adorno had to say about law is to push his negative dialectics further in the direction of a critical realist dialectics than Adorno himself would have wanted to go.

The chapter has four sections. In the first, I introduce three views of law to be found within *Negative Dialectics*. I show how the first and second views contradict each other, and how the third view (concerning the freedom that underlies law) is open to two competing and contradictory interpretations. In anatomising Adorno's conflicting views of law, this section raises the question why his philosophy should disclose such difficulties. In the second section, I briefly introduce the difference between realist and idealist approaches to philosophy, drawing upon Bhaskar's philosophy. I focus on his argument that modern philosophy, including its critical varieties, is caught in a tension between an implicit realism, and an explicit idealism.[1] The argument is advanced as a prelude to examining in a third section how *Negative Dialectics* handles this tension. Finally, the fourth section argues that the tension between realism and idealism underpins Adorno's conflicted account of law, and that it makes best sense when the historically realist direction present in his philosophy (see the first prefatory quotation for an example of this) is emphasised in relation to his view of law.

Freedom and law in modern society: Adorno's three views

In this section, I discuss three views of freedom in Adorno's reading of Kant and law in *Negative Dialectics*. In the first, modern freedom is viewed negatively as an emanation of what he calls 'identity thinking'. In the second, it is viewed more positively. Here liberal forms of freedom are given a degree of approval in a reaction against the negative identitarian critique Adorno has himself developed. A third view is at a deeper level, and concerns the profound impulse to freedom that Adorno finds hidden in the Kantian account of modern freedom, and therefore in the modern law. Adorno views this deeper level in two different, conflicting, ways, and I describe both here. My aim in this section is to map the multiple and conflicting views of freedom and the juridical to be found in Adorno, with a view to understanding, in later sections, what these conflicting views import, and how best they can be brought together.

First (negative) view: freedom as identity

In his magisterial discussion of Kant's philosophy of freedom, and elsewhere in *Negative Dialectics*, Adorno makes it clear that the ideas that go into modern thinking about freedom and its legal expression, ideas like those of responsibility, equality, the free act and the just punishment, are central to the wholly problematic form of thought that he calls 'identity thinking'. Such thinking involves a 'subsumptive logic' that draws things under concepts that can never be adequate to them, and this leads to a suppression of what is not subsumed. What is suppressed does not, however, go away; rather it remains as a contradiction attached to the thing under its identitarian concept:

> The name of dialectics says no more, to begin with, than that objects do not go into their concepts without leaving a remainder, that they come to contradict the traditional norm of adequacy. Contradiction … indicates the untruth of identity, the fact that the concept does not exhaust the thing conceived … Dialectics is the consistent sense of non-identity. (Adorno, 1973, p 5)

---

1 'Hegel would not have been wrong if he had described the history of philosophy as that of explicit idealism and implicit realism' (Bhaskar, 1993, p 308). For different accounts of Adorno's work, see Rose, 1978; Jarvis, 1998; Bernstein, 2001. The argument here is based on a close reading of Adorno's *Negative Dialectics* rather than his work as a whole, and is therefore provisional.

In this light, a juridical claim emanating from Kantian thinking about freedom, such as that embodied in the idea of equality under law, is no more than the identitarian principle in action. Formal legal equality is a mode of exclusion, a form of 'equality-mongering':

> It is precisely the insatiable identity principle that perpetuates antagonism by suppressing contradiction. What tolerates nothing that is not like itself thwarts the reconcilement for which it mistakes itself. The violence of equality-mongering reproduces the contradiction it eliminates. (*Ibid*, pp 142–43)

In the following longer passage, the link between identity thinking and law is made explicit:

> In large measure, the law is the medium in which evil wins out on account of its objectivity and acquires the appearance of good ... Law is the primal phenomenon of irrational rationality. In law the formal principle of equivalence becomes the norm; everyone is treated alike. An equality in which differences perish secretly serves to promote inequality; it becomes the myth that survives amidst an only seemingly demythologised mankind. For the sake of an unbroken systematic, the legal norms cut short what is not covered, every specific experience that has not been shaped in advance; and then they raise the instrumental rationality to the rank of a second legality *sui generis*. The total legal realm is one of definitions. (*Ibid*, p 309)

Formal (legal) egalitarianism is the form in which inequality is promoted. Though counter-intuitive to liberal thought, such a view is not unique in critical thought.[2] It is the stringent way in which Adorno pursues it that is arresting:

> These [legal] bounds, ideological in themselves, turn into real violence as they are sanctioned by law as the socially controlling authority, in the administered world in particular. In the dictatorships they become direct violence; indirectly, violence has always lurked behind them. (*Ibid*, p 309)

Formal legality, then, represents a form of real but indirect violence, and what separates such legality from dictatorship is not essentially the form of law, but whether the violence used is 'direct' or 'indirect'. Both legal rule and dictatorship represent forms of violence, as does the search for equality. What is true of legal equality is also necessarily true of the freedom that underlies it, as well as its other expressions such as concepts of responsibility and punishment. All of them are forms of identity thinking and as such expressive of an underlying cruelty:

> But the paradoxical character of Kant's doctrine of freedom strictly corresponds to its location in reality. Social stress on freedom as existent coalesces with undiminished repression, and psychologically, with coercive traits. Kantian ethics, antagonistic in itself, has these traits in common with a criminological practice in which the dogmatic doctrine of free will is coupled with the urge to punish harshly, irrespective of empirical conditions. (*Ibid*, p 232)

> On the side, Kant's inwardly brittle ethics retains its repressive aspect. He glories in an unmitigated urge to punish ... In its contempt for pity, pure practical reason agrees with the 'Grow hard!' of Nietzsche, its antipode. (*Ibid*, p 240)

---

2 For example: 'And this universal language (law) comes just at the right time to lend a new strength to the psychology of the masters: it allows it always to take other men as objects, to describe and condemn at one stroke. It is an adjectival psychology, it knows only how to endow its victims with epithets, it is ignorant of everything about the actions themselves, save the guilty category into which they are forced to fit' (Barthes, 1973, p 45).

Identity is about suppression, equality is about inequality, freedom and responsibility in the Kantian doctrine are about repression. Virtuous Kantian concepts concerning freedom turn into their negative opposites before our eyes. Since it is of their very nature to act in this way, there is little room for a nuanced view. Modern forms of freedom viewed through the identitarian critique are not what they seem: they are a means of repression.

Second (positive) view: a liberal reaction

The above uncompromising attack on the modern 'Kantian-juridical complex' is certainly prominent in Adorno's *Negative Dialectics*.[3] However, it is not the only view there present. It is important to note that there are other passages which have a less negative view of law and its correlative terms. For example, here is a passage on law's formal equality which contrasts with the dismissal of such equality seen above; indeed, law is held up here in a strong positive contrast to the rule of (fascist) dictatorship:

> Though failing to provide us with a positive casuistry for future action, this [juridical] formalism humanely prevents the abuse of substantial-qualitative differences in favour of privilege and ideology. The German critics who found Kantian formalism too rationalistic have shown their bloody colours in the fascistic practice. (Adorno, 1973, p 235)

There is a qualification in this support for Kantian formalistic freedom: it fails to provide a 'positive casuistry', a guide to what should be done. Nonetheless, the distinction between Kantian formalism and fascistic 'substantivism' clearly contradicts the identitarian critique. No longer is the former seen as 'indirect' violence in comparison with its fascist 'direct' form. They are seen as opposed rather than as points on a continuum of violence. The same is true in the following longer quotation, which finds positive things to say about Kantian freedom and responsibility. In this longer quotation, Adorno calls Kant's discussion of the will a 'cover concept' (*Oberbegriff*). This is a negative comment aligned with the critique of identity: such a concept 'covers' by hiding an underlying state of affairs. However, having said that, Adorno still sees the Kantian will as 'progressive' and as an 'assist to freedom'. Through the Kantian philosophy, the subject becomes 'moral for itself' and 'protected from the violence' of a hierarchical society. Despite its layer of falseness, the Kantian will is also the basis for the important gain for freedom of individual moral conscience:

> The will [is] the cover concept of acts or their moment of unity ... In what thus happens to it theoretically, however, *there is some truth despite all flagrant contradictions* ... The individual impulses' objectification in the will that synthesises and determines them is their sublimation, their successful, delaying, permanence-involving diversion from the primary goal of the drives. Kant faithfully circumscribed this by the rationality of the will ... *The discovery was [nonetheless] progressive*: it kept the judgment about particular impulses from being made casuistically any longer ... *This was an assist to freedom. The subject becomes moral for itself*; it cannot be weighed by standards that are inwardly and outwardly particular and alien to the subject. Once the rational unity of the will is

---

3 It is the position Bowring (2002) argues for and from in his review of my *Punishment, Responsibility and Justice* (Norrie, 2000).

> established as the sole moral authority, the subject is *protected from the violence done to it by a hierarchical society* – a society which … would judge a man's deeds without any previous acceptance of its law by his own consciousness … Kant's relegation of ethics to the sober unity of reason *was an act of bourgeois majesty despite the false consciousness in his objectification of the will.* (*Ibid*, pp 238–39, emphasis added)

This is a difficult passage, but its tendency is clear. While there are qualifications, Adorno affirms the progressive character of Kant's account of modern free will. Thus, his work reveals not just the identitarian, negative, critique of modern freedom, but also a certain positive support for it. Taking these two sides together, we see that Adorno has a conflicted view of the Kantian-juridical complex. There is an opposition between seeing the concepts of legality under the critique of identity as exclusionary and repressive, and seeing them, in a more positive, recognisably liberal way, as enabling and expressive. Comparing Adorno's two views, one could suggest that they indicate a limit in his philosophy, one represented by just the kind of antinomial thinking found in the Kantian tradition he himself criticises. Before we make any judgments, however, we must recognise that alongside these two views of Kantian freedom, Adorno develops a third.

Third (underlying) view: the impulse to freedom

In the following passages, Adorno links the Kantian free will and ego, foundations of law, to an underlying conception of freedom. It is first presented as possessing a mysterious 'pre-temporal' or 'archaic' quality:

> The dawning sense of freedom feeds upon the memory of the archaic impulse not yet steered by any solid I. The more the I curbs that impulse, the more chaotic and questionable will it find the pre-temporal freedom. (Adorno, 1973, p 221)

Adorno speaks here, somewhat mystically, of a protean originary moment when 'the untamed impulse that precedes the ego' was 'banished to the zone of unfree bondage to nature' (*ibid*, p 222), but he insists that this inchoate, primal, banished impulse still echoes in the modern juridical idea of free choice. Later, he links this idea to Kant, whose ideas of freedom are held to evade, and yet to reflect, this underlying impulse. In the following passage, Adorno contrasts what he calls the 'jolt' of freedom within willed action with Kant's emasculation of the will as either the phaenomenal expression of an act in a causal chain in nature, or as the noumenal pure reason. Neither view captures the essential quality of free will:

> The subject's decisions do not roll off in a causal chain; what occurs is a jolt (*ein Ruck erfolgt*) … Consciousness, rational insight, is not simply the same as [the] free act. We cannot flatly equate it with the will. Yet this is precisely what happens in Kant's thought. To him, the will is the epitome of freedom … because it contracts into that necessity which coincides with reason … As the pure *logos*, the will becomes a no-man's land between subject and object. (*Ibid*, p 228)

The idea of a 'jolt', or an 'impulse', is the underlying, truly human, element in Kant's metaphysics, but it is caught in neither the account of phaenomenal nor noumenal freedom. It is nonetheless the true moment of human free will that lies behind Kant's causal ('phaenomenal') and rational ('noumenal') accounts. While it is passed over in Kantian doctrine, it is also implicit as its best moment, the 'heartbeat of the *res cogitans*', the 'addendum' both in and beyond Kantian theory:

> The impulse, intramental and somatic in one, drives beyond the conscious sphere …
> With [it], freedom extends to the realm of experience … Its phantasm … is the phantasm
> of reconciling nature and the mind … It is a flash of light between the poles of
> something long past, something grown all but unrecognisable, and that which some day
> might come to be. (*Ibid*, p 229)

What it means to be truly human is there in Kant as absence and as immanent
presence, as that which Kant seeks to suppress, but implies despite himself. The
idea of an 'impulse', a 'jolt', a 'flash of light between the poles' is reflected, but as a
trace ('something long past', 'archaic', 'pre-temporal'), in current notions of
freedom. This is central to Adorno's thinking, but it is not easy to grasp. It leads to a
range of questions: what is the provenance of this underlying freedom, what is its
purpose, what is its status in the story of human being?

One way of getting at these questions is to consider the relationship between the
impulse to freedom and history. We have seen how, for Adorno, it is something 'pre-
temporal' – a residue of a time before thinking and the separation between thought
and action. However, Adorno is not clear about this. Elsewhere, he suggests that the
impulse has to be understood as a matter of mediated historical development, and
in this, he gives it a more concrete, time-specific, instantiation. When speaking, for
example, of Kant's exclusion of 'the impulse', he contrasts Kant's account of
freedom with Shakespeare's depiction of Hamlet's plight. Adorno praises the
specific force given to the impulse to be a free individual in the play. He sees this as
indicating the 'self-emancipating modern subject's self-reflection', with a resulting
sense of the reflexive 'divergence of insight and action' (*ibid*, p 228) in modern
human being. 'To be or not to be,' the existential decision at the play's heart, is a
matter of real choice, of jumping into history, not a result of either cogitative,
noumenal, reason or causal, phaenomenal, determination in Kantian terms. The
choice, and the freedom it expresses, is, however, profoundly related to a particular
historical period:

> Whole epochs, whole societies lacked not only the concept of freedom but the thing …
> Likewise, freedom, which without impairment can only be achieved under social
> conditions of unfettered plenty, might be wholly extinguished again, perhaps without
> leaving a trace. (*Ibid*, p 218)

In this view, freedom and unfreedom, together with the forms freedom takes, are an
emergent property of an historically developing social system, which expresses both
the developing potential of human being and the ways it is blocked under modern
conditions:

> Freedom is a moment … not to be isolated, and for the time being it is never more than
> an instant of spontaneity, a historical node, the road to which is blocked under present
> conditions. (*Ibid*, p 219)

In summary, we have seen that Adorno gives us three different views of law and
freedom, that the first two are in conflict, and that the third admits of two different,
and also conflicting, interpretations. Deploying Adorno's critique of freedom, of
Kant and of law is thus no easy matter. How are the first and the second (negative
and positive) views of freedom to be held together, and how is the conflict between
the pre-temporal and historical account in the third underlying view to be resolved?
My answer has two parts. The first is that drawing these three views together

depends upon understanding why there are conflicting pre-temporal and historical approaches to the third. The historical approach is to be preferred. The second is to argue that coming to terms with the conflict in the third view of freedom involves an enquiry into the underlying philosophical premises of the negative dialectics. That in turn involves an engagement with dialectical critical realism which will bring out the conflicting realist and idealist directions in Adorno's philosophy and also in his account of law. I start with the latter part: the underlying philosophical conflict in *Negative Dialectics*, which I start to approach in the next section.

Realism and idealism: the need for a depth ontology

In this section, I will introduce a key distinction from Roy Bhaskar's account of critical realism between realist and idealist philosophy. While the former insists that human knowledge relates to objects beyond itself, the latter stresses the independence of the human mind in its construction of an object world. I will emphasise what Bhaskar sees as the tension within modern Western philosophies, including critical theory, between an implicit realism and an explicit idealism. My argument in the following section will then be that Adorno's negative dialectics reflect this tension, but we need first to understand what the tension is, and how it might arise in modern critical philosophy.

Three standpoints in the philosophy of science

Bhaskar's argument is that Western philosophy is generally governed by idealist forms that rest in tension with tendencies towards realism. The result is 'compromise formations' incorporating idealist and realist strains which he terms 'irrealist'. These formations typically involve realist inflected forms of idealism, or inadequate forms of realism which are governed by a dominant idealism. The key element missing in such philosophies is a sense of the world's ontological depth. Critical realism's main claim is to be able to theorise such depth.

Bhaskar developed his philosophy initially in the form of what he called a 'transcendental realism' which he later renamed as 'critical realism' (Bhaskar, 1989, pp 189–92), and then developed further in a dialectical form as dialectical critical realism (Bhaskar, 1993). While there are significant changes in the move to dialectical critical realism, the underlying theory has in important ways remained constant. It starts from the view that in the philosophy of science, two major standpoints have dominated, competed with each other, and at the same time complicitly excluded a third. The two dominant standpoints are empirical realism (for example, in forms of positivism) and transcendental idealism (in Kantian and post-Kantian philosophy). What has been excluded is the third transcendental (critical) realist position.[4] Critical realism developed out of an understanding of the philosophy of science. It stresses the need for theory building in order to identify and to explain the generative mechanisms, causes and structures[5] which underlie

---

4   The argument is first made in Bhaskar (1975). Compare Bhaskar (1986), Chapter 1 and (1994), Chapter 1.

5   Bhaskar (1993, p 226) explains the relationship between these terms as follows. Generative mechanisms are 'the causal powers of structurally efficacious things'. This means that 'causality begins with the concept of the transfactual efficacy of the generative mechanism or the causal powers of a structure' (*ibid*, p 240).

empirical reality. That theory building is linked to a conception of the ontologically real distinguishes it from all forms of subjectivism and idealism in the philosophy of science. That it emphasises the depth-explanatory nature (Bhaskar, 1989, pp 189–92) of scientific enquiry, reflecting the layered and structured character of both natural and social relations, marks its difference from all forms of empiricism and empirical realism. The aim of such enquiry is to get beneath the surface of things to what lies underneath and animates them. This could be, for example, to uncover the tectonic plates which cause geological upheaval in the natural world, or to identify the causes of poverty or violence which cause upheaval in the social world.[6] Getting beneath the surface of things involves the idea of ontological depth as a real feature of the natural and social world, and therefore of any theory that will be adequate to it.

Let us explore the consequences of these three approaches to the philosophy of science in some more detail. As regards (Kantian) transcendental idealism, critical realism agrees that theory building involves subjective mental activity, but insists that this involves an engagement with objects of a world that is real and can be known. Epistemological relativism is a feature of all knowledge, but is offset by an ontological realism which grounds, but does not guarantee, such knowledge. As regards empirical realism (positivism, empiricism), critical realism agrees that experience of a real world is possible and necessary, but, against it, insists that this is not a sufficient basis for scientific understanding. Knowledge requires active theory building and testing in order to provide depth explanations of the stratified reality that underlies the surface forms given to experience. Critical realism sees both transcendental idealism and empirical realism as inadequate to explain a world that involves ontological depth. This leads them to collaborate in unstable formations of ideas. Thus Kant, the transcendental idealist, ends up conceding that he is at the same time an empirical realist.[7] What is missing in this combination, however, is any sense of the ontological depth that underlies the empirical, and which transcendental enquiry should be directed to excavate, elucidate and explain. A focus on subjective forms of knowledge combined with direct empirical means of accessing the world (transcendental idealism plus empirical realism) will not cure this absence. All it can do in fact is to marginalise attempts to place ontological depth at the core of our understanding of how knowledge and explanation work.

Critical realism is thus opposed both to idealism and to inadequate forms of realism (like empirical realism), and to their combination. Such combinations have a tendency, just because they are inadequate and shallow forms of realism, to fall back into idealism, and to merge with idealism in different unstable mixes. This combination of inadequacy and instability is what characterises philosophies of the natural and social sciences as they reach inconsistently between alternative positions, none of which are adequate to an account of how knowledge develops. In the process, what gets squeezed is the idea of a theorised understanding of

---

6   There are, of course, important differences as well as similarities between investigations of things in the natural and social world, just as there are important differences and similarities in the things of these worlds. Bhaskar (1979) is directed at coming to terms with both kinds of difference.

7   This is one of the points on which Bhaskar and Adorno agree. Adorno also sees Kant's empirical realism as a sign of the failure of his idealist philosophy. I discuss this in the next section.

ontological stratification and depth, squeezed between an over-reliance on subjective knowledge on one side and a purely positive and empirical account of the world on the other (Bhaskar, 1994, pp 54–62).

It is these forms of idealist and empiricist knowledge, forcing out an understanding of both subjective theory construction and objective ontological depth, that Bhaskar terms 'irrealist'. The terms 'idealism' and 'irrealism' overlap but are not quite the same. Irrealist forms of philosophy include both those that are explicitly idealist, plus those which illicitly splice together forms of idealism and inadequate forms of realism, such as the 'empirical realism' Kant endorses alongside his 'transcendental idealism'. For Bhaskar, a standard irrealist pattern in philosophy is to combine idealism with a weak compensatory realism.

Irrealist compromise formations

These basic ideas were elaborated by Bhaskar in his pre-dialectical writing, but they are given strong expression in his dialectical thinking, where he speaks more explicitly about the travails of irrealism. Irrealism is specifically characterised by unstable combinations of forms of subjective idealism and empirical realism so long as it operates in the absence of depth explanatory realism. Without that, philosophy either directly endorses, or falls back into, irrealism, and the problem with irrealism is that it *lacks*. It lacks in essence the concept of ontological depth, a sense of what lies under (or traverses – 'transfactually') the fact patterns of the world, and which can be addressed through constructing theoretical knowledge. What is crucially missing is an understanding of 'the transfactuality of relatively enduring causal structures and generative mechanisms in open systems' (Bhaskar, 1994, pp 54–62).

This leads to what Bhaskar (1993, p 402) calls the 'primal squeeze' on 'empirically controlled scientific theory and natural necessity alike'. If we lack a concept of ontological stratification, of the depth and endurance of causal structures, we lose a sense of the working of causes (natural necessity) in the natural and social worlds, and in their place we substitute a fall-back reliance on either forms of idealism or forms of empirical realism or both. If we cannot grasp depth, we fall back to surface (empirical realism), and from surface, we fall back to subjective mind (idealism) and the knowing subject. The empirical, insufficiently grasped as expression of underlying cause, slides inexorably into alignment with the workings of subjective mind. Natural necessity and causal explanation get squeezed between the domains of metaphysics, where idealism dominates, and the empirical, where positivism dominates. Given that the result of the squeeze on structure and depth is the formation of unstable philosophical compromises, Western philosophy is marked by swings between idealist and inadequately realist modes of thinking.

It is this process of fall-back, of splicing forms of idealism and incomplete realism, that I now want to argue runs through Adorno's *Negative Dialectics*, first in his general account of how social knowledge operates (next section), then as it affects his account of law and the Kantian view of modern freedom (final section).

Realism and idealism in *Negative Dialectics*

This section identifies two different and conflicting views in *Negative Dialectics*, representing realist and idealist tendencies in Adorno's work. I consider them sequentially, in the process comparing and contrasting Adorno's standpoint with Bhaskar's. My argument will be that Bhaskar and Adorno have much in common, but that Adorno's strong realist dimension is not pushed far enough, and that in ultimately decisive ways, he reverts to an idealist standpoint. The predominant character of his negative dialectics thus becomes its compromise irrealist form. The realist side of his thought is summarised in his insistence on what he calls 'the preponderance of the object' (Adorno, 1973, p 183), the idealist side in his view of the dominance of 'the concept' in shaping social life. My strategy will be to highlight first the realist aspects of Adorno's philosophy, then its idealist side.

Adorno as realist: 'preponderance of the object'

Ostensibly, there is much to commend Adorno as a realist and in this section I will highlight five different aspects: Adorno's accounts of 'referential detachment', 'depth ontology', 'primal squeeze', essence and appearance, and reification. (While the terms in inverted commas are Bhaskar's rather than Adorno's, I will argue that these realist concepts do important work in *Negative Dialectics*.)

Referential detachment

Like Bhaskar, Adorno sees referential detachment as a first step in thinking. This is the recognition that the knowing subject presupposes an object to be known, distinct from itself. Bhaskar describes this as 'the detachment of the act of reference from that to which it refers', establishing 'the existential intransitivity of a being and the possibility of another reference to it'. This, he says, 'is a condition of any intelligible discourse at all' (Bhaskar, 1994, pp 52–53). In Adorno, existential intransitivity is described, less elevatedly, as the 'indissoluble something':

> There is no Being without entities. 'Something' – as a cogitatively indispensable substrate of any concept, including the concept of Being – is the utmost abstraction of the subject-matter that is not identical with thinking, an abstraction not to be abolished by any further thought process. (Adorno, 1973, p 135)

Thinking presupposes the thought, which presupposes the object which is to be thought: 'Without specific thoughts, thinking would contravene its very concept, and these thoughts instantly point to entities' (*ibid*, p 136). Thus the entwinement of (thinking) subject and (thought) object is the entwinement of epistemology and ontology[8] for Adorno, just as it is for Bhaskar. Referential detachment is a crucial starting point in any realist understanding of the nature of knowledge and its relationship to what is known.

---

8 Ontology in the sense of a realist understanding of being and the limits of the present. This is part of what Adorno (1973, Part 1) calls the 'ontological need' that he finds expressed in Heidegger, albeit in a false, sublimated, form.

Depth ontology

To separate knowledge of a thing from the thing itself is only a first step. Next comes the question how knowledge appropriates the real, and here again there is an essentially realist understanding brought to bear by Adorno. It includes a depth ontology of causes, conditions, structures and their generative mechanisms, which theoretical knowledge identifies and explains. For Adorno, as for Bhaskar, the bankruptcy of Kantian philosophy is seen in the split that allows Kant to say that 'the "transcendental idealist" is also an "empirical realist"'. This is an admission of defeat. Kant's acceptance of this point 'paralyses the specifically philosophical impulse to blast a hidden truth out from behind the idols of conventional consciousness' (Adorno, 1973, pp 72–73). The impulse to bring something hidden into view is central to Adorno's negative dialectics, just as it is caught in Bhaskar's critical realism. Recall that Bhaskar opposes both transcendental idealism and empirical realism as a pair blocking the possibility of 'hidden truths' that could be revealed by depth explanatory enquiry. It is just this impulse, indeed, that drove Bhaskar to formulate the idea of transcendental, or critical, realism. Both philosophers embrace the notion of ontological depth which knowledge strives to grasp and understand.

Primal squeeze

Again, the term is Bhaskar's, but its sense is identified in Adorno. It is the idea of a structured, transfactual world that gets squeezed between forms of subjective philosophy and shallow empirical conceptions of the real. The result is a failure to see both ontological depth and the significance of theoretical enquiry in grasping such depth. Like Bhaskar, Adorno attacks empirical realism (positivism, empiricism). Insisting on the ontological significance of the object, he nevertheless refuses to grant it the form of pure immediacy such as empiricism would suggest. Empiricism registers something of what Adorno calls 'the object's preponderance', but it does so in what he calls a 'sensualist reduction of things' (Adorno, 1973, p 187) that fails to see that the object is 'more than pure factuality'. There is more to the world in its objectivity than just the facts that paper its surface. There is also, however, more to facts, as it were, on their subjective side. The idea of a 'factuality without definitions', or of a world composed separately of 'factuality and concept' is impossible. Putting these together, knowledge involves both construction of theory and excavation of the world's depth: 'what we may call the thing itself is not positively and immediately at hand. He who wants to know it must think more, not less' (ibid, p 189), but at the same time 'the thing itself is by no means a thought product' alone (ibid, p 189). These comments about a world expressed by, but being more than, the factual, and requiring theoretical reflection to appropriate it, anticipate critical realism. Similarly, Adorno foreshadows Bhaskar's criticism of the way empirical realism folds back into idealism, through its 'sensualist reduction of things', whereby 'the thing' is falsely understood as 'immediately to hand' (ibid).

Essence and appearance

These are all philosophical points stated in the abstract. Adorno gives more concrete expression to his realism in his discussions of the relation between essence and appearance and the concept of reification. As for the former, he distances his use of these categories from Hegel's. Essence and appearance, he warns, are categories derived from 'traditional philosophy', but in Adorno's own account, 'their directional tendency is reversed'. Essence can 'no longer be hypostatised as the pure, spiritual being-in-itself'; rather it becomes what 'lies concealed beneath the façade of immediacy, of the supposed facts, and which makes the facts what they are'. Essence is 'the law of fate (*Verhängnis*) thus far obeyed by history, a law the more irresistible the more it will hide beneath the facts'. It is only recognised 'by the contradiction between what things are and what they claim to be' (Adorno, 1973, p 167). The search for 'essence' is a search for ontological depth, for what 'makes the facts what they are', for the 'fatefulness' of a historical development. It is a reaction to a flat, empiricist, conception of ontology which Adorno refers to as 'appearance'. Again, Adorno and Bhaskar's positions are close.

Critique of reification

As for reification, Adorno links the surface discussion of the concept (its 'empirical' manifestation) to the underlying socio-historical conditions which generate and explain it. He argues that 'thingness' relates not to a 'subjectively errant consciousness' but rather is 'objectively deduced from the social a priori, the exchange process' (Adorno, 1973, p 190). This process 'has real objectivity and is objectively untrue at the same time', but reification as a 'form of consciousness' is the 'reflexive form of false objectivity' and must be understood in a depth ontology underlying condition and cause:

> The trouble is with the conditions that condemn mankind to impotence and apathy ...; it is not primarily with people and with the way conditions appear to people ... Reification is an epiphenomenon. (*Ibid*, p 190)

To summarise, these comments reflect an ontological understanding in which depth explanation of a stratified world is sought, the need for theory as the means to explain that world is argued for, and a critique of irrealism is begun. A convincing case can be made for seeing Adorno as a critical realist *avant la lettre*. However, that is not the whole story. There are other aspects of Adorno's thought in which his realism is supplemented by strongly irrealist tendencies, to which I now turn.

Adorno as idealist: predominance of the concept

In the positions we have considered, Adorno has endorsed a realist ontology as the basis for understanding the human world and knowledge of it. However, he does not sustain it, and this is seen in two crucial areas. First, it is seen in his further discussion of the logic of scientific explanation where he explains the process of theory building in terms of a weak subjective notion of the 'constellation'. Here he falls back (with qualification) to a Weberian neo-Kantian methodology to explain the relationship between concepts and history. Secondly, it is seen in the idealist trap that he sets for himself at the end of *Negative Dialectics* in terms of his understanding of the impasse in which critique finds itself. I will discuss these two points in three subsections dealing with: the role of the 'constellation' in theory building and explanation; Adorno's use of Weber as the key exemplar of constellational thinking; and the ultimate impasse in his work concerning the possibility of critique. In these arguments, Adorno's ability to sustain the standpoint of referential detachment or of a depth ontology is called into question. His own insistence on the 'preponderance of the object' (Adorno, 1973, p 183) is undercut by a reversion to the subjectivity of the concept. He himself falls back to idealism, and becomes a victim of his own 'primal squeeze'.

Constellations and theory building

Adorno has argued for an ontology of structures and depth which it is the task of knowledge to grasp, to 'blast a hidden truth out from behind the idols of conventional consciousness'. How is this to be achieved? The nub of his position on the process of scientific explanation concerns the idea of a 'constellation' within which subjective concepts operate, and which Adorno wants to represent as linking such concepts to 'the object' of knowledge. However, there is an obvious problem for Adorno in establishing such a linkage if we recall the central blocking role that concepts play in his philosophy. Concepts are in this view the devices by which 'identity thinking' operates. They are part of a 'classifying procedure' that obstructs knowledge of the object. This is a fundamental element in his thought: that we are trapped by conceptual thinking never to see what lies beyond our concepts, which serve to exclude the truth of things. Now, however, a tension: we have also seen that Adorno believes in referential detachment. This involves the existence of an objective world beyond our subjective concepts, which our concepts explain, and which is not reducible to them. How can he reconcile his belief that concepts explain the objective world with the view that they block that world from us? Adorno's answer to this problem is the idea of the constellation. As well as their blocking role, concepts can 'enter into a constellation [… which] illuminates the specific side of the object'. Constellations of concepts 'represent from without what the concept has cut away within'. They gather 'around the object of cognition' and in so doing, they 'potentially determine the object's interior': they 'attain in thinking what was necessarily excised from thinking' (Adorno, 1973, p 162). While the concept blocks, concepts in constellation illumine.

This move against the blocking power of the concept is surely too easy. The concept by itself cannot but formalise, exclude, freeze, identify, but, it transpires, all that is necessary is that concepts be grouped together and the problems of identity thinking evaporate before the explanatory power of the constellation. What the concept alone actively denies, the combination of concepts actively promotes. The constellation may be made up of subjective concepts involving identity thinking, but this does not stop it revealing the objective conditions blocked by such thinking. Thinking constellationally involves being aware that 'something individual is objective as sedimented history', that is understanding its ontological depth as real history. Yet, the constellation is also the group of concepts by which the thing is identified and its truth obscured. In order to reconcile these irreconcilable positions, the process of scientific enquiry assumes a mysterious, blind aspect:

> Becoming aware of the constellation in which a thing stands is tantamount to deciphering the constellation which … it bears within it … Cognition of the object in its constellation is cognition of the process stored in the object. As a constellation, theoretical thought circles the concept it would like to unseal, hoping (*hoffend*) that it might fly open like the lock of a well-guarded safe-deposit box: in response, not to a single key or a single number, but to a combination of numbers. (*Ibid*, p 163)

To say that structured conceptual (theoretical) investigations can map the structures of the world is a reasonable claim from a realist standpoint. But if the constellation-in-thought really deciphers the constellation-in-the-object, why is the problem of the concept of identity thinking so fundamental for Adorno, as it plainly is? In addition, if the constellation-in-thought performs the function of deciphering reality, why only the 'hope' that the lock might fly open, rather than the knowledge that, knowing the code, it will? Either the constellation-in-thought reflects the problems of individual concepts or it is a genuine tool for scientific enquiry and method. It is hard to see that it can be both, but Adorno's twin accounts of identity thinking and the need for real historical knowledge establish a real tension in his negative dialectics.

Given the importance of the critique of identity thinking to Adorno, sustaining the emphasis on real historical discovery becomes difficult, and it is the first view that ultimately prevails. Adorno, however, still wants some sense of how scientific knowledge – through concepts – is possible. The concept has to play a double and contradictory role in his thought, to which the idea of the constellation purports to be a solution. What emerges here, however, is a strong idealist tendency in the negative dialectics, which posits a fundamental gap between subjective concept and objective world. Adorno's deployment of the notion of the constellation is a means of reconciling the 'explicit idealism' of his idea of the concept with the 'implicit realism' which wants to affirm the scientific value of concepts, and which informs all the positions discussed in the previous section. The tension around the constellation reveals both tendencies at play in his work.

Weber versus Marx

Pursuing this conception of the constellation, it is hard to see how it can reflect the problems of surface and depth, essence and appearance and other realist distinctions with which Adorno otherwise works. If concepts represent 'surface', or appearance – what thinking obscures – then their combination can also only reflect surface. To 'constellate' surface appearances is not to achieve depth. That there is a problem here is indicated by the example of constellational thinking he gives. Despite his obvious substantive and methodological debts to Marx, seen in the discussion of essence and appearance, in the role of commodity exchange in positing reification, and generally in the objective history of concepts, it is Max Weber's neo-Kantian ideal-typical method that Adorno uses to illustrate constellational thinking. Adorno acknowledges that Weber was of 'positivistic bent' and also a 'subjectivist' in epistemology (ie, he embodied aspects of both subjective idealism and empirical realism), but he holds that Weber understood ideal types as 'aids in approaching the object'. While Weber was a 'nominalist' in his use of concepts, Adorno argues that 'some of the nature of the thing will come through' in his sociology. Adorno applauds Weber because he 'explicitly rejected the delimiting procedure of definition ... and asked instead that sociological concepts be "gradually composed" from "individual parts to be taken from historical reality"'. Weber's method of 'composing' concepts may look 'only at the subjective side, at cognitive procedure', but the 'subjectively created context – the "constellation" – becomes readable as sign of objectivity' (Adorno, 1973, p 165).

My aim here is not to deny the validity of Adorno's assessment of Weber, but to point to the limited nature of the Weberian position from a realist standpoint. One can agree that Weber's ideal-type model does indeed represent an advance in terms of its insistence on building concepts out of historical material. However, it is also seriously limited by its failure to contemplate notions of generative mechanism, or underlying cause and structure, those crucial elements which make up a structural depth ontology. In short it does not look for causal structure and depth, though it may hint at such things, and is ultimately ontologically shallow. As Bhaskar (1979, p 39) puts it, it is 'constrained by [a] continuing commitment to an empiricist ontology'. Adorno's use of Weber to exemplify the constellation thus raises the question why he ignores Marx at this point, when he uses him so frequently for his substantive theoretical understanding. Here is Bhaskar's critical realist comparison of Marx's methodology with that of Weber: whereas Weber is caught between empiricism and idealism, Marx's approach:

> is not a one-sided accentuation in thought of an equivalent aspect of an undifferentiated empirical reality, but an attempt to grasp what is really accentuated (or, as it were, lop-sided) in reality; and its focus is causal, not taxonomic. (*Ibid*, p 167)

In remaining, despite reservations, at the level of Weber's ideal-typical method, Adorno confirms the counter-tendency to his own realism. In the constellation, thinking and explanation are not rooted in the structured nature of things, but remain at the level of concepts. Subjective (conceptual) thinking is given primacy here, despite Adorno's conflicting insistence elsewhere in *Negative Dialectics* on the 'preponderance of the object'.

Impasse in negative dialectics

At the most fundamental level, and against the grain of the depth realism in his work, Adorno's theory of knowledge is unable to go beyond an empiricist conception of reality. His constellational theory is a 'flat' theory of the structure of concepts and how they map onto reality. This leads to a revindication of idealist thought, for the failure to think ontological depth ultimately supports reversion to subjective, conceptual thinking. This is seen in the famous sense of impasse that characterises the final part of *Negative Dialectics*. Adorno (1973, p 145) had said that to 'criticise … immanently means to criticise … from outside as well' and that the 'possibility of internal immersion requires … externality' (*ibid*, p 163). He insists on the 'preponderance of the object' and the 'indissoluble something' as the basis for understanding the problems of conceptual thinking. However, in the end, Adorno acknowledges the trap laid by his idealist view of the concept: that there can be no externality or outside. Dialectics accordingly 'is obliged to make a final move … it must now turn even against itself'. 'Contrary to its own tendency,' critique must 'remain within the medium of the concept' and 'can reach no further than [the] claim of identity' (*ibid*, p 406). From being a way of reaching beyond the concept, dialectics becomes involuted and self-devouring. The idea of dialectics ruthlessly criticising itself certainly has a pleasingly radical sound to it, and it is indeed true that dialectics must remain self-critical. However, Adorno's acknowledgment that it is impossible to go beyond the concept is the price exacted by his irrealism. It turns dialectics into a self-defeating proposition:

> Dialectics is the self-consciousness of the objective context of delusion; it does not mean to have escaped from that context. Its objective goal is to break out of the context from within. (*Ibid*, p 406)

This is paradox dressed up as dialectics. How can dialectics be the consciousness of the 'objective context' if it has not in some way 'escaped'? How can it possess an 'objective' goal, if it is located essentially 'within'? Dialectics in this contradictory framework has to be both hermetically caught within the realm of the concept and able to break out of it. It is both subjective awareness that cannot go beyond the concept and a view of its objective context. It is knowledge only of the concept and knowledge of it as delusion. It is both required to remain within identity and to go beyond it. Adorno does not explain how these paradoxical requirements are to be sustained. Ultimately *Negative Dialectics* is reduced to incoherence.

Why should this be so? My argument is that this is the result of the conflict between realist and idealist tendencies in Adorno's thought. The problem is that the subjectivist problematic of the concept, even when constellationalised, is sustained. Adorno himself fails to 'break out' from the concept, yet this is precisely what is required by his substantive positions on 'referential detachment', the 'preponderance of the object', a 'depth ontology', the 'primal squeeze' in philosophy, the realist significance of essence and appearance, the critique of reification, and the references to real historical development throughout the text. A conception of a stratified, depth ontology is required in order to reposition subject and concept fully in the subject-object dialectic. Adorno knows this but is blocked[9] from theorising it. He insists in principle upon the 'preponderance of the object' over the subject, he insists on the historical understanding of essence, and the link between philosophical form (identity thinking) and social and historical practice. However, his theory of knowledge and being reflects a limit in his philosophy, with the result that his dialectics find their ultimate structure in their own dilemmatic antinomy, an unresolved dialectic of the internal and the external, the subject and the object, the real and the ideal. Adorno's implicit realism, then, does not go far enough in its attack on the idealism and consequent irrealism that ultimately govern *Negative Dialectics*.

We have now identified a conflict between realist and idealist tendencies in Adorno's thought. Ultimately, the latter gets the better of things, making negative dialectics an uneasy compromise formation, ensuring its tense and contradictory forms and its ultimate impasse. I now want to move on to consider the significance of this instability, this fall back into irrealism, for Adorno's account of Kantian freedom and the juridical under modern conditions with which we started.

Understanding modern freedom: realism and idealism in Adorno's three views

When discussing Kant, human freedom and its modern juridical forms, Adorno was divided between, first, a negative view subsuming these under the terms of his critique of identity thinking; secondly, a positive reaction against his own

---

9 Adorno's own term (1973, pp 384–90) to denote a self-imposed limit, particularly in the Kantian philosophy.

identitarian critique in qualified defence of liberal terms; and, thirdly, a view of the way originary human freedom underlay, and was expressed inchoately in, modern social forms. This third view was expressed contradictorily in both ahistorical and historical terms. How are we to understand these different views, and achieve a sense of the overall import of Adorno's position?

The initial problem is to consider the contradiction between seeing juridical freedom as a form of violence and as a defence against violence. At a political level, the antinomialism in the first two views of freedom probably stems from a conflict between the dominant critique of identity thinking in his philosophy and his reflection on the differences between liberal modernity and fascism. How could Adorno, who lived through the experience of Nazi Germany, not reflect on the differences between liberal capitalism and fascism? The identitarian critique comes uncomfortably close to failing to distinguish the different forms of political life under capitalism. However, the conflict between the critique and the liberal recoil against it only makes prominent the antinomy immanent in his argument, it does not create it. Underlying these two approaches was a third which sought to link discussion of freedom to a basic impulse of the human condition. On the nature of this, Adorno remained ambivalent. In places, he described it as pre-temporal and pre-social, something lost to humankind but still somehow echoing in its practices. In other places, he linked it to the nature of human species being as it has evolved socially and historically. He describes the impulse to freedom as emerging in limited and attenuated forms under modern social conditions. In this final section, I will consider the implication of this ambiguity in Adorno's third view of freedom. I will link it to the tension between realist and irrealist standpoints in his philosophy, and argue that we best understand the relationship between his three views of freedom if we adopt the realist standpoint that is present but incomplete in his work.

Pre-temporal or historical freedom?

Let us first consider the consequence of linking the negative and positive views of freedom in the first two approaches to the third in either its historical or its ahistorical form. Whether taken historically or pre-temporally, the impulse to freedom has an inchoate quality. It lacks completion, lurking as a trace element that is experienced but not given proper expression within modern conceptions. In the pre-temporal view, this inchoateness is doubled by the mysterious absence of a ground from which such freedom could emerge. All that we know is that true freedom echoes from a time before time, before society, where the 'untamed impulse' resides. When was this time, and how was it possible? It is not at all clear that any plausible answer could be given to such questions. In the historical view, in contrast, the mystery of freedom is not so mysterious, for its inchoateness in the present is understood within the social and historical development of human species being. Both its emergence and its limited form are accounted for by the nature of subject-object relations under modern social and economic conditions. While modern freedom retains its latency and partiality, this can be explained according to an historical analysis of its structural emergence under modern social conditions, in terms of an historico-anthropological account of human natural and social evolution. The freedom expressed in modern juridical forms remains blurred and incomplete, but its ground of existence does not, and it owes nothing to a questionable metaphysics of the pre-temporal.

This difference between the two views of the underlying nature of freedom is important because it reflects the conflict between realism and idealism in Adorno's work, explored in the middle sections of this chapter. The pre-temporal view is aligned to the idealist argument that it is impossible to overcome the dominance of the concept. If identity thinking subsumes all thinking and practice within its ambit, then any genuine moment of freedom (however unformed) *must* be one of pure origin, a protean moment or element precedent to the social and historical first steps of the species. As soon as one moves into the social and temporal, one moves into language and therefore the prison house of concepts. Any element of social positivity involves bringing human life into the realm of the historical, and therefore subsumptively within identity-thinking and under the concept. Adorno's lengthy critique of Heidegger's metaphysics makes it clear that he is alert to the problems of an originary moment (Adorno, 1973, Part 1). However, he himself falls prey to it, albeit in his characteristically allusive fashion, with his idea of pre-temporal freedom. This idea fits with the idealist conception of the inescapability of the subsumption of being to thought. If thinking predominates, then the concept has priority and all conceptions of freedom must be brought under the identitarian critique. If concepts dominate human being and act repressively towards it, where could Adorno find the basis for an underlying genuine, if fragile, freedom save in echoes from a time before concepts? In providing such a moment, Adorno's idealist reliance on the identitarian critique forces him to have recourse to the kind of foundational metaphysics he otherwise condemns.

In contrast to the idealist side of Adorno's philosophy, the discussion of an underlying, emergent, freedom that is consistent with the historical development of human being under given social relations reflects the realist tendency in *Negative Dialectics*. This finds its place in all those aspects of his approach discussed in the first half of the third section above: arguments for referential detachment and for a depth explanatory realism, the identification of the problem of primal squeeze, the recasting of the relationship between essence and appearance, the critique of reification, the insistence on the 'preponderance of the object'. It is present in his consistent linking of historical forms and social relations to forms of thought. All these elements are reflected in a view of a latent potential for human freedom, glimpsed 'through a glass darkly' in its actually existing forms under modern social conditions. Even though he did not sustain it, his arguments for the social, historical and anthropic bases of the pulse of freedom under modern conditions express the depth realism that lies within *Negative Dialectics*. However, they remain in conflict with an ultimately dominant idealist insistence on the supremacy of the concept (in effect, the 'preponderance of the subject') that coexists there, and which is given expression in the pre-temporal conception of the pulse to freedom.

Relating the three views of freedom

The reason for labouring the conflict between idealism and realism in Adorno's philosophy relates to the question how we may best bring together his three views of freedom: the identitarian critique, the liberal reaction, and the underlying view (in what we now see to be its realist and idealist forms). If we take the antinomy of freedom represented by the first two opposing views, we need some way of understanding how these views could be held together in Adorno's account. The third underlying view of freedom is potentially the way to move towards a more complete understanding of the way freedom works under modern conditions. However, this is so only if we adopt the realist, historical approach in *Negative Dialectics*, eschewing the idealist, pre-temporal one.

If the underlying impulse to freedom is given an idealist, pre-temporal cast, it cannot bring the first two views into a cogent relation with each other. If the underlying freedom represented in the 'jolt', the 'impulse', the 'flash of light', is simply an echo from a time before time, it can only be an 'accidental' addendum to modern antinomial practices. In themselves, these would have to be seen, as the identitarian critique stipulates, as devoted entirely to the predominance of subsumptive logic and identity, to unfreedom. Because of the dominance of identity and its exclusion of everything beyond it, there would be no ground, other than that of a supplementary, unwarranted assertion, on which to base anything positive within the modern conception of freedom. There is no way of linking the traces of a 'lost' freedom in a time before time to a valued temporal freedom today. Were this possible, Adorno would have to limit the writ of the concept in his identitarian critique, which means giving the critique up. He cannot say that the positive aspects of modern freedom in his second view embody the pre-temporal pulse to freedom without undermining the negative critique in his first view. In aligning a pre-temporal pulse of freedom to freedom within the modern juridical complex, he would have to concede that his argument concerning identitarian logic is one-sided and incomplete. At the same time, politically, it would be foolish and irresponsible for one who lived through the Nazi period to deny the validity of liberal forms of freedom, limited though they may be.

The point is that this political need cannot be reflected in Adorno's philosophy so long as he maintains the idealist insistence on the scope of identity thinking expressed in his first negative view of modern freedom. That view cannot explain an intrinsic, although troubled, link between freedoms past and present, and would therefore need to resort to an extraneous sense of 'the political' on which to base itself. It cannot theorise the importance of modern freedom, limited though it may be, as brought out in Adorno's second, positive view.

By contrast, deploying the realist side of Adorno makes it possible to hold both the identitarian critique and the qualified defence of liberal forms within the juridical complex together in a dialectically fuller perspective. To put it shortly, it is of the essence of freedom in its various modern forms, to which Kant gave philosophical expression, that it, first, embodies limited forms of freedom, and that, secondly, these forms are also in fundamental ways turned into their opposite, forms of oppression, under modern conditions. These are the contradictory legal effects of modern subject-object relations. Thus, the freedom to exchange becomes the necessity to sell one's labour; the respect for individual responsibility becomes the repression of state punishment. However, at the same time, the declarations of freedom retain their importance as a limited means of opposing arrogatory power. They permit a level of *expression* of the interests of individuals, as well as establishing a means for their *repression* (see further Norrie, 1993a, 2001b, Chapter 11).

The problem with modern (bourgeois) society in this view is neither that it excludes all freedom (the negative identitarian critique) nor that it directly embodies freedom (the second, positive, view: the view of liberalism). Rather, it is that modernity delivers freedom in a limited and alienated way. Freedom is denied in the moment and in the forms in which it is expressed, although expressed it still is. Kantian theory, when approached critically and read for its absences as well as for what it says, is the most sophisticated philosophical statement of this position. 'Freedom,' says Adorno, 'is a moment [...] not to be isolated, and for the time being it is never more than an instant of spontaneity, a historical node, the road to which is blocked under present conditions' (Adorno, 1973, p 219). This is a situation where Kantian subjective freedom, which has its own points of purchase on the world, turns into its opposite because subjective freedom is shaped by the objective world of which it is a part. A constant theme of *Negative Dialectics*, on its realist side, is what Adorno calls the 'preponderance of the object', the insistence on reading the subjective within the objective:

> In ourselves ... we discover neither a positive freedom nor a positive unfreedom. We conceive both in their relation to extra-mental things: freedom as a polemical counter-image to the suffering brought on by social coercion; unfreedom as that coercion's image ... Whether or not there is autonomy depends upon its adversary and antithesis, on the object which either grants or denies autonomy of the subject. (*Ibid*, p 223)

However, what is expressed as a limited freedom under modern conditions, for all its problems, also participates in something deeper, a social and historical evolution of the quality of being human. Such a vision of the human condition, latent and unfulfilled, speaks through the limits of the existing forms in which freedom is expressed. What lies underneath those forms and is signalled by their presence is the promise of a real autonomy. This presses at the limits of what is expressed or understood as actually existing autonomy, as something inchoate within the present: something already there, but also still 'to come'.

Human freedom is expressed in modern Kantian accounts of the free subject, but only in a partial way. Its underlying quality, expressed in, and turned against itself through, modern social relations is brilliantly caught by Adorno's complex and conflicted account of negative dialectics. A realist reading of the potential for human freedom in its socio-historical contexts brings out Adorno's argument because it links the underlying impulse to freedom within modern society to an appraisal of its contradictory and limited forms in the here and now. An idealist reading to the contrary leaves us with a sense of the contradictions in modern forms of freedom, but no understanding of what holds these conflicts together. In resorting to a mystical past that could not in truth be known in the present, it only adds to the mystification that already surrounds the subject.

Pushing Adorno's 'implicit realism' against the 'explicit idealism' of his identitarian critique brings out the grounded historicity of the dilemmas and incompleteness of modern freedom. It helps us to see how freedom 'lies' in a double sense under modern conditions. First, it lies in a structural and objective sense within an anthropo-historical context that shapes and forms the possibilities for freedom available to human beings under particular social conditions. Secondly, it lies in the different subjective sense that it misstates the nature and limits of human freedom. Read through a realist lens, Adorno's negative dialectic of law sheds brilliant light on how far humanity has travelled, and how far it still has to go, in its pursuit of freedom.

Chapter 10
Law and the Beautiful Soul

Bliss was it in that dawn to be alive ...
When reason seemed the most to assert her rights,
When most intent on making of herself
A prime Enchantress ...
Not favoured spots alone, but the whole earth,
The beauty wore of promise ... (Wordsworth)

The type of spiritual life cultivated by the Moravians ...
and popular with sentimentalists in Hegel's day. (Hegel, 1952, p 345)

Introduction

This chapter is about Hegel, the moral expressivism of the Enlightenment, and the nature of law. It takes as its focus Hegel's diverging analyses of the Beautiful Soul[1] in his early and mature work, arguing that the transition from the former to the latter involves a move to legitimate modern law. In doing so, something important is lost, and the loss can be briefly described by contrasting my two prefatory quotations. Wordsworth's famous lines on the French Revolution ('As it Appeared to Enthusiasts at its Commencement') express the full idea of the Beautiful Soul as it was born in the time of the revolutionary Enlightenment, in its promise to remake the world in the image of enlightened reason. While the first line has become something of a cliché, to be treated ironically as romantic naivety, it is worth recalling the moral passion, conviction and hope for a better world it reflects. The second quotation is TM Knox's summation of the Beautiful Soul as it is treated in Hegel's *Philosophy of Right* (1821) and his earlier *Phenomenology of Spirit* (1807). From being a spirit to move the times, the Beautiful Soul is forced, in a very short period of time, into a by no means exalted Moravian exile. What caused this transition in its fortunes, what does it tell us about Hegel, and what about the nature of modern law? These questions are asked as we move from a discussion of the idea of moral expressivity to Hegel, and thence to law. This is the direction of the chapter as a whole, and is developed as an outline argument in the rest of this section. Let us take things one step at a time: moral expressivism, Hegel, law.

---

1   For a discussion of the general importance of the Beautiful Soul in 18th century aesthetic morality, see Norton, 1995, which describes Hegel's changing treatment of the figure and how he came to put an end to its hundred year history. My original interest was triggered by the discussion in Bhaskar's *Plato Etc* (1994, pp 1–7, 116–19). The essay shares some themes with Gillian Rose's *Hegel Contra Sociology* (1981), probably the most prominent recent critical discussion of the topic. In particular, I share the sense of an 'unfinished' Hegel (*ibid*, p 203) linked to the property form in modern liberal society. In the penultimate section, I argue like Rose (*ibid*, p 184) for a legacy of conflicted theory which Hegel bequeathed to modernity. I do not, however, discuss Rose's work here. On the early Hegel, see Lukacs, 1975; Taylor, 1975; Pinkard, 2000; Plant, 1983.

Moral expressivism

Charles Taylor, whose account I initially follow, has written that it 'is evident that the expressivist conception of man is of more than merely historical interest' (Taylor, 1975, p 29). The expressivist approach to morality involved a strong belief in the perfectibility of human being. It stressed a sense of the self-unfolding of individual human life, at ease with itself, with nature and with a moral community. Taylor describes it as entailing an anthropology of free expression and discovery by each individual of their uniqueness: 'man comes to know himself by expressing and hence clarifying what he is and recognising himself in this expression' (*ibid*, p 17). This flowering from within of the qualities of individual life is at the same time a 'passionate demand for unity and wholeness' (*ibid*, p 23) through overcoming the modern dichotomies of mind and body, reason and feeling, desire and calculation. It insists on freedom not in terms of autonomy from interference, but in terms of authentic self-expression, an awareness of self in communion with both nature and other human beings. Moral expressivism 'responds with dismay and horror to the Enlightenment vision of society made up of atomistic, morally self-sufficient subjects who enter into external relations with each other' (*ibid*, p 28). It seeks a 'deeper bond of felt unity which will unite sympathy between men with their highest self-feeling'. Such self-feeling is 'woven into community life rather than remaining the preserve of individuals' (*ibid*). This view was popular in Germany in the last decades of the 18th century. Its leading thinkers included Herder, Goethe, Schiller and the poet Hölderlin. Hölderlin was an old college friend of Hegel's, and he was to be a strong influence on the young Hegel, coming to philosophical life in the 1790s. However, alongside this personal link, moral expressivism was part of the spirit of the times. It reflected the optimism that was unleashed by the French Revolution as well as a reaction against the narrow materialist ideology that had preceded it. There was a sense of the possibility of changing the world radically, of overcoming the negativity and deathly quality of the present in favour of a future of self-actualisation, harmony and community.

Moral realism and ethical naturalism

What is the nature of such a moral argument? I want to take it in two different ways: as (i) a direct ethical demand for a state of moral completeness; and (ii) as an emergent social and historical expression of the promise of the modern world and the forms of moral development of which it was believed to be capable. Both the intrinsically moral and the socio-historical points are important. The first involves a form of *moral realism*: a claim about the real moral possibilities available for human being. It is a deontological claim in the same way as Kant's philosophy is deontological. There is a sense of what morally ought to be the case, but the claim is the more radical for surpassing Kantian notions of reason and duty. Moral expressivism was essentially critical of Kant for his abstract and monadic moralism and his failure to think widely enough about the nature of ethical being. Kantianism was a barrier to moral completion from the expressivist standpoint, but moral expressivism maintained a strong ethical sense of what the world ought to become. The second involves a form of *ethical naturalism*: a descriptive-explanatory claim about the way in which moral feelings come into being. Against deontologists, ethical naturalists see morality in terms of how it expresses the way human beings are. Thus, Adam Smith could write of the moral instincts in his 'Theory of the moral sentiments' in terms of a natural sympathy amongst human beings to put themselves in the place of each other. Moral realism is concerned with the intrinsic ethical status of moral concepts, ethical naturalism is concerned with explaining how such concepts come about.[2]

The idea of ethical naturalism is important in order to relate the emergence of a moral standpoint to a particular historical moment, as emergent from a specific social context. While ethical naturalism has lent itself to individual psychologistic accounts of moral feelings (as in the case of Smith), it can also be given a strong social and historical reading. For example, Kathryn Dean argues that in what she terms the early bourgeois period, roughly when Hegel became a philosopher, a new form of public-spirited 'worldliness' became possible. This took the form of a belief in the possibility of a new moral world with a genuinely unifying public sphere and an ethical sense of community (*sensus communis*). It involved 'a worldly form of strongly individuated subjectivity' (Dean, 2003, p 57). Such a world would be one envisaged without the splits and oppositions that would later pervade the actually existing world of modern capitalism. Dean distinguishes between an early bourgeois mentality in the late 18th century and a completed capitalist mentality in the 19th. The latter period pursues the processes of economic development already present in the former, but inaugurates a more confined moral viewpoint in which the idea of *sensus communis* and a strong commitment to disinterested public spiritedness is under threat and may be lost.

Her argument can only be sketched here,[3] but it is important because it develops a sociological and historical dimension to ethical naturalism. I want to start with the idea of an historically and socially grounded, emergent, expressive ethical way of seeing the world, a promise of the way the world could be as real historical event and as imagined possibility. A moral charge was set loose in modernity by Enlightenment and revolution, even if it was one that was not redeemed in the ensuing historical development. Inherent in this is a view of the way in which the real moral categories of the western world are developed out of and shaped by the underlying social relations of which they are a part. It is in the tension between an historically emergent demand for human perfectibility and freedom (the ideal moral pulse or charge of the Enlightenment) and the actual historical relations as they developed from the period of revolutionary change into the modern capitalist world that the modern moral, and ultimately legal, cloth is cut. We can see this

---

2 The distinction between moral realism and ethical naturalism is drawn from Bhaskar (1993). Although I draw the two terms here as contrasting, ultimately, like Bhaskar, I see them as complementary. Louis Irwin explains the pair of concepts as follows: 'Ethical naturalism is at the level of moral rules designed to guide actions, and these change over time with changes in our ethical concepts (for example, "slave", "person"). Underlying these is a moral realism which grounds our ethics and which can be rationally discovered via analysis of the changing nature of ourselves, our needs, and our society … It is moral realism that prevents ethical naturalism from being an arbitrary matter internal to a culture.' See http://philosophy.consumercide.com/irwin-bhaskar.html; my thanks to Bill Bowring for drawing this to my attention. On the moral realist claim of a critical realist ethics, see above, Chapter 8, and Hostettler and Norrie, 2003.

3 Dean's book synthesises writings exploring the social and historical underpinnings of modern subjectivity as well as its psychoanalytical explanation. She draws imaginatively on the early Habermas, Norbert Elias, and Hannah Arendt as well as Freud and Lacan.

tension, I shall argue, articulated in Hegel's philosophy, in particular in his changing account of the Beautiful Soul, and then in his account of law and the legal subject.

Hegel

I have already mentioned Hegel's links to moral expressivism, his friendship with Hölderlin, his youthful enthusiasm for the French Revolution. This enthusiasm (and its waning) can be read and charted in his philosophy via the concept of the 'Beautiful Soul' and its counterpart, the 'Unhappy Consciousness'. The beautiful soul was an idea with general currency in Germany in Hegel's time. It is introduced into Hegel's thinking in one of his early theological writings, an essay called 'The Spirit of Christianity and its Fate', written about 1799. This is a pivotal work for developing an expressive moral theory for modern society, and its use of the Beautiful Soul is linked in particular with the example of Jesus. As a Beautiful Soul, Jesus can find no moral home with his people. He must deal with this either by giving up beauty of soul and surrendering, like them, to the baseness of the actual world, or by withdrawing from them, and in so doing challenging their way of life. This leads to a state of isolation and withdrawal, which is the state of unhappy consciousness that accompanies beauty of soul. As a result, Jesus ends up an outsider, and his fate as a Beautiful Soul is to be crucified.

Taylor describes Hegel's use of the Beautiful Soul in this and his other early theological writings as 'basically the same' as in his later treatment in the *Phenomenology*, a work which was published in 1807, only eight years or so later (Taylor, 1975, p 62). However, there is quite a marked difference in approach between the two treatments. While there is a critical edge to Hegel's treatment of Jesus in the early essay, there is also a strong sense of his moral rectitude and tragic fate, a fate that was to have an epochal effect upon the Christian church thereafter.[4] In the *Phenomenology*, by contrast, the Beautiful Soul is treated much more negatively, as a form of failed moral being in the world. There is a difference here, and one that I shall argue is important for thinking about the nature of modern moral experience. In particular, I will suggest that the tension between a radical demand for moral perfectibility and a reconciliation with actually existing moral relations based upon private property and capitalism informs the change in Hegel's account of the Beautiful Soul. The move from ambivalence to thorough negativity reflects Hegel's shifting view. What happened to Hegel's thinking between the early theological writings and the *Phenomenology* reflects something of the historical change Dean charts in the development of modern bourgeois society. The change in Hegel's approach to the Beautiful Soul is reflected in his developing account of law for it transpires that the turn against the Beautiful Soul is a turn towards the forms embodied in modern law such as private property, exchange relations and legal subjectivity. This move, I then argue, has an importance that goes beyond Hegel himself, and this relates to the nature of modern law.

---

4 Taylor notes Hegel's ambivalence to Jesus in the early essay, which foreshadows the treatment in the *Phenomenology*. This is true, though my argument is that the later treatment reveals a much more decisively negative attitude. Cf Norton (1995, pp 264–82). One could say that in the early writings, the Beautiful Soul becomes through force of circumstances an Unhappy Consciousness, whereas in the *Phenomenology*, to be a Beautiful Soul is in itself to be an Unhappy Consciousness.

The nature of law

The main aim of this chapter is to chart the life and death of the Beautiful Soul in Hegel's philosophy and its significance for his account of modern institutions such as law. A secondary aim is to indicate, albeit briefly, what the broader significance of Hegel's shifting accounts might be for law and critical legal method. My starting point, drawing on my previous work, is the claim that law is persistently antinomial in its forms. Legal concepts generally hunt in pairs, in the sense that law is essentially dichotomous. It consists of a series of antinomies. There are, first, antinomies which establish law itself: the 'ideal' and the 'actual', the 'internal' and the 'external', the 'positive' and the 'moral', the 'formal' and the 'informal', 'autonomy' and 'heteronomy', the 'legal' and the 'popular' (see above, Chapters 2–4; Norrie, 1998b). Secondly, there are antinomies which seek to establish the workings of a particular area of law. In criminal justice, for example, these would include the 'individual' and the 'community' (or the 'social'), the 'criminal' and the 'victim', 'form' and 'content' (or 'substance'), the 'universal' and the 'particular' (see above, Chapters 4–7; Norrie, 2000). Thirdly, there are specifically legal antinomies, as it were transmitted inwards from those already mentioned. In criminal law, these would include 'character' and 'capacity', 'motive' and 'intention', the 'subjective' and the 'objective', the 'honest' and the 'reasonable', the 'orthodox subjectivist' and the 'morally contextualist', the 'direct' and the 'indirect', 'foresight' and 'foreseeability'.[5]

I will suggest that what underlies the difference in treatment of the Beautiful Soul in Hegel's theological writings and his *Phenomenology* is connected with the nature of law as an antinomial discourse. Law as a modern social and historical phenomenon has certain central characteristics. Hegel is an archetypal modern social, political and legal philosopher, and as such, what he has to say in theory has something important to tell us about legal forms and practice. His handling of the problem of the Beautiful Soul involves wrestling with a grounding antinomy: the relationship between the ideal (the moral charge of Enlightenment and revolution) and the actual (actually existing social relations). In the early theological writings, this antinomy lies raw, open and unresolved, its existence linked to the clash between an ideal moral standpoint and emergent modern social institutions such as private property. The change in Hegel's attitude to the Beautiful Soul in the *Phenomenology* stems from the attempt to reconcile this antinomy. However, the reconciliation is only achieved superficially, so that the antinomy remains in place, and returns to haunt Hegel in his later work, in particular, the *Philosophy of Right*. A focal point for the attempted resolution of antinomy is the idea of the individual moral-legal subject whose recognition leads to the marginalisation of the Beautiful Soul. This subject's universality is supposed to reconcile the ideal and the actual, and it is this focus that provides the connection with law. The subject in legal discourse is modernity's attempt to reconcile the ideal and the actual, and its failure to achieve this leaves us – in the law, as in Hegel's philosophy of law – with a world rippling with antinomy. I will return to this argument briefly after a close examination of Hegel's changing treatment of the Beautiful Soul and what it signals for his philosophy of law.

---

5   For detailed discussion of antinomies in particular areas of law, see above, Chapters 4, 5 and 7; Norrie, 1999, 2001a and 1993a, 2001b.

Travels and travails of a Beautiful Soul

In this section, I contrast Hegel's early writings with his first mature work, the *Phenomenology*, on the Beautiful Soul. My argument will be that the later negative and marginalising treatment reflects Hegel's attempt to reconcile (and thereby to control) the inchoate, radical impulse of Enlightenment thinking (which becomes 'the ideal') with the actually existing/developing social relations and institutions of Western society (which becomes 'the actual').

The early theological writings

In his early theological writings, Hegel developed the kind of expressive morality described by Taylor in the previous section. He gave an account of the morally good as entailing non-alienated human being and relations within nature. This involved a sense of a morally expressive unity. The idea was for a whole, integrated life in which human beings were at one with themselves and each other. The age was one of human division and repression, and Hegel's vision was that human beings should not be ruled by dead formulae, but by the immediate spontaneity of *agape*, brotherly and reasonable love, as seen in the original teachings of Jesus. Thus what was needed in contemporary Germany was a moral regeneration that would combine autonomous Enlightenment reason, a recreation of what was best in the Greek spirit, and a recovery of the pure teachings of Jesus.

Hegel's position had strong implications for the moral judgment of contemporary religion, law, and institutions such as private property. Hegel regarded Christianity as a 'positive' religion, meaning one that had fallen away from the original teachings of Jesus. It had ceased to be a religion that expressed spontaneous love and morally expressive unity, taking refuge in a set of 'posited' norms that were simply received by the community. Its moral commands were regarded as coming from outside the individual, its conception of religion as private vocation was seen as alienating. It reflected a situation in which there was no moral unity between people but rather domination of man by man and by man of nature. This gave rise to a situation of 'unhappy consciousness', and the message of Jesus was 'to restore the lost unity, to replace the law which commands from outside and divides men from nature and each other with the voice of the heart' (Taylor, 1975, p 59). Similarly, the positive law of society represented the process of separation of man from man. To live under the law was not to live in freedom because the law was profoundly alienating. To be punished under posited law was not to be reconciled with a broader moral standpoint but to submit oneself to that which denied such a standpoint. 'Law cannot overcome transgression because to be under law is already to be guilty of the essential trespass, that against the unity of life' (*ibid*, p 61). Similarly, private property, whose presence was strongly reflected in modern law, was essentially alienating because its insistence on the absolute dominion of the owner set each against the other, and ran counter to the deeper unifying needs of love.

In this situation, the resulting moral position was that of the Unhappy Consciousness. The moral person could only feel a sense of not belonging, but it was hard to break down the alienations that existed, and to try to do so was to set oneself at odds with society. To stand up for moral completeness was to stand outside the norms and to risk ridicule, chastisement and worse. The person prepared to give everything up for the morally good life was the Beautiful Soul, of which the classic example was Jesus. Jesus could only react to the ways of his people by withdrawing from them into himself. The result was inevitable and tragic, that he would find himself in violent conflict with his people, leading of course to his death on the cross.

In discussing the fate of Jesus, Hegel is talking of an historical figure, but he sees Jesus's example as of central relevance to modernity. The modern conflict between the ideal and actuality is in effect Jesus's and his disciples' problem. Hegel's early vision is of a Jesus-like, totalising, moral love that transcends division, be it of law, of property, or of a Kantian style philosophy of duty, but the vision must compete with the divisiveness of the modern world. Faced with this, Hegel's attitude is one of ambivalence about the value of the Beautiful Soul. On the one hand, his retrieval of a morality of the Beautiful Soul indicates a moral force, a moral possibility and direction for modernity with which Hegel strongly identifies. He feels this force and it drives his thinking. On the other, he admits that the conditions of modern society cannot permit its adoption. In places, Hegel seeks to use the idea of universal love as a means of reconciling the effects of modern institutions. For example, in his discussion of punishment, he plays with the idea that love and fate can reconcile the wrong in punishment with the wrong in crime (Hegel, 1948, pp 238–39). In other places, he renounces the standpoint of reconciliation. The problem is that modern social institutions do not permit a universal love to rule. Private property stands in opposition to unconditional togetherness, since it is against the rule of love. From the standpoint of such a love, it is necessary to condemn private property. However, Hegel does not do so. Of the biblical difficulty concerning the rich man entering the Kingdom of Heaven, Hegel is frankly dismissive: 'there is nothing to be said [of it]; it is a litany pardonable only in sermons and rhymes, for such a command is without truth for us. The fate of property has become too powerful for us to tolerate reflections on it, to find its abolition thinkable' (*ibid*, p 221). However, he also acknowledges that the possession of riches allows 'of no whole, of no complete life' so that 'Wealth at once betrays its opposition to love, to the whole'. At best, all that it provides is some particular 'duties and virtues' that are 'of necessity linked with exclusion' (*ibid*). While such duties and virtues are not to be rejected out of hand, they nonetheless run counter to the demands of a universal love, to the morality of the Beautiful Soul.

Similarly, considering what happened to Jesus's disciples after his death, Hegel writes that they shared the same fate of marginalisation as their master. Either they maintained their beauty of soul at the cost of isolation in small groups, or they became absorbed into society's mainstream. Hegel notes that some of those following the first route 'wholly abolished property rights against one another', yet this kind of life was necessarily in conflict with modern times, wherein a 'large group' of people must live and share together (*ibid*, p 279). An irredeemable conflict was thereby established between the community of love and that 'prodigious field of objectivity which claims activity of many kinds and sets up a fate whose scope extends in all directions' (*ibid*, p 280). The abstract language hardly obscures its object, the contemporary growth of a civil or market society in which relations are distant and cool, based upon multiple dealings between self-interested individuals (*ibid*, p 279). The fate of a religion of love in the modern world was therefore to fail to embrace that world so that 'church and state, worship and life, piety and virtue, spiritual and worldly action, can never dissolve into one' (*ibid*, p 301). The community of love, which drove the young Hegel morally and emotionally, could not exist under modern conditions.

In terms of the contrast drawn in the introduction to this chapter between moral realism and ethical naturalism, one could say that the radical deontological (moral realist) claim of the expressive morality begins to run into the sand as the revolutionary historical (ethical naturalist) context in which it emerges begins to fade, both in itself and for Hegel. 'The Spirit of Christianity and its Fate' sets up a radical moral claim as to how humanity ought to be which stems from the emergent historical impact of Enlightenment and revolution. Opposed to it is an irreconcilable actual world, in which, Hegel comes to realise, it cannot find itself. The essay represents an historical impasse between the radical expressive moral unity unleashed by Enlightenment and the way the actually developing world is associated with modern private property and its attendant social relations. In this period, Hegel is still strongly drawn to the radical vision, but he has also begun to accept its other, the actually existing world. This explains his empathy with Jesus's tragic fate, but also his turning away from it. This shift away from the Beautiful Soul increases, I will now argue, as Hegel develops his mature position.

The Phenomenology

The *Phenomenology* of 1807 is widely regarded as Hegel's first major work. It establishes the themes that were to preoccupy him for the rest of his life. It is the story, in the frame of dialectical reason, of the process of logical and moral evolution that the individual undertakes as he moves from self-consciousness to an understanding of his place in the 'universal mind' ('Spirit', *Geist*), a place that he always occupied, though he did not understand that this was so. In two places, the ideas of the Unhappy Consciousness and the Beautiful Soul are deployed to explain the nature of this process: in relation to the development of, first, self- and then moral consciousness. The latter is the more significant, but the former will be dealt with briefly first.

Unhappy Consciousness and the emergence of self-consciousness

Self-consciousness represents an important early stage in the development of the *Phenomenology*. It arises out of an attitude of Unhappy Consciousness as the individual moves towards consciousness of self and awareness of the universal he represents. The Unhappy Consciousness is on the verge of the state of self-consciousness. It 'holds together pure thinking and particular individuality', but it has not yet reconciled the two. It involves a 'movement *towards* thinking', ie, towards the rational, but it has not gone far enough. It is groping for awareness through thought that is 'no more than the chaotic jingling of bells, or a mist of warm incense, a musical thinking that does not get as far as the Notion' (Hegel, 1977, pp 130–31). Comparing this with the theological writings, the Unhappy Consciousness is a staging post in the development of self-consciousness towards reason. The intrinsic linkage in the *Phenomenology* is with reason rather than with love so that the concept of a 'religion of love' is no longer foregrounded. Hegel does not give up on love, but it plays a background role. The Unhappy Consciousness is linked to the idea of the 'pure heart', but it is the aim of the pure heart to know its object so that it becomes synonymous with 'a pure *thinking* which thinks of itself as a particular individuality' (*ibid*, p 131, emphasis added). In this development, the Beautiful Soul/Unhappy Consciousness pair is being subsumed in the dialectic of rational self-consciousness that is the philosophical core of the *Phenomenology*. The significance of this move from love to reason becomes clearer when Hegel returns to the Beautiful Soul in connection with moral consciousness.

The Beautiful Soul and moral consciousness

The 'pure heart' emerges again towards the end of the *Phenomenology*, when Hegel again discusses self-consciousness, this time of the moral kind. The Unhappy Consciousness at this point is the individual moral consciousness that declines to take up the intrinsic link between itself and the whole, the link with universal Spirit. This takes the form of a vain and immature purity wherein the individual refuses to take his place in the world. Such a consciousness is one that 'exists in its poorest form, and the poverty which constitutes its sole possession is itself a vanishing' (*ibid*, p 399). The certainty of self as moral consciousness in action is lost in an inwardness in which the self 'finds itself … changed immediately into a sound that dies away … and only the echo … returns to it' (*ibid*). The Unhappy Consciousness:

> lives in dread of besmirching the splendour of its inner being by action and an existence; and, in order to possess the purity of its heart, it flees from contact with the actual world, and persists in its self-willed impotence to renounce its self which is reduced to the extreme of ultimate abstraction … The hollow object which it has produced for itself now fills it, therefore, with a sense of emptiness. (*Ibid*, p 400)

Its activity 'is a yearning which merely loses itself', it becomes 'devoid of substance' and 'finds itself only as a lost soul'. As an 'unhappy, so-called "Beautiful Soul"', its light dies away … and it vanishes like a shapeless vapour that dissolves into thin air'. It becomes a form of 'the evaporated life' (*ibid*). Slightly later, things get even worse:

> The 'beautiful soul', lacking an *actual* existence, entangled in the contradiction between its pure self and the necessity of that self to externalise itself and change itself into an actual existence … is disordered to the point of madness, wastes itself in yearning and pines away in consumption. (*Ibid*, p 407)

Comparing this with 'The Spirit of Christianity', much more than ambivalence to the Beautiful Soul is reflected here. Jesus, the Beautiful Soul in the earlier account, is a tragic figure caught in a fate he cannot escape, and it is the impossibility of escape that is his tragedy as world-historical figure. While a critical undertone is deployed by Hegel, there is also a strong sense of an essentially admirable figure, whose plight is epochal for the early Christian communities, the Christian Church, and modern society as a whole. The Beautiful Soul's tragedy becomes the historical fate of the modern world in which reason and faith, religion and state, ethical whole and social practice are inherently apart. Splitting is modernity's tragic fate because virtue becomes 'of necessity linked with exclusion, and every act of virtue is in itself one of a pair of opposites' (*ibid*, p 221). Morality is not abandoned under modern conditions, but it is limited, and this is expressed in its antinomialism (a point I will develop below). In the *Phenomenology* in contrast, the Beautiful Soul and the Unhappy Consciousness are only negative staging posts on the way to a more complete synthesis that *can* be achieved. With regard to moral consciousness, they reveal wrongheaded attitudes that deserve only our contempt.

In dialectical terms, is there not something positive in the negative for Hegel? The attitude struck by the Beautiful Soul with regard to moral consciousness stems from the recognition of the moral nature of our acts in the world. It emerges at a point of development that is necessary to a more complete moral consciousness. It could therefore be said that its attitude is carried forward into the moral wisdom that comes from recognising the unity between universal and individual moral consciousness that is the conclusion of the argument. We can only recognise the richness of moral activity by always holding in mind the alternative negativity to which maintaining beauty of soul would lead. In that sense, the Beautiful Soul is not just taken negatively within Hegel's account. Nonetheless, the move beyond the Beautiful Soul is in a real sense forced by its intrinsic negativity, by the dread consequence of doing otherwise. To be this figure is to be 'empty', 'hollow', 'evaporated', 'mad', 'impotent' and 'consumptive'. From such negativity, nothing positive is to be maintained, except the need to move beyond it.

Transcending the Beautiful Soul in the *Phenomenology* is thus premised on a warning of its awfulness, which is both to be pitied and despised. It involves a pathology of moral being, a failure to see things as they are, and this establishes a contrast with the earlier theological writings. Previously, the moral failing had been in the world the Beautiful Soul confronted: it was the world's failure to measure up to the ideal moral consciousness that led to the tragic fate of Jesus. Now the failing is in the Beautiful Soul itself, which has lost its earlier tragic character and become, in today's language, a 'loser' who needs to 'get a life'. The problem is in it; the world itself is vindicated.[6] There is a crucial transition here, and one, I shall now argue, that is emblematic of a broader change in Hegel's thought as he came to write his mature philosophy. Disparaging the Beautiful Soul was Hegel's way of coming to terms with the institutions of modernity, and of turning the revolutionary demands of an expressive morality into an ethical means of reconciling himself to the present. In so doing, it was also a way of recognising the antinomialism at the core of modern life and seeking to overcome it.

Legitimating modernity: the ideal in the actual

In this section, I will argue that the broader significance of this change in view of the Beautiful Soul represented a shift towards a legitimation of modern forms of individual moral subjectivity, private property and law. At the core of this move was the identification of a gap between (what became) 'the ideal' and 'the actual', a foundational antinomy for modernity and law which Hegel would seek (without success) to overcome dialectically. I begin by discussing the antinomy of the ideal and the actual and then trace its significance through Hegel's discussion of moral

---

6 Cf Hegel's later comments (1952, pp 103, 230). At p 230, he writes 'However "beautiful" such a disposition may be, it is nevertheless dead'.

consciousness, private property and the 'legal standpoint' in the *Phenomenology*, ending with discussion of the relation between the ideal and the actual in the later *Philosophy of Right*.

The ideal and the actual

Generally, the shift from the early to the mature works involves a channelling and controlling of the revolutionary spirit of the times through dialectical philosophy.[7] In the 1790s, Hegel was an enthusiast of the French Revolution, albeit he was a political moderate. His youthful enthusiasm at the philosophical level found its place in the moral expressivism of the early theological writings. In backward Germany, he imagined the possibility of a world made new through radical social and moral change. The result would be the kind of ideal community presaged by Jesus and the early Christian community. This was the (ambivalent) message of 'The Spirit of Christianity', but also of an earlier essay entitled 'The Positivity of the Christian Religion', written around 1796 (Hegel, 1948). In that work, Hegel was more optimistic about the possibility of real moral change under modern conditions. By the turn of the century, in 'The Spirit of Christianity', his position had become more conflicted. As we have seen, while he still held to moral expressivism, he was now more aware of the problems of bringing an ideal community into existence in the modern world. Modern society's relations were too widespread and cool, too much infected with private property, for this to be possible. Thus 'The Spirit of Christianity' is poised between a radical demand and a historical impossibility. When faced with the social relations of modern life, the radical morality becomes increasingly seen as an ideal confronting a wide gulf with what actually exists. There emerges a fundamental opposition between how things ought to be and how they are, which becomes an antinomy of the ideal and the actual.

This was an uncomfortable, unresolved, position, but Hegel's remarks in favour of private property – implicitly against love – indicate the direction in which he was moving, that is towards embracing the actual. Add to this that, for Hegel, the ideal seemed at this point to pose a threat, for an ideal conception of freedom, left without a place to be in the world, led in his view to danger and destruction. It would become a purely negative freedom, which Hegel associated with the terror that followed the French Revolution.[8] If this, now dangerous, gap between the ideal and the actual could not be overcome in practice, it could perhaps in theory, and Hegel's response to the impasse of his early writings was to immerse himself more fully in the philosophy of German Idealism, in the thought of Kant, Fichte and Schelling (Pinkard, 2000, pp 153–69).

---

7 Cf the early, more radical Habermas (1974, p 121): 'in order not to sacrifice philosophy to the challenge posed by the revolution, Hegel elevated revolution to the primary principle of his philosophy. Only after he had fastened the revolution firmly to the beating heart of the world spirit did he feel secure from it.'

8 Hegel's well known comments on the potential destructiveness of modern freedom in the *Phenomenology* and the *Philosophy of Right* are anticipated in the early theological writings (Hegel, 1948, pp 281, 288).

The details of this immersion are beyond the scope of this chapter, as are the biographical reasons which also directed him (Pinkard, 2000, pp 81–88). My interest is in how the moral and political impasse in which he found himself expressed itself as an antinomy of the ideal and the actual which could be overcome in thought, where it could not be directly overcome in the world itself. The *Phenomenology* is only about eight years after 'The Spirit of Christianity', but it has a different political, moral and philosophical agenda. Hegel was shifting politically towards acceptance of modern bourgeois society from the more radical, if inchoate, ethical standpoint of his youth. The way that this was achieved was by seeking to resolve the gap between the ideal and the actual so that the latter itself became the expression of the ideal, not its antinomial 'other'. Morally, this involved underpinning modern social relations with an ethical purpose. Philosophically, this was achieved through the tracing of dialectical reason as it brought together what was 'rational' (ideal) with what was 'real' (actual). However, this idealisation of the actual was necessarily incomplete and conflicted, and therefore in danger of breakdown.

Modern moral consciousness

In making the Beautiful Soul into a mere nothing, the 'evaporated life', Hegel is clearing the ground for a new moral subject to take its place, a strong individual confident in its own moral outlook. Aware of itself as a moral subject, it accepts its place in a community of like-minded individuals. However, these moral subjects share only the *form* of subjectivity, for the *content* of moral conscience remains particular to the individual:

> In calling itself *conscience*, it calls itself ... a universal knowing and willing which recognises and acknowledges others, is the same as them ... In the will of the self that is certain of itself ... lies the essence of what is right ... [This universal self] is not universal in the *content* of the act, for this ... is intrinsically an indifferent affair: it is in the form of the act that the universality lies. (Hegel, 1977, p 397)

Conscience 'puts whatever content it pleases into its knowing and willing', and is therefore a 'solitary divine worship [which] is at the same time essentially the divine worship of a community' (*ibid*). No attempt is made to reconcile further one this-worldly conscience with another, though, despite this, all appears well with the world:

> the declaration of [moral] *conscience* affirms the certainty of [the self] to be ... a universal self. On account of this utterance ... the validity of the act is acknowledged by others. The spirit and substance of their association are thus the mutual assurance of their conscientiousness, good intentions, the rejoicing over this mutual purity, and the refreshing of themselves in the glory of knowing and uttering, of cherishing and fostering, such an excellent state of affairs. (*Ibid*, p 398)

The subject recognises itself as moral being and recognises this in others too, but no deeper moral togetherness is posited. This is a self-confident, happy, moral subject, but one that, in terms of Hegel's previous moral expressivism, is shallow, formal and isolated in its own specific projects. The position is surprisingly Kantian in its assertion of the sufficiency of individual moral consciousness. Further reconciliation of form and content at the level of moral self-consciousness is not offered. True, it eventually arrives through the further mediations of religion and philosophy at higher and different levels. However, while these involve a further embedding of moral subjectivity, they do not change its actual form. The divine, into which self-consciousness passes, remains, as Terry Pinkard puts it, 'only the way in which the world embodies within itself the potential for *Geist*, for our "mindedness" and "like-mindedness"' (Pinkard, 2000, p 219), ie, for our recognition of self and other as rational and moral self-consciousness in the way this has previously been laid out. The further moves do not actively address the split between form and content with which Hegel leaves us at the end of his analysis of moral consciousness. They provide rather an 'other-worldly' reconciliation of what remains otherwise unreconciled at the level of moral practice and awareness.

The role of private property

In the passages on moral consciousness, private property plays an intriguing role. It is defended as an actual content of moral consciousness even though, on Hegel's account, any particular content of moral consciousness should be irrelevant. Being a moral subject entails no particular project, as we have seen, but increasing one's property, we now also learn, is a real moral duty! That 'an individual increases his property in a certain way' and 'is aware that this is a duty ... directly contained in his certainty of himself' is a desirable state of affairs. Others may attack what he does as 'violence and wrongdoing' or as 'cowardice', but increasing property both preserves one's life and assists others, so those who criticise the property accumulator themselves ignore their own duty, and are 'guilty of ineptitude, of being immoral'. Knowing 'what he does to be a duty, and ... moral obligation, [the property owner] is thus recognised and acknowledged by others' (Hegel, 1977, p 392).

With these comments, Hegel has it both ways in the *Phenomenology*. He has maintained that the mere fact of a sense of moral duty is sufficient for one to be acknowledged as a moral person, but now he introduces an argument about the content of such duty, one in favour of private property. Recalling the tension in 'The Spirit of Christianity' between an ideal morality and the modern actuality of private property, it is striking that *this* should be the particular content Hegel is now prepared to defend. Note also that he does so while advancing a seemingly content-less theory of moral consciousness. There is no doubt something illicit in this argument; nonetheless the message is clear. The modern 'actual' has been endorsed as part of the philosophical 'ideal'. In the process, the property owning moral individual, in effect the legal subject, is given a central place in the philosophy.

Legal status

This position seems puzzling in its own terms, but also in terms of an earlier discussion in the *Phenomenology* on the nature of 'legal status', which seems to run counter to the formalism that emerges at this point (*ibid*, pp 290–94). It will be helpful to consider Hegel's argument at the earlier stage before moving on to discuss the *Philosophy of Right*. In considering legal status, Hegel criticises the (in effect) legal notion of personality we have just examined precisely for its formalism, for the '*empty unit* of the person' it endorses, for its inherent contingency 'that comes to no lasting result' (*ibid*, p 291). In consequence, Hegel says, 'to describe an individual as a "person" is an expression of contempt' (*ibid*, p 292). The crucial problem for legal subjectivity, he says in this earlier passage, is precisely that it lacks content, so that its concepts of 'possession' and 'property' are ethically inadequate:

> The formalism of legal right ... finds before it a manifold existence in the form of 'possession' and ... stamps it with [an] abstract universality, whereby it is called 'property'. (*Ibid*)

These comments on the nature of legal status indicate that Hegel was explicitly against the formalism and abstraction that crop up later in the discussion of moral self-consciousness. In this earlier section, Hegel refuses to see property and legal subjectivity as valid in themselves precisely because they are developed out of formal law, and represent a content that lacks full universality. Why should he then have returned to formalism at the higher level of morality after rejecting it at the lower level of legal personality?

The contradiction between the earlier and later passages in the *Phenomenology* can be understood if we return to the problem bequeathed by the early theological writings, and recall how Hegel sought to address it in the *Phenomenology*. In the early writings, a moral ideal ran up against the limits imposed on ethics by modern private property, a domain of 'particular' ethical duties. The *Phenomenology* is an attempt to reconcile such an ideal ethics with the actuality of modern social institutions, so it locates private property within a universalising ethics. The earlier passage on legal status shows Hegel embedding the individual legal subject and property owner within an ethical form of life that will 'sublate' (transcend but also preserve) it. This will lead ultimately to further dialectical moves including the recognition of moral consciousness (and then religion and philosophy). Legal status is not condemned as such, but is seen as involving only an abstract universality which requires englobing in a wider ethical perspective. From that point of view, legal status is a necessary, although inadequate, form of ethical life, and property must be dialectically rationalised in a wider ethical whole. The later passage on moral consciousness then shows Hegel configuring the nature of such an englobing moral subjectivity, but this has to be in a way compatible with modern individual relations. From that point of view, individualism is preserved as a matter of formal moral willing, and the defence of private property becomes its obvious, though 'supplementary', content. What Hegel renounces at the lower level, abstract subjectivity as legal status, he affirms at the higher, abstract subjectivity as moral consciousness.

Looking at this through the analysis presented here, the juxtaposition of the two passages on legal status and moral consciousness reveals what the young Hegel had himself understood. Any attempt at the sort of expressive ideal morality based upon love as originally envisaged would necessarily find itself compromised by the most basic form of modern morality: individual private property relations. In the tension between the passage on legal status, where Hegel demands that the actual be idealised, and the account of moral self-consciousness, where he (implicitly) acknowledges the limits of the actual as ideal, this underlying conflict is affirmed but not resolved.

Law in the Philosophy of Right

In Hegel's later work, the *Philosophy of Right* (1821), the process of embedding liberal legal forms in the ethical continued, but in a developed, significantly different way. The work, which is in three parts, begins with self-consciousness ('Abstract Right') and proceeds to moral consciousness ('Morality') before ending with the idea of an 'Ethical Life' in which self- and moral consciousness are englobed in modern forms and institutions that are at once ideal and actual. Throughout, the process of ideal rational development is concretely linked to legal and social forms associated with modern civil society. The forms of Abstract Right are developed as a dialectic of self-consciousness in its links with property, contract and civil and criminal wrongdoing. These then find a universal ethical setting in the categories of modern civil society, as Hegel sees them: a 'system of needs', the administration of justice, institutions of police and corporations, the state itself. Ethical Life is then further assured by systems of international law and 'world history'.

This rich contextualisation of liberal legality makes Hegel a difficult philosopher to place in terms of modern labels (Taylor, 1975, pp 449–61). To see him as a liberal meets the objection that his idea of a supervening Ethical Life with institutions limiting individual freedom runs counter to liberal tenets. On the other hand, his articulation of the development of self-consciousness through the forms of liberal law and into a regulated form of civil society reveals how much an emergent liberal, bourgeois form of society lies at the heart of his philosophy. From that point of view, the *Philosophy of Right* confirms the political progression we identified from the early theological writings to the *Phenomenology*. Hegel increasingly endorses the actuality of individualist private property as the basis for his social philosophy. The moral expressivism of the early writings, which stood against law and property, becomes the ethical philosophy of Spirit which englobes and endorses institutions which he had initially seen as giving rise to separation and alienation. As for the Beautiful Soul, it is relegated to an addition to a passage on Morality (Hegel, 1952, p 103), in which Hegel refers the reader back to the rough treatment it receives in the *Phenomenology*. In a philosophy which synthesises a concrete-rational (ideal-actual) order out of subjective conviction and objective condition (as Knox describes it, *ibid*, p 345), the idea of the Beautiful Soul can only be of the most limited and negative significance. Knox's description of it as a regional curiosity, a Moravian speciality, amply reflects this.

The concretisation of the forms of ethical life in the *Philosophy of Right* adds, however, a final twist to the conflict between moral expressivism and the forms of modernity, between the ethical ideal and modern actuality. The ideal has now been channelled through actual social forms, so that these become its expression. However, those social forms have not lost their original problematic character just because they have been endowed with a sense of the ideal. Such forms are now part of an ethical progression, but they also have to be viewed as they are, according to their practical implications and effects. The conflict between the ideal and the actual accordingly re-emerges as a conflict between the ways in which existing legal forms ideally should participate in a sense of an ethical whole and the troubling qualities of modern life with which the ideal is supposedly synthesised, but in fact finds itself out of phase. Thus, Hegel's account of the ideal of self-consciousness moving into property and then progressing into the wider ethical life of civil society runs into problems of poverty and injustice occasioned by the existence of private property. Hegel observes how the division of labour leads to 'the dependence and distress of the class tied to [unskilled] work' and to an 'inability to feel and enjoy the broader freedoms and especially the intellectual benefits of civil society' (*ibid*, pp 149–50). There develops 'a large mass of people [which] falls below a certain subsistence level', and it becomes apparent that civil society is unable 'to check excessive poverty and the creation of a penurious rabble'. In this situation, the very terms of justice are called into question. Right and wrong are no longer perceived as logical stages in the ideal dialectic of individual right, for poverty leads to a 'loss of the sense of right and wrong', shaking the terms of the ideal to its roots:

> Against nature man can claim no right, but once society is established, poverty immediately takes the form of a wrong done to one class by another. The important question of how poverty is to be abolished is one of the most disturbing problems which agitate modern society. (*Ibid*, pp 277–78)

To this question, Hegel had no real answer. The conflict between the ideal and the actual, which had wound its way from the early theological writings through the *Phenomenology* into the *Philosophy of Right* remained unresolved. Where Hegel had originally portrayed the gap between the ideal and the actual as a gap between morality and modernity, his later ethical idealisation of modernity did not make that gap go away. Confronted with modern social conditions, the *Philosophy of Right* reproduces it as a gap between the ideal way in which the modern world should work, and the way things happen in it.[9] In resolving the gap between the ideal and the actual, Hegel only reinstates it as a gap between the idealised actual and actuality. The antinomy of the ideal and the actual remains in place.

The Beautiful Soul and the law

Hegel's aim in his mature work was to inscribe social forms such as the individual moral and legal subject and private property within an ideal ethical framework. In order to do this, he had to confront what he had originally thought as a young man growing up in a period of radical ferment, under the influence of a strongly perfectionist moral doctrine. Under that doctrine, the social institutions he wanted in his maturity to endorse were inherently problematic. The young Hegel had claimed:

> this at least is to be noticed, that the possession of riches, with all the rights as well as all the cares connected with it, brings into human life definitive details whose restrictedness prescribes limits to the virtues, imposes conditions on them, and makes them dependent on circumstances. Within these limitations, there is room for duties and virtues, but they allow of no whole, of no complete life ... (Hegel, 1948, p 221)

Individual wealth, he wrote as a young man, 'betrays its opposition to love, to the whole, because it is a right caught in a context of multiple rights' (*ibid*). While it possessed its own virtue of honesty as well as 'the other virtues possible within its sphere', these were fatefully limited. They were 'linked with exclusion', so that

---

9 For analysis of the gap between ideal and actuality in Hegel's theory of punishment, see Norrie, 1991b. For analysis of Hegel's *Philosophy of Right* that sees Hegel as a *critic* of modern society on the basis of the gap between the ideal and the actual, see Fine, 2001, Chapters 2–4.

'every act of virtue is in itself one of a pair of opposites' (*ibid*). Individual wealth thus engendered an antinomial morality, one which would refuse a sense of ethical wholeness. In contrast, the aim of the *Phenomenology* and then the *Philosophy of Right* was to place these limited antinomial forms at the core of an overall ethical progression towards totality. What had stood in the way of the expressive ideal was now to be a significant part of its expression. The antinomy between ideal and actual was to be sublated in a dialectical philosophy that would idealise the actual and thus actualise the ideal. In the *Phenomenology*, however, the antinomial fate of modernity is preserved in the formalism of moral consciousness, despite Hegel's critique of legal status, while the illicitly introduced content is that of private property. In the *Philosophy of Right*, the dynamics of a social system based on private property yield a fatal antinomy between individual and social justice from the idealisation of the actual.

These antinomies of form and content and of individual and social justice look familiar in light of the previous chapters in this book. Chapter 7 identifies the split between form and substance at the core of criminal law theory, where 'orthodox subjectivists' and 'moral substantivists' battle over the moral character of the law. Underlying this antinomy, it was argued, is the deeper antinomy of individual and social justice. The antinomial patterning of the law described in the Introduction to this chapter begins to take its place in a larger philosophical setting. Let us see how this works. Every 'virtue' associated with legal form, as the young Hegel put it, is 'linked with exclusion' (Hegel, 1948, p 221). As regards law's antinomies, the positing of a discourse 'internal' to law establishes an 'outside' excluded from it; the identification of a positivised sphere of law points to a moral realm that somehow exists beyond it; the existence of formal legal argument indicates a sphere of being that is in a sense 'informal'; formal legality proposes a distinction between what is within legal form and a content or substance that is extraneous to it; while universality of laws invites reflection on the particular not caught within it. The problem with the partiality and one-sidedness in each of the 'law terms' in these pairs (internality, positivism, formalism, form, universality) is seen in that they are never enough in themselves to do the law's work. The external, the moral, the informal, context or substance, the particular are also invoked within and by legal argument. The excluded returns so that law's discourse becomes intrinsically antinomial, just as the young Hegel had said it was. In so saying, he spoke not only against law but against his own mature philosophy, and that is why we see a close parallel between the antinomies of the *Phenomenology* and the *Philosophy of Right* and those of modern legal theory and practice. Where the mature Hegel sought to overcome antinomy by combining the ideal and the actual, modern legal theory and practice seek to ground systems of legal reasoning in a set of legal terms that constitute a legal totality: a kind of positivised ideal that makes law 'law'. However, the antinomies keep forcing this idealised actual that is the law beyond itself.

Tracing the trajectory of the Beautiful Soul in Hegel's work has a broader importance than the 'merely' philosophical. It not only takes us into Hegel's philosophy of law, but also beyond it, into the theory and practice of the modern law. Hegel would have approved of this general trajectory from philosophy to practice, though not perhaps its particular conclusions. Reading the young against the mature Hegel gives us a negative, sceptical critique of the forms (the antinomies) of modern law and their limits, one that ties the historical structuring of antinomy to the ethical perversions wrought by the dominance of private property. There is, however, another side to the critique, one which is represented by the expressive morality of the young Hegel, and which was born out of the revolutionary enthusiasm with which modern society began. This stands as both an historical moment in our experience of the modern (its 'ethical naturalist' side) and an intrinsic moral claim as to how the world ought to be (its 'moral realist' side). In the face of individual, social and natural alienation, expressive moral demands for self-actualisation and oneness of humankind with itself and nature remain on the horizon of modern life. Forced to play the role of the 'ideal' in the face of modern 'actuality' in Hegel's mature work, this radical ethics still permeates his system even if it is required to perform menial work, to get its hands more than a little dirty.

Is the same not also true of modern law-based justice? We are aware of the social injustices that law perpetuates, which necessarily work their way into its own systems and practices, and many of the chapters in this collection have reflected on how this happens. However, when the law seeks in its own terms to do justice, even on a terrain of injustice, when it moves back and forth between the antinomies which constitute it, does it not also reach towards a justice that lies beyond it, and that echoes inchoately within it? Might this not be the remnant of that expressive morality on which modernity was founded, but which was repressed by being channelled into the social forms through which humankind lives today? Perhaps there is then a sense in which the ghost in the corridors of the law is that of the Beautiful Soul, the harbinger of an expressive morality that once seemed a real human possibility. Almost 200 years ago, Hegel took decisive steps to banish it, to force it into oblivion. If we now recall it from its Moravian[10] exile, we may be reminded of what is morally, socially and politically at stake in the modern law.

---

10 See my second prefatory quote.

Bibliography

Abel, R (1992) *The Politics of Informal Justice*, London: Academic Press

Abrams, P (1968) *The Origins of British Sociology: 1834–1914*, Chicago: University of Chicago Press

Adorno, TW (1973) *Negative Dialectics*, London: Routledge

Adorno, TW (1993) *Hegel: Three Studies*, Cambridge, Mass: MIT

Albrow, M (1975) 'Legal positivism and bourgeois materialism: Max Weber's view of the sociology of law' 2 *British Journal of Sociology of Law* 14

Alexy, R (1989) *A Theory of Legal Argumentation*, Oxford: Oxford University Press

Allison, J (1990) 'In search of revolutionary justice in South Africa' 18 *International Journal of the Sociology of Law* 409

American Friends Service Committee (1971) *Struggle for Justice*, New York: Hill and Wang

Archer, M (1995) *Realist Social Theory: The Morphogenetic Approach*, Cambridge: Cambridge University Press

Archer, M, Bhaskar, R, Collier, A, Lawson, T and Norrie, A (1998) *Critical Realism: Essential Readings*, London: Routledge

Arendt, H (1961) *Between Past and Future*, London: Faber

Arlidge, A (2000) 'The trial of Dr David Moor' *Criminal Law Review* 31

Ashworth, A (1976) 'The doctrine of provocation' 35 *Cambridge Law Journal* 292

Ashworth, A (1987) 'Belief, intent and criminal liability' in Eekelaar, J and Bell, J (eds), *Oxford Essays in Jurisprudence: Third Series*, Oxford: Oxford University Press

Ashworth, A (1989) 'Criminal justice and deserved sentences' *Criminal Law Review* 340

Ashworth, A (1991) *Principles of Criminal Law*, Oxford: Clarendon

Ashworth, A (1994) *The Criminal Process*, Oxford: Oxford University Press

Ashworth, A (1996) 'Criminal liability in a medical context' in Simester, A and Smith, A (eds), *Harm and Culpability*, Oxford: Oxford University Press

Ashworth, A (1999) *Principles of Criminal Law*, Oxford: Oxford University Press

Ashworth, A (2000) *Sentencing and Criminal Justice*, London: Butterworths

Austin, J (1861) *The Province of Jurisprudence Determined*, London: John Murray

Barnett, S (1998) *Hegel After Derrida*, London: Routledge

Barron, A (1993) 'The illusions of the "I": citizenship and the politics of identity' in Norrie, A (ed), *Closure or Critique: New Directions in Legal Theory*, Edinburgh: Edinburgh University Press

Barthes, R (1973) *Mythologies*, St Albans: Paladin

Beccaria, C (1964) *Of Crimes and Punishments*, Oxford: Oxford University Press

Bentham, J (1975) *Theory of Legislation*, New York: Oceana

Benton, T (1977) *Philosophical Foundations of the Three Sociologies*, London: Routledge

Bernstein, J (2001) *Adorno: Disenchantment and Ethics*, Cambridge: Cambridge University Press

Beyleveld, D and Brownsword, R (1986) *Law as a Moral Judgement*, London: Sweet & Maxwell

Beyleveld, D and Brownsword, R (1993) 'The dialectically necessary foundation of natural law' in Norrie, A (ed), *Closure or Critique: New Directions in Legal Theory*, Edinburgh: Edinburgh University Press

Bhaskar, R (1975) *A Realist Theory of Science*, Leeds: Leeds Books

Bhaskar, R (1979) *The Possibility of Naturalism*, Brighton: Harvester

Bhaskar, R (1986) *Scientific Realism and Human Emancipation*, London: Verso

Bhaskar, R (1989) *Reclaiming Reality*, London: Verso

Bhaskar, R (1993) *Dialectic: The Pulse of Freedom*, London: Verso

Bhaskar, R (1994) *Plato Etc*, London: Verso

Bhaskar, R (1997) *A Realist Theory of Science*, 2nd edn, London: Verso

Bhaskar, R (1998) *The Possibility of Naturalism*, 3rd edn, London: Routledge

Bhaskar, R and Norrie, A (1998) 'Introduction: dialectic and dialectical critical realism' in Archer, M, Bhaskar, R, Collier, A, Lawson, T and Norrie, A (eds), *Critical Realism: Essential Readings*, London: Routledge

Bird, G (1995) 'Kantianism' in Honderich, T (ed), *Oxford Companion to Philosophy*, Oxford: Oxford University Press

Blom-Cooper, L (1995) 'Social control and criminal justice: an unresponsive alliance', paper delivered at the British Society of Criminology Conference

Bourdieu, P (1988) *Homo Academicus*, Cambridge: Polity

Bower, T (1997) *Blind Eye to Murder*, London: Warner

Bowring, W (2002) 'Review essay' 29 *Journal of Law and Society* 521

Boyle, C (2000) 'Judges and gender' in Doran, S and Jackson, J (eds), *The Judicial Role in Criminal Proceedings*, Oxford: Hart

Braithwaite, J (1989) *Crime, Shame and Reintegration*, Cambridge: Cambridge University Press

Brittain, V (1994) 'A state remade to the United Nations' design' *The Guardian*, 6 August

Bronitt, S and McSherry, B (2001) *Principles of Criminal Law*, New South Wales: Law Book Co

Burman, S and Scharf, W (1990) 'Creating people's justice: street committees and people's courts in a South African city' 24 *Law and Society Review* 695

Burnside, J and Baker, N (1994) *Relational Justice*, Winchester: Waterside Press

Butler, J (1987) *Subjects of Desire: Hegelian Reflections in Twentieth Century France*, New York: Columbia University Press

Cain, M (1985) 'Beyond informal justice' 9 *Contemporary Crises* 335–73

Carter, A (1977) *The Passion of New Eve*, London: Gollancz

Cohen, S (1979) 'Guilt, justice and tolerance: some old concepts for a new criminology' in Downes, D and Rock, P (eds), *Deviant Interpretations*, Oxford: Martin Robertson

Collier, A (1994) *Critical Realism*, London: Verso

Collins, H (1981) *Marxism and Law*, Oxford: Oxford University Press

Cornell, D (1992) *The Philosophy of the Limit*, London: Routledge

Cornell, D (1995) *The Imaginary Domain*, London: Routledge

Cornell, D, Rosenfeld, M and Carlson, DG (1991) *Hegel and Legal Theory*, London: Routledge

Corrigan, P and Sayer, D (1985) *The Great Arch*, Oxford: Basil Blackwell

Cotterrell, R (1983) 'English conceptions of the role of theory in legal analysis' 46 *Modern Law Review* 481

Cotterrell, R (1989) *The Politics of Jurisprudence*, London: Butterworths

Cotterrell, R (1993) 'Sociological perspectives on legal closure' in Norrie, A (ed), *Closure or Critique: New Directions in Legal Theory*, Edinburgh: Edinburgh University Press

Cotterrell, R (1995) *Law's Community*, Oxford: Oxford University Press

Criminal Law Commissioners (1839) XIX *Parliamentary Papers, Fourth Report*

Criminal Law Commissioners (1843) XIX *Parliamentary Papers, Seventh Report*

Cross, R (1978) 'The reports of the Criminal Law Commissioners (1833–1849) and the abortive Bills of 1853' in Glazebrook, P (ed), *Reshaping the Criminal Law*, London: Stevens

Cullen, B (1979) *Hegel's Social and Political Thought*, Dublin: Gill and Macmillan

Darian-Smith, E and Fitzpatrick, P (1999) *Laws of the Postcolonial*, Ann Arbor: University of Michigan Press

Davies, M (1996) *Delimiting the Law*, London: Pluto

de Sousa Santos, B (1992) 'State, law and community in the world system: an introduction' 1 *Social and Legal Studies* 131

Dean, K (2003) *Capitalism and Citizenship*, London: Routledge

Dennis, IH (1997) 'The critical condition of criminal law' 50 *Current Legal Problems* 213

Derrida, J (1977) *Of Grammatology*, Baltimore: Johns Hopkins University Press

Derrida, J (1978) *Writing and Difference*, London: Routledge

Derrida, J (1986) *Glas*, Lincoln, Nebraska: University of Nebraska Press

Derrida, J (1990) 'Force of law: the "mystical foundation of authority"' 11 *Cardozo Law Review* 919

Derrida, J (1994) *Specters of Marx*, London: Routledge

Derrida, J (1999) 'Marx and sons' in Sprinker, M (ed), *Ghostly Demarcations*, London: Verso

Dews, P (1979) 'The *nouvelle philosophie* and Foucault' 8 *Economy and Society* 127

Dignan, J (1992) 'Reintegration through reparation: a way forward for restorative justice?' Fulbright Colloquium on Penal Theory and Penal Practice, University of Stirling

Douzinas, C and Warrington, R (1995) *Justice Miscarried: Ethics, Aesthetics and the Law*, Brighton: Harvester Wheatsheaf

Duff, RA (1986) *Trials and Punishments*, Cambridge: Cambridge University Press

Duff, RA (1990) *Intention, Agency and Criminal Liability*, Oxford: Blackwell

Duff, RA (1996) 'Penal communications' in Tonry, M (ed), *Crime and Justice: A Review of Research*, Chicago: University of Chicago Press

Duff, RA (1998) 'Principle and contradiction in the criminal law: motives and criminal liability' in Duff, R (ed), *Philosophy and the Criminal Law*, New York: Cambridge University Press

Durkheim, E (1964) *The Division of Labour in Society*, New York: Free Press

Durkheim, E (1973) 'Two laws of penal evolution' 2 *Economy and Society* 307

Dworkin, R (1977) *Taking Rights Seriously*, London: Duckworth

Dworkin, R (1986) *Law's Empire*, London: Fontana

Eagleton, T (2001) *The Gatekeeper: A Memoir*, London: Penguin

Egero, B (1987) *Mozambique: A Dream Undone*, Uppsala: SIAS

Engels, F (1968) 'Ludwig Feuerbach and the end of classical German philosophy' in Marx, K and Engels, F (eds), *Selected Works in One Volume*, London: Lawrence & Wishart

Ferri, E (1901) *The Positive School of Criminology*, Chicago: Kerr

Fine, R (1993) 'The "rose in the cross of the present": closure and critique in Hegel's Philosophy of Right' in Norrie, A (ed), *Closure or Critique: New Directions in Legal Theory*, Edinburgh: Edinburgh University Press

Fine, R (2001) *Political Investigations*, London: Routledge

Fish, S (1993) 'The law wishes to have a formal existence' in Norrie, A (ed), *Closure or Critique: New Directions in Legal Theory*, Edinburgh: Edinburgh University Press

Fitzpatrick, P (1982) 'The political economy of dispute settlement in Papua New Guinea' in Sumner, C (ed), *Crime, Justice and Underdevelopment*, London: Heinemann

Fitzpatrick, P (1987) 'The rise and rise of informalism' in Matthews, R (ed), *Informal Justice?*, London: Sage

Fitzpatrick, P (1991a) 'The abstracts and brief chronicle of the time: supplementing jurisprudence' in Fitzpatrick, P (ed), *Dangerous Supplements: Resistance and Renewal in Jurisprudence*, London: Pluto

Fitzpatrick, P (1991b) *Dangerous Supplements: Resistance and Renewal in Jurisprudence*, London: Pluto

Fitzpatrick, P (1992a) 'The impossibility of popular justice' 1 *Social and Legal Studies* 199–215

Fitzpatrick, P (1992b) *The Mythology of Modern Law*, London: Routledge

Fitzpatrick, P (1995a) 'Missing possibility: socialisation, culture and consciousness', paper delivered at the Law and Society Association Summer Institute

Fitzpatrick, P (1995b) 'Passions out of place: law, incommensurability and resistance' 6 *Law and Critique* 95

Foucault, M (1972) *The Archaeology of Knowledge*, London: Tavistock

Foucault, M (1977) *Discipline and Punishment*, Harmondsworth: Peregrine

Foucault, M (1980) *Power/Knowledge: Selected Interviews and Others Writings*, Brighton: Harvester Wheatsheaf

Foucault, M (1981) *History of Sexuality*, Harmondsworth: Penguin

Foucault, M (1982) 'Afterword: the subject and power' in Dreyfus, H and Rabinow, P (eds), *Michel Foucault: Beyond Structuralism and Hermeneutics*, Brighton: Harvester Wheatsheaf

Foucault, M (1984) 'What is Enlightenment?' in Rabinow, P (ed), *The Foucault Reader*, Harmondsworth: Penguin

Foucault, M (1991) *The Foucault Effect*, London: Harvester Wheatsheaf

Frank, J (1963) *Law and the Modern Mind*, New York: Anchor

Fuller, L (1969) *The Morality of Law*, New Haven: Yale University Press

Gardner, J (1998) 'On the general part of the criminal law' in Duff, R (ed), *Philosophy and the Criminal Law*, New York: Cambridge University Press

Gardner, J and Jung, H (1991) 'Making sense of *mens rea*: Antony Duff's account' 11 *Oxford Journal of Legal Studies* 559

Gardner, J and Macklem, T (2001a) 'Compassion without respect? Nine fallacies in *R v Smith*' *Criminal Law Review* 623

Gardner, J and Macklem, T (2001b) 'Provocation and pluralism' 64 *Modern Law Review* 815

Garland, D (1985) *Punishment and Welfare*, Aldershot: Gower

Garland, D (1990) *Punishment and Modern Society*, Oxford: Oxford University Press

Giddens, A (1979) *Central Problems in Social Theory*, London: Macmillan

Giddens, A (1991) *Modernity and Self Identity*, Oxford: Polity

Goff, R (1988) 'The mental element in murder' 104 *Law Quarterly Review* 30

Goodrich, P (1986) *Reading the Law*, Oxford: Blackwell

Goodrich, P (1993) 'Fate as seduction: the other scene of legal judgement' in Norrie, A (ed) (1993), *Closure or Critique: New Directions in Legal Theory*, Edinburgh: Edinburgh University Press

Goodrich, P (1995) *Oedipus Lex: Psychoanalysis, History and Law*, Berkeley: University of California Press

Guha, R (1987) 'Chandra's death' in Guha, R (ed), *Subaltern Studies*, Oxford: Oxford University Press

Gundersen, A (1992) 'Popular justice in Mozambique: between state law and folk law' 1 *Social and Legal Studies* 257

Habermas, J (1974) *Theory and Practice*, London: Heinemann

Habermas, J (1984) *A Theory of Communicative Action*, London: Heinemann

Habermas, J (1987) 'The entry into modernity: Nietzsche as a turning point' in Habermas, J (ed), *The Philosophical Discourse of Modernity*, Cambridge, Mass: MIT

Habermas, J (1989) *Moral Consciousness and Communicative Action*, Cambridge: Polity

Hale, M (1972) *Pleas of the Crown*, London: Professional Books

Halevy, E (1972) *The Growth of Philosophic Radicalism*, London: Faber

Hall, CG (1985) 'The Right Honourable Lord Edmund-Davies of Aberpennar: an appreciation' 16 *Cambrian Law Review* 18

Hall, S (1977) *Policing the Crisis*, London: Macmillan

Hanlon, J (1984) *Mozambique: The Revolution Under Fire*, London: Zed Press

Harré, R (1983) *Personal Being*, Oxford: Blackwell

Harré, R (1998) *The Singular Self*, London: Sage

Harré, R, Clarke, D and De Carlo, N (1985) *Motives and Mechanisms*, London: Methuen

Hart, HLA (1961) *The Concept of Law*, Oxford: Clarendon

Hart, HLA (1968) *Punishment and Responsibility*, Oxford: Clarendon

Hay, D (1977a) 'Poaching and the game laws on Cannock Chase' in Hay, D, Linebaugh, P, Rule, J, Thompson, EP and Winslow, C (eds), *Albion's Fatal Tree*, Harmondsworth: Peregrine

Hay, D (1977b) 'Property, authority and the criminal law' in Hay, D, Linebaugh, P, Rule, J, Thompson, EP and Winslow, C (eds), *Albion's Fatal Tree*, Harmondsworth: Peregrine

Hay, D, Linebaugh, P, Rule, J, Thompson, EP, and Winslow, C (1977) *Albion's Fatal Tree*, Harmondsworth: Peregrine

Hegel, G (1948) *Early Theological Writings*, Chicago: University of Chicago Press

Hegel, G (1952) *The Philosophy of Right*, Knox, TM (trans), Oxford: Oxford University Press

Hegel, G (1956) *The Philosophy of History*, New York: Dover

Hegel, G (1975) *Logic*, Oxford: Oxford University Press

Hegel, G (1977) *Phenomenology of Spirit*, Oxford: Oxford University Press

Higgins, A (1995) 'Land and freedom' *The Guardian*, 17 October

Hobbes, T (1968) *Leviathan*, Harmondsworth: Penguin

Honderich, T (1995) *The Oxford Companion to Philosophy*, Oxford: Oxford University Press

Horder, J (1992) *Provocation and Responsibility*, Oxford: Oxford University Press

Horder, J (2000) 'On the irrelevance of motive in criminal law' in Horder, J (ed), *Oxford Essays in Jurisprudence: Fourth Series*, Oxford: Oxford University Press

Horton, J and Mendus, S (1994) 'Alasdair MacIntyre: after virtue and after' in Horton, J and Mendus, S (eds), *After MacIntyre*, Cambridge: Polity

Hostettler, N and Norrie, A (2003) 'Are critical realist ethics foundationalist?' in Cruickshank, J (ed), *Critical Realism: The Difference it Makes*, London: Routledge

Hudson, B (1998) 'Doing justice to difference' in Ashworth, A and Wasik, M (eds), *Fundamentals of Sentencing Theory*, Oxford: Clarendon

Hume, D (1888) *A Treatise on Human Nature*, Oxford: Clarendon

Hume, D (1898) 'Of the original contract' in Hume, D and Miller, E (eds), *Essays, Literary, Moral and Political*, London: Longman

Hunt, A (1978) *The Sociological Movement in Law*, London: Macmillan

Inwood, M (1992) *A Hegel Dictionary*, Oxford: Blackwell

Irigaray, L (1993) *Je, Tu, Nous: Towards a Culture of Difference*, London: Routledge

Isaacman, A and Isaacman, B (1982) 'A socialist legal system in the making: Mozambique' in Abel, R (ed), *The Politics of Informal Justice*, New York: Academic Press

Jameson, F (1971) *Marxism and Form*, Princeton: Princeton University Press

Jarvis, S (1998) *Adorno: A Critical Introduction*, Cambridge: Polity

Kamenka, E and Erh-Soon Tay, A (1975) 'Beyond bourgeois individualism: the contemporary crisis in law and legal ideology' in Kamenka, E and Neale, R (eds), *Feudalism, Capitalism and Beyond*, London: Arnold

Kant, I (1965) *The Metaphysical Elements of Justice*, Indianapolis: Bobbs Merrill

Kant, I (1993) *Critique of Pure Reason*, London: Everyman

Kant, I (1997) *Groundwork of the Metaphysics of Morals*, Cambridge: Cambridge University Press

Kelman, M (1981) 'Interpretive construction in the substantive criminal law' 33 *Stanford Law Review* 591

Kelman, M (1984) 'Trashing' 36 *Stanford Law Review* 293

Kelman, M (1987) *A Guide to Critical Legal Studies*, Cambridge, Mass: Harvard University Press

Kelsey, J (1993) *Rolling Back the State: Privatisation of Power in Autorea/New Zealand*, Wellington: Bridget Williams

Kenny, CS (1902) *Outlines of Criminal Law*, Cambridge: Cambridge University Press

Kramer, M (1994) 'False conclusions from true premises: warnings to legal theorists' 14 *Oxford Journal of Legal Studies* 111

Lacey, N (1985) 'The territory of the criminal law' 5 *Oxford Journal of Legal Studies* 453

Lacey, N (1988) *State Punishment*, London: Routledge and Kegan Paul

Lacey, N (1993a) 'A clear concept of intention: elusive or illusory?' 56 *Modern Law Review* 621

Lacey, N (1993b) 'Closure and critique in feminist jurisprudence: transcending the dichotomy or a foot in both camps?' in Norrie, A (ed), *Closure or Critique: New Directions in Legal Theory*, Edinburgh: Edinburgh University Press

Lacey, N (1996) 'Normative reconstruction in socio-legal theory' 5 *Social and Legal Studies* 131

Lacey, N (1998a) 'Contingency, coherence and conceptualism' in Duff, R (ed), *Philosophy and the Criminal Law*, New York: Cambridge University Press

Lacey, N (1998b) *Unspeakable Subjects*, Oxford: Hart

Lacey, N, Wells, C and Meure, D (1990) *Reconstructing Criminal Law*, London: Butterworths

Land, N (1993) 'After the law' in Norrie, A (ed), *Closure or Critique: New Directions in Legal Theory*, Edinburgh: Edinburgh University Press

Lechte, J (1994) *Fifty Key Contemporary Thinkers*, London: Routledge

Llewellyn, K (1951) *The Bramble Bush*, New York: Oceana

Locke, J (1960) *Two Treatises on Government*, Cambridge: Cambridge University Press

Lukacs, G (1975) *The Young Hegel*, London: Merlin

Lukacs, G (1971) *History and Class Consciousness*, London: Merlin

Lyotard, J (1993) 'The other's rights' in Shute, S and Hurley, S (eds), *On Human Rights*, New York: Basic Books

MacCormick, DN (1976) 'Challenging sociological definitions' 3 *British Journal of Law and Society* 88

MacCormick, DN (1978a) 'Dworkin as pre-Benthamite' 87 *Philosophical Review* 585

MacCormick, DN (1978b) *Legal Reasoning and Legal Theory*, Oxford: Clarendon

MacCormick, DN (1983) 'Contemporary legal philosophy: the rediscovery of practical reason' 10 *Journal of Law and Society* 1

MacCormick, DN (1989) 'The ethics of legalism' 2 *Ratio Juris* 184

MacCormick, DN (1993) 'Reconstruction after deconstruction: closing in on critique' in Norrie, A (ed), *Closure or Critique: New Directions in Legal Theory*, Edinburgh: Edinburgh University Press

MacIntyre, A (1967) *A Short History of Ethics*, London: Routledge and Kegan Paul

MacIntyre, A (1985) *After Virtue*, London: Duckworth

MacIntyre, A (1988) *Whose Justice? Which Rationality?*, London: Duckworth

MacIntyre, A (1990) *Three Rival Versions of Moral Enquiry: Encyclopedia, Genealogy, Tradition*, London: Duckworth

Marcuse, H (1941) *Reason and Revolution*, London: Routledge and Kegan Paul

Marx, K (1954) *Capital*, London: Lawrence & Wishart

Marx, K (1968) 'Critique of the Gotha Programme' in *Selected Works*, London: Lawrence & Wishart

Marx, K (1973) *Grundrisse*, London: Harmondsworth

Marx, K (1975) 'Critique of Hegel's doctrine of the state' in Colletti, L (ed), *Early Writings*, Harmondsworth: Pelican

Marx, K and Engels, F (1968) 'The Communist Manifesto' in Marx, K and Engels, F (eds), *Selected Works in One Volume*, London: Lawrence & Wishart

McBarnet, D (1981) *Conviction*, London: Macmillan

McColgan, A (1993) 'In defence of battered women who kill' 13 *Oxford Journal of Legal Studies* 508

McLellan, D (1969) *The Young Hegelians and Karl Marx*, London: Macmillan

Merry, S and Milner, N (1993) *The Possibility of Popular Justice*, Ann Arbor: University of Michigan Press

Moore, M (1997) *Placing Blame*, Oxford: Oxford University Press

Murphy, J (1979) *Retribution, Justice and Therapy*, Dordrecht: Reidel

Murphy, WT (1993) 'The bondage of freedom: Max Weber in the present tense' in Norrie, A (ed), *Closure or Critique: New Directions in Legal Theory*, Edinburgh: Edinburgh University Press

Neumann, F (1957) *The Democratic and the Authoritarian State*, Glencoe, Illinois: Free Press

Neumann, F (1986) *The Rule of Law*, Leamington Spa: Berg

Neumann, F and Kircheimer, D (1987) *Social Democracy and the Rule of Law*, London: Allen & Unwin

Norrie, A (1982) 'Pashukanis and the commodity form theory: a reply to Warrington' 10 *International Journal of the Sociology of Law* 49

Norrie, A (1989a) 'Oblique intention and legal politics' *Criminal Law Review* 793

Norrie, A (1989b) 'Review of Goodrich, *Reading the Law*' *Juridical Review* 222

Norrie, A (1990a) 'Locating the socialist Rechtsstaat: underdevelopment and criminal justice in the Soviet Union' 18 *International Journal of Sociology of Law* 343

Norrie, A (1990b) 'Review of Lacey, *State Punishment*' 18 *International Journal of the Sociology of Law* 112

Norrie, A (1991a) 'A critique of criminal causation' 54 *Modern Law Review* 685

Norrie, A (1991b) *Law, Ideology and Punishment*, Dordrecht: Kluwer

Norrie, A (1992) 'Subjectivism, objectivism and the limits of criminal recklessness' 12 *Oxford Journal of Legal Studies* 45

Norrie, A (1993a) *Crime, Reason and History*, London: Weidenfeld & Nicolson

Norrie, A (1993b) 'Criminal justice, the rule of law and human emancipation: an historical and comparative study' in Adelman, S and Paliwala, A (eds), *Law and Crisis in the Third World*, London: Hans Zell

Norrie, A (1997) 'Between structure and difference: law's relationality' in Bergalli, R and Melossi, D (eds), *The Emergence of Law Through Economy, Politics and Culture*, Onati: Onati Papers

Norrie, A (1998a) 'Critical legal studies' in MacCormick, D and Brown, B (eds), *The Philosophy of Law*, London: Routledge

Norrie, A (1998b) '"Simulacra of morality"? Beyond the ideal/actual antinomies of criminal justice' in Duff, R (ed), *Philosophy and the Criminal Law: Principle and Critique*, New York: Cambridge University Press

Norrie, A (1999) 'After *Woollin*' *Criminal Law Review* 532

Norrie, A (2000) *Punishment, Responsibility and Justice*, Oxford: Oxford University Press

Norrie, A (2001a) 'The structure of provocation' 54 *Current Legal Problems* 307

Norrie, A (2001b) *Crime, Reason and History*, 2nd edn, Cambridge: Cambridge University Press

Norrie, A (2001c) 'Criminal justice, judicial interpretation, legal right: on being sceptical about the Human Rights Act 1998' in Campbell, T, Ewing, K and Tomkins, A (eds), *Sceptical Essays on Human Rights*, Oxford: Oxford University Press

Norrie, A and Adelman, S (1989) '"Consensual authoritarianism" and criminal justice in Thatcher's Britain' 16 *Journal of Law and Society* 112

Norris, C (1991) *Deconstruction: Theory and Practice*, London: Routledge

Norton, R (1995) *The Beautiful Soul*, Ithaca: Cornell University Press

Nourse, V (1997) 'Passion's progress: modern law reform and the provocation defence' 106 *Yale Law Journal* 1331

Nozick, R (1975) *Anarchy, State and Utopia*, Oxford: Blackwell

O'Donovan, K (1991) 'Defences for battered women who kill' 18 *Journal of Law and Society* 219

Ollmann, B (1993) *Dialectical Investigations*, London: Routledge

Outhwaite, W (1987) *New Philosophies of Social Science*, London: Macmillan

Pashukanis, EB (1978) *General Theory of Law and Marxism*, London: Ink Links

Pinkard, T (2000) *Hegel: A Biography*, Cambridge: Cambridge University Press

Plant, R (1983) *Hegel: An Introduction*, Oxford: Blackwell

Radzinowicz, L (1948) *A History of the English Criminal Law*, London: Stevens, Vol 1

Radzinowicz, L and Hood, R (1986) *A History of the English Criminal Law*, London: Stevens, Vol 5

Rawls, J (1972) *A Theory of Justice*, Oxford: Oxford University Press

Rawls, J (1985) 'Justice as fairness: political not metaphysical' 14 *Philosophy and Public Affairs* 219

Reiner, R (1992) *The Politics of the Police*, London: Harvester Wheatsheaf

Rorty, R (1991) *Philosophy and the Idea of Freedom*, Oxford: Blackwell

Rose, G (1978) *The Melancholy Science*, New York: Columbia

Rose, G (1981) *Hegel Contra Sociology*, London: Athlone

Rose, G (1984) *Dialectic of Nihilism*, Oxford: Blackwell

Rosenblum, N (1978) B*entham's Theory of the Modern State*, Cambridge, Mass: Harvard University Press

Russell, B (1973) *The Problems of Philosophy*, Oxford: Oxford University Press

Sachs, A (1985) 'The two dimensions of socialist legality' 13 *International Journal of Sociology of Law* 133

Sachs, A and Welch, G (1990) *Liberating the Law*, London: Zed Press

Salter, M and Shaw, J (1994) 'Hegel and constitutional law' 21 *Journal of Law and Society* 464

Sanders, A and Young, R (1994) *Criminal Justice*, London: Butterworths

Sandland, R (1998) 'Seeing double? Or, why "to be or not to be" is (not) the question for feminist legal studies' 7 *Social and Legal Studies* 307

Sayer, A (1992) *Method in Social Science: A Realist Approach*, London: Routledge

Sayer, D (1987) *The Violence of Abstraction*, Oxford: Blackwell

Scharf, W and Ngcokoto, B (1990) 'Images of punishment in the people's courts of Cape Town 1985–1987: from prefigurative justice to populist violence' in Manganyi, C and du Toit, A (eds), *Political Violence and the Struggle in South Africa*, London: Macmillan

Schlag, P (1990) '"Le hors de texte, c'est moi": the politics of form and the domestication of deconstruction' 11 *Cardozo Law Review* 1631

Schlag, P (1991) 'The problem of the subject' 69 *Texas Law Review* 1627

Schlag, P (1997) 'The empty circles of liberal justification' 96 *Michigan Law Review* 1

Schluchter, W (1981) *The Rise of Western Rationalism*, Berkeley: University of California Press

Sereny, G (1995) *Albert Speer: His Battle with Truth*, London: Picador

Smith, JC (1987) 'Law reform proposals and the courts' in Dennis, I (ed), *Criminal Law and Justice*, London: Sweet & Maxwell

Smith, JC (1989) *Justification and Excuse in the Criminal Law*, London: Stevens

Smith, JC (1995) 'Comment on *Morhall*' *Criminal Law Review* 890

Smith, JC and Hogan, B (1992) *Criminal Law*, 7th edn, London: Butterworths

Smith, JC and Hogan, B (1999) *Criminal Law*, 9th edn, London: Butterworths

Spitzer, S (1982) 'The dialectics of formal and informal control' in Abel, R (ed), *The Politics of Informal Justice*, New York: Academic Press

Stein, D (1988) 'Burning windows, burning brides: the perils of daughterhood in India' 61(3) *Pacific Affairs* 465–85

Steintrager, J (1977) *Bentham*, London: Allen & Unwin

Stewart, A (1995) 'Debating gender justice in India' 4 Social and Legal Studies 253–74

Strauss, L (1953) *Natural Right and History*, Chicago: University of Chicago Press

Summers, R (1984) *Lon L Fuller*, London: Edward Arnold

Taylor, C (1975) *Hegel*, Cambridge: Cambridge University Press

Teubner, G (1987) '"Juridification": concepts, aspects, limits, solutions' in Teubner, G (ed), *Juridification of Social Spheres*, Berlin: De Gruyter

Therborn, G (1976) *Science, Class and Society*, London: New Left Books

Thompson, EP (1975) *Whigs and Hunters*, Harmondsworth: Peregrine

Thompson, EP (1991) *Customs in Common*, London: Penguin

Turner, B (1974) *Weber and Islam*, London: Routledge and Kegan Paul

Unger, RM (1976) *Law in Modern Society*, New York: Monthly Review Press

Utting, P (1989) *From 'Orthodoxy' to 'Reform': Experiences of Dependent Transitional Economies*, United Nations Research Institute for Social Development

von Hirsch, A (1993) *Censure and Sanctions*, Oxford: Oxford University Press

Waldron, J (1987) *Nonsense Upon Stilts: Bentham, Burke and Marx on the Rights of Man*, London: Methuen

Warrington, R (1981) 'Pashukanis and the commodity form theory' 9 *International Journal of the Sociology of Law* 1

Weber, M (1978) *Economy and Society*, Berkeley: University of California Press

Weber, M (1991) *From Max Weber: Essays in Sociology*, London: Routledge

Wells, C (1982) 'Swatting the subjectivist bug' *Criminal Law Review* 209

Wells, C (2000) 'Provocation: the case for abolition' in Ashworth, A and Mitchell, B (eds), *Rethinking English Homicide Law*, Oxford: Oxford University Press

White, G (1983) *Revolutionary Socialist Development in the Third World*, Brighton: Harvester Wheatsheaf

White, G (1988) 'Riding the tiger' in Saith, A (ed), *The Re-Emergence of the Chinese Peasantry*, London: Croom Helm

Williams, G (1961) *Criminal Law: The General Part*, 2nd edn, London: Stevens

Williams, G (1981) 'Recklessness redefined' 40 *Cambridge Law Journal* 252

Williams, G (1983) *Textbook of Criminal Law*, 2nd edn, London: Stevens

Williams, G (1987) 'Oblique intention' 46 *Cambridge Law Journal* 417

Williams, G (1988) 'The unresolved problem of recklessness' 8 *Legal Studies* 74

Wolff, RP (1973) *The Autonomy of Reason*, New York: Harper

Wootton, B (1963) *Crime and the Criminal Law*, London: Stevens

Zedner, L (1994) 'Reparation and retribution: are they irreconcilable?' 57 *Modern Law Review* 1

Index